The Church Plate
of the Diocese of Bangor

PLATE I.

LLANDUDWEN, CARNARVONSHIRE.
Pre-Reformation Silver Chalice, Parcel-Gilt.
Date : *circa* 1500.

The
Church Plate
of the
Diocese of Bangor

BY

E. Alfred Jones

AUTHOR OF

" *Old English Gold Plate* "

" *The Old Church Plate of the Isle of Man* "

" *An Illustrated Catalogue of the Gutmann Collection of Foreign Plate* "
(Now the property of Mr. J. Pierpont Morgan)

" *The Old Silver Communion Vessels of Foreign Protestant
Churches in England* "

" *An Illustrated Volume on Mr. Leopold de Rothschild's Collection of Plate* "

AND

" *Old English Plate in the possession of the Czar of Russia* " etc.

London

BEMROSE AND SONS LIMITED, 4 SNOW HILL, E.C.

AND DERBY

1906

MOST of the Plate in Anglesey and Carnarvonshire has been photographed by Mr. Wickens, of Bangor, who spared no pains to give satisfaction. Other Plate has been photographed by Mr. J. Clay, Holyhead; Mr. Edge, Llandudno; Mr. P. G. Thomas, Penrhyndeudraeth; Mr. Gaffron, Dolgelley; Miss Mathew, Towyn; Mr. E. Davies, Newtown; Mr. G. Thomas, Llanfairfechan; and Mr. A. T. Hughes, Llanrwst.

PREFACE

I WISH to record my thanks to the Lord Bishop of the Diocese for his kindly interest in this work; to Colonel O. Lloyd J. Evans for valuable help; to the Rev. E. Evans, Rector of Llansadwrn, for notes as to the donors of plate; to Mr. A. Ivor Pryce, M.A., for assistance in the search for old terriers and other documents in the Diocesan Registry; to those clergy who helped by taking the plate to be photographed; and to my friend, Mr. K. A. R. Sugden, B.A., sometime demy of Magdalen College, Oxford, who rendered services in various directions. I am also under obligation to Mr. C. J. Jackson's invaluable volume, recently published, *English Goldsmiths and their Marks*.

E. ALFRED JONES.

LIST OF ILLUSTRATIONS

INTRODUCTION

THE scattered Welsh diocese of Bangor, with its numerous churches, has lost many of its possessions of plate and other objects of interest and value to the archæologist and the antiquary, the ecclesiologist and the historian. There still, however, fortunately remain several valuable specimens of plate, the earliest dating from the fifteenth century, which will be found fully described, and in many instances illustrated, in the following pages.

The earliest piece of plate, whether secular or ecclesiastical, that has been found by the author, is the Mazer Bowl (Plate II.), of dark maple-wood, mounted in silver-gilt, with a Latin inscription meaning "Jesus of Nazareth, King of the Jews, Son of God, have mercy upon me," dating from the last quarter of the fifteenth century. It was long used as an Alms-dish in the ancient church at Clynnog, in Carnarvonshire, and is believed to be the sole surviving relic in the form of plate from the religious house at that place.

Among the numerous forms of drinking vessels in use in England from the thirteenth to the sixteenth centuries, the commonest of all, and the one most highly esteemed by prince and baron, monk and peasant, was the Mazer Bowl. The name is said to be applied to the material from which it is constructed rather than to its use as a drinking vessel, and is believed to be of old Low-German origin. The most popular wood was maple, and particularly the spotted variety known as bird's-eye maple, which was highly polished. No better evidence of the great popularity of the Mazer among all sections of the people in England can be adduced than the wills of private persons and the inventories of monasteries and other corporate bodies. From records still extant, it would seem that in the frater at Canterbury, in the year 1328, there were one hundred and thirty-eight Mazers; at Battle, a century or so later, there were thirty-two; Durham in 1446 could boast the possession of forty-nine; and Westminster in 1540 contained forty. The Mazers of the richer folk were embellished with bands and mountings in silver, and occasionally even in gold, while those of the poorer members of the community remained entirely unmounted, or had, perhaps, merely a simple band of metal. In the absence of hall marks, the dates of many of the mounted Mazers can be determined, as in the Clynnog bowl, by the style of the lettering in the interesting inscriptions which several of them carry on the bands. Inscriptions worthy of mention are:—"In the name of the Trinity drink to me"; that on the well-known great Mazer formerly belonging to the Guild of Corpus Christi at York, and now in the Minster there, which has an inscription in English granting an indulgence of forty days by Richard Scrope, Archbishop of York, "to those truly penitent and confessed who should drink of this cup soberly yet with moderation, and not excessively nor according to the will, but with a pure mind"; and the inscription (in Latin) of the well-known verse from the first chapter of S. Luke's Gospel: "Hail, thou that art highly favoured, the Lord is with thee: blessed art thou among women," on a bowl in the possession of the Ironmongers' Company.

The supposition has frequently arisen from the scriptural inscription on the Clynnog Mazer that these bowls were exclusively for use in the service of the Church; but while here and there they may have been used in post-Reformation times as Chalices or Alms-dishes, just as other equally domestic utensils have been, and are, used for such purposes, contemporary writings establish beyond doubt the secular character of the Mazer. For instance, according to the *Rites of Durham*, "every monk had his Mazer severally by himself to drink in, . . . and all the said Mazers were largely and finely edged with silver double gilt"; and at S. Saviour's, Southwark, in 1552, a Mazer was "given to the wardens when they meet to drink in."

An examination of all the existing Mazers reveals the fact that in almost every case they are fitted in the bottom inside with a circular medallion, known as a print, the two earliest remaining specimens—those at Harbledown Hospital, Kent—having in one a silver-gilt plate embossed with a representation of a combat between a lioness and a dragon, and in the other an incident in the life of the famous Guy of Warwick. A fourteenth century Mazer at S. John's Hospital, Canterbury, has a print with the Virgin and Child. The remarkable Mazer, of late fourteenth century date, at Corpus Christi College, Cambridge, has in place of the usual print an unique central ornament in the form of a standing pillar surmounted by a swan enclosed in a battlemented top. Among other devices recorded are the sacred monograms, I.H.S. and I.H.C.; various kinds of flowers, originally enamelled, as in the Clynnog bowl; shields of arms; the Majesty; the Vernicle; the Trinity; the Salutation; engraved figures of S. John the Baptist and S. Andrew; and in the Mazer at All Souls' College, Oxford, the arms and initials of the donor, Thomas Ballard.

Though so numerous during the centuries previously mentioned, the number of these quaint vessels which still exist probably does not exceed fifty, and the preservation of these is doubtless largely due to the fact that no great value was attached to a vessel composed mainly of wood. With the close of the reign of Elizabeth, Mazers were no longer made, being superseded in popularity by the tall silver cups on stems.

The Clynnog Mazer is closely followed in point of age, interest and rarity by the pre-Reformation silver Chalice, date *circa* 1500 (Plate I.), in the remote country church of Llandudwen, also in Carnarvonshire, now brought to light for the first time, and thus making one more addition to the limited number of medieval silver Chalices that have survived not only the spoliation of the cathedral and conventual churches by Henry VIII., and of the parish churches and chantries by Edward VI., but also the injunction of Archbishop Parker that all " profane cups, bowls, dishes or chalices heretofore used at Mass " should be turned into " decent communion cups."

Of the existing pre-Reformation English silver massing Chalices and

3

Patens, Wales can claim only one other Chalice—that at Llanelian-yn-Rhos, in Denbighshire, which is of the same period and almost identical with the Llandudwen Chalice—and a Paten, dated 1535, at Llanmaes, Glamorganshire. The number of these medieval silver Chalices and Patens throughout England and Wales is in all probability not over forty and ninety-five respectively.[1]

The development in the form and decoration of these Chalices has been classified somewhat as follows: From about 1200 to 1250, the bowl is almost hemispherical, broad and shallow, while the stem, knop and foot are circular and plain, as in the earliest existing Chalice from the church of Berwick S. James', Wiltshire, and now in the British Museum. Immediately following this Chalice is probably the finest English medieval silver Chalice yet discovered, namely, the one (date, *circa* 1230) which was found buried some years ago in the parish of Llanelltyd, Merionethshire, which deserves special notice here from the fact of its discovery in this diocese. It has a low, plain bowl, with slightly-curved lip, supported by a short stem engraved with stiff-stalked leaves, and divided by a large knop, which is separated into twelve lobes, alternately beaded and plain. The broad, circular foot has twelve plain lobes with pointed trefoil terminations, radiating downwards from the knop, and below these are trefoiled lobes, exquisitely engraved with characteristic Early English foliage, while the spaces between the points reaching to the edge of base are engraved with similar foliage. The foot is inscribed—

NICOL'VS MꞒ | FꞒCIT DꞒ ҺꞒR | FORDIꞒ,

from which it will be seen that the Chalice was wrought by one Nicholas of Hereford. The Chalice, which is of unusually massive proportions, is $7\frac{1}{4}$ ins. high, and is only exceeded in height by the English medieval

---

[1] At S. David's Cathedral are two highly interesting plain Chalices and fragments of a Paten, all of silver, found with a crosier head and part of another crosier, described as of copper-gilt, and two episcopal rings of gold set with sapphires, found in the tombs of two bishops of the See of S. David's, Richard de Carew (1256-1280) and his successor, Bishop Beck (1280-1293). The custom of burying a Chalice and Paten with ecclesiastics was introduced about the twelfth century. They are frequently of pewter and latten as well as of silver.

Chalices at Leominster and Trinity College, Oxford. The Paten found with this Chalice is the largest English specimen known. It has two depressions, one plain and circular, the other sexfoil, with spandrels engraved with foliage and symbols of the four Evangelists. The centre is occupied by an engraved figure of the Saviour, seated on a seat, His right hand raised in blessing, His left hand holding a closed book. The figure is surrounded by this inscription—

✠ IN NOMINE : PATRIS : ET FILII : ET SPIRITVS SANCTI AM.

Its diameter is $7\frac{5}{16}$ ins.

It has been suggested that this Chalice and Paten originally belonged to the Cistercians of Cymner Abbey, which is in this parish, and that they were hidden in times of peril. Both were sold at Christie's in 1892 for £710, and are now in a private collection.

In the succeeding type, 1250-1275, the bowl and foot remain much the same, but a considerable difference can be observed in the stem and knop, the knop in one example being octagonal, and in two others eight-lobed. Of Chalices prevailing during the last quarter of the same century, three specimens have come down to the present day, and the special feature of this type is the enrichment of the foot, which consists of a series of lobes radiating from below the stem over the foot; the stem in one instance is octagonal, and in the other two circular, with the same variation in the knop.

The Chalice which is next to be considered (dating from 1300 to 1350) is of singular interest, for it is distinguished not only from the fact that it is the only specimen of its kind remaining extant, but also because it is the first English Chalice with the crucifix engraved on the foot. This example, which is at York Minster, is somewhat taller than those already described, and the bowl shows a distinct change, being deeper and conical in form; the foot continues to be circular, and the stem is circular, taller, and more slender, the knop being eight-lobed.

With the extension in the fourteenth century of the custom of laying the Chalice on its side on the Paten to drain at the ablutions at mass, the circular-footed Chalice disappears in favour of one with a curved-hexagonal or mullet-like foot. The earliest of this form is that at Hamstall Ridware, in Staffordshire, and its date is about the middle of the fourteenth century; its bowl is deep and conical, while the knop and the short stem are circular, the former being spirally twisted, the latter ribbed.

In the next stage which is observed in the development, the stem changes from circular to hexagonal, with a six-sided knop, the letters **iɧc** being engraved on the foot.

Following this type is that with a similar form of deep and conical bowl, supported by a plain, hexagonal stem, which is divided by a large knop, usually formed of six lobes, terminating in masks of angels, lozenge-shaped ornaments decorated with roses or other flowers, which were generally enamelled, the spaces between the lobes being pierced in the majority of cases. There are, it need scarcely be pointed out, departures from these decorative details, as in the Leominster Chalice, the stem of which is enriched with applied tracery and the angles buttressed. The foot of the foregoing type, which prevailed from about 1450 to 1510, remains six-sided, and in the later specimens, as in that at Llandudwen, the points terminate in small pierced ornaments, added, it is believed, to prevent the sharp points of the foot from digging into the cloths, etc., used in the service of the Mass. The usual decoration of the compartment of the foot is a crucifix of various forms, though other devices are known, namely, **iɧc** and **xpc**, while the donors' names are engraved on the feet of two Chalices, and this inscription on the bowls of two others—" Calicem salutaris accipiam et nomen Domini invocabo." (Psalm cv. Sarum Breviary.)

The well-known Chalice and Paten with London date-letter for 1479 at Nettlecombe, Somerset, are the earliest pieces of plate in existence, either ecclesiastical or secular, with a hall-mark.

At the beginning of the sixteenth century another type is introduced; the bowl changes from conical to nearly hemispherical, and while the shape of the stem and the knop remain much the same as in the preceding type, the knop is not pierced in every instance. The form of the foot now becomes quite different, the curved hexagonal or mullet shape giving way to a sexfoil, but the engraved crucifix being still retained. The most interesting and valuable example of this type is the unique gold Chalice, dated 1507-8, given, with a gold Paten and a magnificent silver Crosier, which are still preserved there, to Corpus Christi College, Oxford, by its founder, Richard Foxe, Bishop of Winchester. In addition to the crucifix, the compartments on this gold Chalice are filled with saints, etc.

The final form of the pre-Reformation Chalice, of which five examples have survived, dating from 1525-6 to 1536-7, may be summarised as follows: the bowl continues to be shallow and broad at the bottom, and in every case but one is inscribed with a legend, as is also the foot. The stem of the Chalice at Trinity College, Oxford, has beautiful quatrefoil tracery from top to bottom, and cables run along the angles; two others have plain unpierced stems; another is buttressed at the angles. The knop remains similar in type but flatter and without the traceried openings. At the junction of the stem with the foot is a pierced gallery with a vase-shape buttress at each angle. The border of the foot is described as a wavy-sided hexagon, though in one example the sexfoil form has been retained and without the crucifix. The legends on the bowls vary, the most general being that from Psalm cv. Sarum Breviary, previously referred to.

The main characteristics of the pre-Reformation silver Paten may be briefly summarised in the following manner:—

The earliest type, dating from about 1180 to 1260, has the lower depression quatrefoil. Among the notable examples of this type is one at Chichester Cathedral, found in the grave of a bishop, which has a rude engraving of the Holy Lamb in the centre, surrounded by this inscription:—"Agnus Dei qui tollis peccata mundi miserere nobis"; and another with a figure of a bishop in vestments, the right hand raised in the act of blessing, the left holding a crosier, discovered in the grave of the famous Bishop Grostete of Lincoln. A variation from this type is the Paten found in Merionethshire, which has already been described.

The next type, which appears to have prevailed from about 1260 to 1300, has a lower depression or single depression octofoil or multifoil.

The most interesting specimen of this kind is undoubtedly the one at Wyke Church, near Winchester, which has the Agnus Dei as a central device sunk in a circular depression, the other depression being octofoil. A legend is engraved on the border:—" + Cunta creo. virtute rego pietate reformo." Another remarkable Paten of this period is that at York Minster, the only known example where the first and not the second depression is multifoil.

The features of the third type, 1300 to 1350, are a lower sexfoil depression with the spandrels plain, the central device usually being the Manus Dei.

In the next type, the lower depression still remains sexfoil, but the spandrels are filled with a rayed ornament, and the central device is most frequently the vernicle.

The sexfoil now gives way to the single circular depression in this fifth type, and the centre is more generally occupied by the sacred monogram ihc or ihs.

The succeeding Paten is an elaboration of the previous type, which it resembles in general form, but the central device, which is various, has a glory of long rays filling the field, and the rim bears an engraved legend.

In the final stage of the pre-Reformation silver Paten, 1510-1535, the single circular depression still remains, with the central device surrounded by a glory of long rays, and the rims bearing engraved legends. In the Paten dated 1535 at Llanmaes, Glamorganshire, however, the centre is sexfoil, and the vernicle is engraved, while the rim is plain.

A beautiful example of a Paten of *circa* 1520 is at Felbrigge, Norfolk, which has in the centre an enamelled plate of S. Margaret of Antioch, the patron saint of the church.

The earliest type of Communion Cup adopted by the reformed Church in the reign of Edward VI., of which only about fifteen are recorded, usually has a plain bowl, unadorned, except for a series of plain dotted lines at the most, and the stem, with its collar or flange close up to the bowl, has some delicate ornamental mouldings. Immediately succeeding the Edwardian Cup is the familiar Elizabethan Cup with its

Paten-Cover, found in abundance throughout England and Wales, and in the main following one model. The bowl, which is characterised by a simple dignity, resembles an inverted bell, and is invariably decorated with an engraved intersecting band of strap-work filled with arabesques, a sprig being carried above and below each intersection. The stem, which is divided by a plain flattened knop, the knop occasionally covered with short incised lines, has a plain, reeded, or other variety of moulding at the junctions with the bowl and the foot, which is always circular. On the edge of the foot is a delicate ovolo moulding, or it may be plain. There are, of course, departures from this orthodox type, but these are generally confined to prescribed areas. In the Norwich pattern the bowl is wider and shallower, and the stem is without a knop; in Leicestershire the stem is often vase-shape, the bowl, too, is occasionally plain; the Cups wrought by the local silversmiths of Exeter also exhibit varying distinctions, and those wrought by the craftsmen of York show a tendency to depart from the usual type.

A very large number of these Elizabethan Cups were transformed from the pre-Reformation Chalices, with the addition of the necessary amount of silver to render the bowls large enough for the administration of the cup to the laity. In the perfect little Chalice at Bottwnog (PLATE XXX., No. 3), which bears a date—1575—contemporary with the time when this living was held by Henry Rowlands, founder of the Grammar School there, and subsequently Dean and Bishop of Bangor, the holding capacity of the bowl remains much the same as the former Massing Chalice, and the hammering marks, and also traces of the original gilding, are plainly visible inside the bowl. Very little, if any, additional metal was used in the re-construction of this interesting piece.

Each of these Chalices was provided with a "cover of silver appointed also for the ministration of the communion bread." These Paten-Covers, which have a circular foot, frequently engraved with a date, and less often with a device of some kind—a Tudor rose appears on the one at Llanddeiniolen—closely fit over the rim of the bowl, and the decoration often follows that on the Chalice.

In comparison with other parts of Wales, this diocese is singularly poor in the number of Elizabethan cups, the total not exceeding 28, 13 of which have their Paten-Covers, 15 without, while there are 2 Paten-Covers without their Chalices. The diocese of Llandaff yields 75—mostly of the year 1576, Cardiganshire about 22, and Pembroke-shire no fewer than 59, the majority dating from 1574-5.

Though these Elizabethan Chalices in the diocese of Bangor appear to vary little in general, no two are exactly alike, each exhibiting some variation, slight though it may be, in the decorative details, even when wrought by the same silversmith. The one at Llangwnadl (PLATE VII., No. 1) has an unusually deep bowl, with a correspondingly short stem, the knop being high up, not in the centre. The Llanelltyd Chalice (PLATE XXVII., No. 2) is also very deep in the bowl, which is quite plain except for the inscription with the name of the parish. The bowls may have the usual plain strap-work band, enclosing sprays of arabesques, generally near the lip, or occasionally in the middle, with the addition of a lower band or series of rows of hyphens; or, as at Penstrowed (PLATE XXII., No. 3), the strap-work band, with a row of hyphens, may remain without the conventional sprays of arabesque work. Considerable variation also occurs in the width of this band. The bowls of the Chalices at Dolwyddelen and Llanbedr-y-Cenin, which are by the same hand, and that at Llanddeiniolen, as well as of that previously mentioned at Llanelltyd, are plain, being engraved only with the name of the parish in English in Lombardic capitals. In the diocese of Llan-daff and other parts of South Wales these inscriptions are in Latin.

The earliest of these Elizabethan Chalices is at Llanfwrog, and bears the London date-letter for 1561-2; there are six others with London mark for 1574-5, with various makers' marks; eight Chalices and two odd Paten-Covers, mostly dated 1574, and one 1578, with only one mark—a bird's head, apparently confined to this diocese and found at five places in Anglesey, as far north as Coedana and Llandyfrydog; at Llanffinan, Llangoed, and Llaniestyn; and at three places in Carnarvon-shire—in the north at Aber, at Clynnog in the south, and at Llanrug. In the absence of a London mark, this unknown maker's sign may be that of a provincial craftsman working at Chester.

Four Chalices are stamped with the initials IL, unaccompanied by any other marks, three of them, which are dated 1574 and 1575, being in adjoining parishes—Bottwnog, Bryncroes and Tydweiliog, and the fourth at Llanbedrgoch in Anglesey. This mark may not improbably represent John Lynglay, one of the Elizabethan goldsmiths at Chester. Six are without marks, and the remaining three are of London make, late in Elizabeth's reign—Llanelltyd, 1591-2; Llanbrynmair, 1595-6; and Llanddeiniolen, 1599-1600.

Three other pieces of plate of the Elizabethan era, which is marked by great progress in the minor arts, such as that of the silversmith, as well as in the wider realms of colonisation and of literature, have survived. One is an elegant Tazza, dated 1570-1, in the historic church of Penmynydd (PLATE XV.). These open form of drinking vessels are, as their name indicates, Italian in origin, and were produced in large numbers by the goldsmiths of the Italian Renaissance for the adornment of the tables of the nobles. The German craftsmen of Augsburg and Nuremberg were not slow to appreciate the decorative value of the Tazza, and many examples of German workmanship, which are noted for their ornateness, were wrought at those famous centres of the silversmiths' craft during the last half of the sixteenth and the early part of the seventeenth centuries. The Tazza spread to Holland, where it became a popular type of drinking cup, and it frequently figures in pictures by Dutch artists of the end of the sixteenth and the seventeenth centuries, for instance in the "Garden Party" by David Vincheebooms, in a painting by Pieter Isaachs, and in works of Pieter and Willem Claesz and others. The English Tazza is small and restrained in its decoration; the bowl is invariably plain except for some interlaced strap-work enclosing arabesques, similar to that on the Elizabethan Chalice, and in the centre of most examples is an embossed medallion of a Roman warrior, after the fashion of the Greek *emblema*, in the style of the Italian Renaissance. The stem is only slightly decorated, and the circular foot is embossed with fruit, foliage, etc.

The Tazza prevailed in England from about 1560 to 1590, though one as late as 1617 is at S. Giles', Cripplegate.

4

The second piece of Elizabethan plate in the Diocese of Bangor is the superb and valuable silver-gilt cup and cover, dated 1573-4 (PLATE III.), at Llanbadrig. The mode of decoration, the sprigs of foliage, short incised lines or hyphens, and the vase-shape knob and the mouldings, are all typical of the period. Radiating from the base of the bowl and the top of the cover are narrow applied strips of plain wire. This Cup has been considered unique, but there is another Cup very similar to it of the year 1570-1, but without its original cover, at Charlton Mackrell, in Somersetshire.

And the other piece of this period, which is at Llanfihangel-Ysceifiog (PLATE VI., No. 2), is a V-shape Cup, chased with flat panels containing vines and roses, supported by a slender baluster stem on a splayed foot, similarly decorated, with London mark for 1601-2. A cover, with similar chasing surmounted by a " steeple " on three scrolled brackets, with date-letter for 1611-12, has been added to the Cup. The " steeple " first makes its appearance on the large standing salts of Elizabeth's reign, and became very popular later as finials for the tall Cups and covers throughout the reign of James I., as a result of that monarch's well-known partiality for obelisks of that kind. The stem of the Cup with steeple-cover is usually vase-shape, on a high bell-shape foot; and a Cup of this kind, embossed with foliage, of the date 1612, though unfortunately the steeple is missing, is at Rhuddlan Church.

One of the most noteworthy pieces of plate in the Diocese of Bangor is the beautiful and unique Chalice of Beddgelert (PLATE VIII.). The bowl, which is in the form of an inverted bell, has been delicately engraved by a contemporary artist with standing figures of Mary the Virgin, Mary Cleophas, and Mary Salome; the Blessed Virgin, with a halo surrounding her head, occupying the central position, and the other two Marys standing with their heads turned towards the Mother of our Lord. The two compressed knops on the stem are enriched with rose and ovolo mouldings, which are repeated on the edges of the foot and the tazza-like cover. The inscription records that this splendid Chalice was given in 1610 to the church of Beddgelert by Sir John Williams, who was born at Hafod Lwyfog in that parish, and forms a worthy gift by a Welshman who enjoyed the distinction of being goldsmith to James I. On the foot of the cover, the donor's arms are engraved. No other English Chalice is known to exist with these figures, and it can only be supposed that their appearance is due to the increasing ritualism in the services of the church at that time, largely the result of the influence of Lancelot Andrewes, Bishop successively of Chichester, Ely and Winchester, who insisted on the doctrines of the Real Presence and the Eucharistic sacrifice, and introduced in his chapel lights and incense, wafer-bread and the mixed Chalice.

The other silver Chalices of the reign of James I. number eleven, and these include three plain V-shape cups on very tall, slender baluster stems, the earliest, dated 1607-8, at Llandinam, one dated three years later at Trefdraeth, and another of 1616-17 at Llanllyfni. To these must be added one of 1607-8 at Llandudno (PLATE XXIX., No. 3), which is similar in every respect, except that the edge of the foot has an ovolo moulding, while the others are plain. In the Cup at Holyhead, date 1610-11 (PLATE XXIX., No. 2), the stem is similar to the others, but the bowl is oviform. A charming Cup of the same form as the Llandudno Cup, embossed with grapes and foliage, and fluted, dated 1614-15, is at Llanrhychwyn (PLATE XXIX., No. 1). There are four other distinct types of this period, namely, one at Abererch, dated 1611, with a Latin inscription within an interlaced strap-work band; and one of 1610-11, engraved with a band of laurel leaves, standing on a slender stem with a moulding in the centre, dated 1610-11, at Llandygwynning (PLATE VII., No. 3). A plain Chalice with deep inverted bell-shape bowl, and delicate ovolo mouldings on the foot, and engraved with an appropriate inscription for ecclesiastical plate, namely, " qui alienarit anathema sit," was given in 1615 to Llangeinwen by the then Rector, Robert White, D.D. (PLATE XXXI., No. 2).

At Llandwrog is a plain Chalice with very deep bowl and short stem, dated 1619 (PLATE X., No. 3), which is very similar in form to the Elizabethan Chalice at Llanelltyd. The Chalice at Bodfean (PLATE VII., No. 2), which has an engraved strap-work band filled with arabesques, distinctly Elizabethan in character, has the name of the parish and the scriptural inscription—" Drink ye all of it," engraved on the bowl. The Paten-Cover, which dates, like the Chalice to which it belongs, from 1623-4, does not overlap the lip of the bowl in the manner of the earlier ones. In this respect it is one of the earliest examples of its class.

The first year of the reign of Charles I. is represented by the plain Chalice and Paten, dated 1625, probably by a provincial silversmith, at Llanfihangel-y-Pennant, Merioneth (PLATE IX., No. 3). Of this reign there are nine of the cups with plain inverted bell-shape bowls on baluster stems, resembling the one at Penmynydd (PLATE XIV., No. 3), which is dated 1638-9, and found in abundance from early in the seventeenth century through the Commonwealth to the reign of Charles II., when the base of the bowl has a tendency to become flatter, as in the example dated 1664-5 at Harlech (PLATE XIV., No. 1).

Another specimen of the Penmynydd type is at Llangybi (PLATE XIV., No. 2), and this is mentioned here because it bears the Dublin date-letter for the same year—1638-9.

There are three of the massive plain Chalices, not unlike those of Edward VI., with bell-shape, or tapering, beaker-shape bowl, on a truncated stem with a collar or flange near the base of the bowl. One of these, of the year 1630-1, is at Rhosbeirio (PLATE XXVIII., No. 2); another, which is complete with its Paten-Cover, dated 1633 (PLATE XXXI., No. 1), is at Llanwnda; and the third, of the same date, is at S. David's, Barmouth.

A Chalice of more than ordinary interest is the one given in 1632 by William Bold, of Tre-yr-ddol, to Llechcynfarwy (PLATE VI., No. 3). The hexagonal stem and the large ornate knop, and the sexfoil foot with the engraved representation of the Crucifixion, follow a pre-Reformation type, while the bowl is distinctly like those found on baluster stems of the reign of Charles I. Here and there throughout the country Chalices with medieval characteristics are found, and the influence of Archbishop Laud may account for their appearance. There are five—the original number was seven—in Derbyshire Churches, given about 1632 by Lady Frances Kniveton; and these have plain bowls supported by hexagonal stems, the knops having angels' heads, while angels' heads and wings project from the corners of the curved hexagonal feet. Another similar Chalice, the gift of the Duchess Dudley in 1639, is at S. Mary's, Acton; and one more is at Ugthorpe Roman Catholic Church, near Whitby, which was used by the well-known Nicholas Postgate, who was hanged at York in 1679 for saying Mass. This taste for Chalices with medieval characteristics was also favoured in the reigns of Charles II. and William and Mary, and two gold Chalices of the latter reign are preserved at the Chapel Royal, S. James's Palace.

Other Chalices of this period are a plain one with a bell-shape bowl on a truncated stem, dated 1638-9 (PLATE IX., No. 2), at Llanfairfechan; one with a deep beaker-shape bowl, inscribed—"As oft as ye shall eate this bread and drinke this cup, ye shew the Lord's death till He come," the gift of Roger Jones, Citizen of London, to his native parish of Llaniestyn, Carnarvonshire, 1634-5 (PLATE IX., No. 1); and the two exceptionally large plain Chalices with Paten-Covers, both almost identically alike, and by the same maker, at Clynnog[1] and Llanaelhaiarn, dated respectively 1636-7 and 1638 (PLATE XI.). The latter is the earliest piece of plate in the Diocese of Bangor with a Welsh inscription—"Rhodd Thomas ap John y Eglwus Ailhaiarn." At Mallwyd is a massive plain Chalice, dated 1628 (PLATE XXVIII., No. 1), thought to be the gift, though there is no direct evidence in support of the suggestion, of the celebrated Welsh lexicographer, Dr. John Davies, then Rector of that place.

Mention must not be omitted of the fine plain silver-gilt service of plate at Bangor Cathedral (PLATE XII.), dated 1637-9, provided during the Episcopate of Bishop William Roberts, a noted loyalist and friend of Archbishop Laud, to whose recommendation he is said to have owed

---

[1] The Will of Oliver Lloyd, the donor of the Chalice to Clynnog Church, has been examined at Somerset House since the printing of the note on page 73, and in the codicil, dated October 9th, 1625, he bequeathed to that Church the sum of five pounds "to be paid at the feast of St. Peter next ensuing," which sum appears to have been expended in the purchase of this Chalice.

his appointment as Bishop of Bangor in recognition of his rescue from destruction of Church goods of the value of £1,000. Though the Bishop complained in a letter to Laud in 1639 that he had not then a " penny of yearly revenue to support the walls (of the Cathedral Church), much less to buy utensils," it is doubtless owing to his zeal and generosity that the Cathedral was provided with this service.

The majority of the Chalices of the Restoration period and the last quarter of the seventeenth century are quite plain, the form of the bowl resembling a beaker—supported by a truncated or trumpet-shaped stem —a type introduced in the reign of Charles I., of which the Clynnog and Llanaelhaiarn Chalices are fine examples. Of these there is one, made between 1660 and 1664, at Llanrhyddlad; one, with its Paten-Cover, given in 1672 to Rhiw by Frederick Wynne, of Bodwythog, then warden of that church. At Llanbedrog there is one (PLATE XVI., No. 2), dated 1693, which was presented by Love Parry, of Cefnllanfair, and there are others at Llangefni, Llanidloes and Waenfawr. To this group belong the two interesting Chalices, with remarkably short stems, wrought by Chester goldsmiths, at Llanfihangel-Bachellaeth (PLATE XVI., No. 1) and Pentraeth, which are stamped with the initials of Nathaniel Bullen, who flourished from about 1668 to 1712, and the word " sterling " in an abbreviated form—a mark used by Chester silversmiths in the seventeenth century, and by Irish silversmiths at Cork and Limerick, as a guarantee of quality, in the succeeding century. Another Chalice of this form, complete with Paten-Cover (PLATE XVI., No. 3), is at Llangian, and this bears the initials PP, representing Puleston Partington or Peter Pemberton of Chester, the sterling mark, and probably the date-letter for 1692-4. At Llansadwrn is another Chalice with Paten-Cover of this " Chester " type (PLATE XVII., No. 2), but differing from the other three in that the bowl is engraved with a narrow band or belt of roses, thistles, and shamrocks— an embellishment obviously suggested by the bands of arabesques on the Elizabethan Chalices with which the eye of the silversmith had no doubt become familiar from the numerous examples existing in his native city and elsewhere. The Llansadwrn Chalice has two marks, the initials T.G.

and " Sta," *i.e.*, sterling, the first standing for Timothy Gardener, who worked at Chester at the end of the seventeenth century, and whose distinctive mark is now, it is interesting to note, recorded for the first time.[1]

This same form prevailed to a very limited extent in the reign of Queen Anne, and examples of this period may be seen at Meillteyrn, where the Chalice appears to have been transformed in 1703 from an earlier one, to the order of " Arthur Williams, Esquire," whose name is inscribed thereon; another of 1710-11 is at Penllech; and late survivals of the same type, with high stems, of 1740 and 1797-8, are at Ynyscynhaiarn and Mallwyd respectively. The two Chalices of 1777 at Bangor Cathedral have the same beaker-like bowl on a truncated stem, with the addition, however, of a beading on the edges of the lip and foot.

The other Chalices of the seventeenth century in this diocese are the following:—At Dolgelley is one of 1683 (PLATE XXI.), with plain beaker-shape bowl, the stem encircled by a moulding, and engraved with the names of the then Rector, Maurice Jones, and the two church-wardens. A similar one, of 1697-8 (PLATE XXIII., No. 3), was given to Penmorfa by Sir Robert Owen, Knt., M.P. for Merioneth, 1681, and for Carnarvon, 1689-98, grandson of the Welsh royalist, Sir Robert Owen. Of quite a different type is the Chalice, dated 1694, at Pentir (PLATE X., No. 2), which has a deep beaker bowl, with a twisted rope

---

[1] Though no trace of a centre of the goldsmiths' craft established in any part of Wales can be found, many distinctly Welsh names appear amongst the Chester silversmiths of the sixteenth and seventeenth centuries, and the lists of enrolments of apprentices, from the year 1632, in the records of the important Goldsmiths' Company of Dublin—the Guild of All Saints—also include the names of four boys and their parents from different parts of Wales, as well as those of the craftsmen to whom they were apprenticed, and the dates, namely—

" 1660. Andrew Presland, son of Richard Presland, of Issaroyd, C°. Denbigh, gent., decd.—apprenticed to Thomas Parnell."

" 1667. Walter Lloyd, son of Jenkin Lloyd, D.D., Treaprise, Pembrokeshire— apprenticed to John Dickson."

" 1675. John Bennett, son of John Bennett, of Kidwelly, Carmarthenshire— apprenticed to John Popkins."

" 1675. John Bulkeley, son of William Bulkeley, of Anglesey, gent.—apprenticed to Walter Lewis."

moulding at the base, and supported by a short vase-shape stem on a plain splayed foot. The rope moulding is seen on several of the Chalices and much of the secular plate of this time; and among other examples which have come under the author's notice are a Chalice of 1674 at Llanllowell, Monmouthshire, and one with an engraved representation of the crucifixion on the bowl at Kirk Andreas, Isle of Man. At Llanfaes is a still earlier Chalice, of 1676-7, with a rope moulding at the top of the stem where it is joined to the bowl. A Chalice of another type is at Llandwrog, which has an exceptionally deep bowl on a very short baluster or vase-like stem, and which is dated 1699-1700; while another of similar type, in a reduced size, of the following year, is at Trefriw.

The main characteristic of the Chalices of the eighteenth century is their absolute plainness, combined with solidarity, the bowl still retaining a beaker-like form, though in many instances shewing a tendency to resemble an inverted bell. The stem is divided by the rudiments of a knop of varying widths and sizes. Many of the earlier Chalices are remarkable for their enormous size, as will be gathered from the dimensions quoted in the descriptive lists in this volume. Examples of these large ones, which vary in date from 1706 to 1715, and in height from $8\frac{1}{2}$ in. to $10\frac{3}{4}$ in., are in use in Anglesey at Holyhead—the legacy of John Owens, of Penrhos, in 1712, at Llandegfan and Llanfair-yn-Nghornwy; in Carnarvonshire at Llandegai, where one of 1714-15 (PLATE XXIII., No. 1) was given with two large silver Patens by Lord Edward Russell (second son of the first Duke of Bedford), who married Frances, daughter and heiress of Sir Robert Williams, Baronet, of Penrhyn; and at Penmachno, where there is a Chalice with Paten, dated 1713 (PLATE XXIII., No. 2), engraved with the arms of the donor, Roderick Lloyd, of Hafodwryd, a generous benefactor to the parish; in Merionethshire at Trawsfynydd; and in Montgomeryshire at Llanwnog, where the Chalice was given in 1707 by Hester Pryce, second daughter of John Thelwall, of Bathafarn Park, and widow of Matthew Pryce, of Park, M.P. for Montgomery in the two last parliaments of Charles II.

There can be no doubt that many of these capacious vessels replaced the smaller Elizabethan Chalices, which had then become too small for the number of communicants at a time when practically all the adult inhabitants attended the parish church at the Easter Festival. The Holyhead Chalice, large as it is, would not be too large even so late as 1776, when the Communicants on Easter Sunday numbered about four hundred, and when some signs are evident of the approaching upheaval in the Church as a result of the spread of Nonconformity in Wales. The parish of Aber succeeded in retaining its valuable Elizabethan Chalice when provided in 1712 with a large silver Chalice, Paten and Flagon (PLATE XIX.) by its pluralist Rector, John Jones, who was also Dean of Bangor. It will be noticed that most of these Chalices are engraved with the sacred monogram, I.H.S., a cross and nails in glory. The later silver Chalices of the eighteenth century follow the same lines as the foregoing in a reduced size, and some fifteen of these, dating from 1716 to 1782, were wrought by members of the well-known Richardson family, of Chester, silversmiths, established in that city for more than a century from the end of the seventeenth until early in the nineteenth century. Five, or perhaps six, members of this family were engaged in the trade of a silversmith—three Richards and two Williams. At Llanerchymedd is a very small Chalice of 1716-17 by the first Richard; at Bettws-y-coed is one which was given in 1731 by the second Duke of Ancaster; and at Festiniog is another Chalice of small size, dated 1782-3, by the third Richard. This important family, as well as other Chester silversmiths, was largely employed by clergy, wardens, and residents in the Dioceses of Bangor and S. Asaph, owing to the proximity of that city to North Wales.

Other pieces of plate in this diocese which may be singled out for mention include a very rare miniature silver Cup of the later part of the seventeenth century, only 3⅜ in. high (PLATE XXXIV., No. 4), at Carngiwch. Miniature articles in silver, such as Porringers, Cups, Goblets and Bowls, were produced in large numbers in the seventeenth, and to a limited extent in the eighteenth, century, as playthings and ornaments for the wealthy. They recall the miniature suits of armour

5

favoured in the reign of James I., and also the quaint old silver toys made by Dutch silversmiths.

An interesting reproduction in the reign of George II., in the year 1736, of an Elizabethan silver Chalice and Paten-Cover, with the well-known decorative embellishments, bands of arabesque work, is at Llangaffo, and was given by the then rector, the Rev. Thomas Holland, of Berw. It is not improbably an exact copy of the original Elizabethan Chalice belonging to that Church which had been rendered unfit for use owing to its dilapidated condition. Such copies of earlier Chalices are occasionally met with, some of them having been wrought by provincial goldsmiths, as is the case with one of 1682-3 at Windermere Parish Church, which was made by a York craftsman.

The silver-gilt Chalice with its Paten-Cover at Jesus College, Oxford, dating from the second year of the Restoration, is a very fine reproduction of an Elizabethan type. Whether this and the massive Flagon of 1670 are copies of the original sacramental plate belonging to the College, it is impossible to say with certainty, though this is highly probable.

A solitary specimen of plate—a large silver-gilt Alms Dish or Credence Paten with embossed gadroon border, of the date 1683-4—decorated with engraved work in the Chinese style, is at Beaumaris, and was given by Viscount Bulkeley in 1734. The taste for Chinese porcelain, which became exceedingly popular in the reign of William III., is largely responsible for the appearance of the Oriental designs on English plate of all kinds in the last quarter of the seventeenth century. The same taste prevailed also in Holland, and the artist Bérain created a fashion for it in France. The Earl of Derby has a gold Cup, with a single handle, decorated in this manner; and the only known silver Chalice and Paten-Cover engraved in the same style, with London hall-marks for 1689, is in the Church of Welsh Newton, in Herefordshire.

A very fine, large silver Loving Cup, with domed cover and two harp-shape handles, standing on a low foot, belongs to the Church of Llanfaglan. This cup, which was made at Dublin in 1723-4 by Thomas Sutton, was given, together with an old silver Salver of London make, of the date 1752-3, by Mrs. Susannah Jones, and is one of the only two pieces of Irish plate in the diocese, the other being the plain Charles I. cup on baluster stem (PLATE XIV., No. 2), probably wrought by William Hampton, Warden of the Goldsmiths' Company of Dublin in 1638-9. The taste for the vase-shape Cups and covers like that at Llanfaglan, which is chased with foliage, scrolls, and scales, was probably introduced into England by the talented group of French silversmiths who sought refuge here on the Revocation of the Edict of Nantes by Louis XIV., and who with their descendants produced so many admirable examples of the silversmiths' art in their adopted country.

Different in form and character is the tall, plain, and graceful Cup and cover, the latter surmounted by a flame-like finial (PLATE XXXII.), of London make of the year 1720-1, presented to Cemmaes Church in the same year by Mrs. Bridgett Mostyn, of Aberhirieth.

Other types of Chalices are to be seen at Bodfean, where the Chalice, which is of goblet form, boldly fluted, of the date 1772, was given by Sir John Wynn, Baronet; and the one of 1810 at Beaumaris (PLATE XX.), given by the seventh Viscount Bulkeley and his wife.

The post-Reformation Patens, as seen in the Elizabethan examples, act also as a cover for the Chalice, and overlap the lip of the bowl, and they are provided with a small X-shape foot or handle with a circular disc at the end which is sometimes engraved with a date. This same type continues in vogue in a lessening degree until the reign of Charles I. As early as the reign of James I., a tendency is noticeable, however, to widen and flatten the rim of the Paten, and not to overlap. The illustrations of the Chalices with Paten-Covers of 1623-4 at Bodfean (PLATE VII.); those of 1637-8 at Bangor Cathedral (PLATE XII.); and that of 1638-9 at Llanfairfechan, provide specimens of this innovation. They almost invariably have only a single depression for the bread, though three exist—the large ones of 1634-5, 1636-7 and 1638 at Llaniestyn (Carnarvonshire), Clynnog, and Llanaelhaiarn, respectively —with a double depression. The Paten-Cover on the unique Chalice at Beddgelert affords an example of quite a different form; it appears to have been modelled after the shallow bowl of the tazza, while the foot is engraved with the arms of the donor, previously referred to. Paten-Covers like those at Bangor Cathedral, but varying slightly in the width of the rim, depth of the depression, and size of the foot, remain in favour throughout the last half of the seventeenth, and a great part of the succeeding, century.

Silver Patens, independent of Chalices, *i.e.*, those which do not act the double part of Covers, are found in large numbers from the last quarter of the seventeenth century. Many of them assume large proportions, and, like the contemporary Chalices, they are invariably plain, except for embossed gadroon borders, and stand on truncated feet. Examples of those with gadroon borders are four in number: one of about 1690 at Llangristiolus; two in silver-gilt of 1699-1700 at Beaumaris (PLATE XX.), which were given in 1810 by the seventh and last Viscount Bulkeley and his wife; and one of the Queen Anne period, dated 1703-4 at Llanddeiniolen (PLATE XVIII.), which is engraved with the arms of the donor, Jane Wynne, wife of the then rector, Robert Wynne. Some of the Patens of the end of the seventeenth century have wide flat rims and very short truncated feet, and one of these is at Aber, the gift in 1677 of the Rev. Richard Fletcher (PLATE XIX.), and a similar one, though perhaps of later date, given in 1736 by Rev. Thomas Holland to Llangeinwen, is illustrated on PLATE XXXI., No. 2. An early Paten with a narrow reeded border on a short truncated foot, dated 1682-3, though given some few years later by Hugh Hughes, Deputy Baron of the Exchequer in North Wales, is preserved with the other valuable plate at Llangoed. A good example of the larger plain silver Patens with narrow moulded borders, standing on high truncated and moulded feet, may be seen at Aber (PLATE XIX.)—the gift in 1794 of the well-known Welsh naturalist, Hugh Davies, who was rector of that place—and an earlier one of 1713, which was a legacy of Thomas Parry, D.D., then rector, is at Machynlleth. At Llannor is a very large Paten of 1717, engraved with the arms of the donor (Bishop Majendie) impaling the arms of the See of Bangor, a Welsh scriptural inscription, and the date of the gift, 1815.

For two centuries or so a little silver Saucer-Dish of the reign of

Charles I. has acted as a Paten to the pre-Reformation silver Chalice in the Church of Llandudwen. This little piece (PLATE XV., No. 2), which is dated 1636-7, is a good representative specimen of those singular little sweetmeat dishes, produced between 1634 and 1655, remarkable for their flimsiness and crudeness, and in striking contrast to the solid and severe plainness of the other plate of this period. The designs usually consist of crude reproductions of fruit or flower-like forms, such as tulips, acorns and thistles, and also flutings, which are punched out with simple tools, and they frequently have two small handles somewhat like escallop shells. Their form is generally circular, though oval ones are known. Many have been given by benefactors to churches for the purposes of Patens and Alms-Dishes, and there is one of 1652 at Llanedeyrn in Glamorganshire.

Not a few domestic silver Salvers are found in use as Patens in several Churches in the diocese of Bangor. There is a charming little Salver, square in form, with shaped corners, standing on four feet, dated 1728-9, at Pennal. There are four with shaped borders, dating from 1742 to 1753, at Llanerchymedd, Trefdraeth, Llanfaglan and Penmorfa; and one of a different pattern, the edge being beaded, of the year 1784-5, belongs to Rhosbeirio.

The small Cruets, for wine and water, of pre-Reformation times, were superseded by large silver flagons, the earliest of which had globular or round bellied bodies. They did not, however, become general in those parishes which could afford the high cost of silver until after the year 1603, when a Canon enacted that the wine should be brought to the communion table " in a clean and sweet standing pot or stoup of pewter if not of purer metal." Examples of Elizabethan Flagons of this shape have survived at Cirencester Church, where there is a pair of 1576. Two of 1583 are at S. Margaret's, Westminster, and a single one of the same date, with a later copy of 1613, is at S. George's Chapel, Windsor. Another fine pair, dated 1592, of the same form, exists at Rendcombe in Gloucestershire, and to these may be added the superb pair of silver-gilt, ornamented with engraved strapwork, of the year 1598, the legacy of the foundress to Wadham College, Oxford.

Several Flagons of this type, decorated with flat repoussé work, varying in date from 1596 to 1612, form part of the remarkable collection of English plate included in the treasures of the Czar of Russia and of the Patriarch of Moscow in the Kremlin—the gifts of English Sovereigns—which will be illustrated and fully described in the author's forthcoming work on that collection.

The "bellied" Flagon gave way to a tall, upright, straight-sided Tankard-Flagon, used for domestic as well as ecclesiastical purposes, and sometimes lavishly decorated with repoussé work, strapwork, flowers, fruit, and medallions filled with marine monsters, etc. Specimens of these of the reign of James I. belong to the Corporation of Norwich of the year 1618, and a pair of the same date are at Bodmin Church. They gradually become plainer and less ornate, except for the retention of the delicate stamped ovolo borders, as seen on a fine pair of Flagon-Tankards of 1608-9, formerly belonging to the destroyed church of All Hallows the Great, E.C., and are finally succeeded by the absolutely plain and solid Flagon with flat cover and a wide splayed base, of which a fine specimen of the year 1638-9 (PLATE XII.) exists in the Cathedral Church at Bangor. This Flagon, which closely resembles two of the same date given to Llandaff Cathedral by Sir Charles Williams, the defender of Llangibby Castle against the Cromwellian forces, is the earliest silver Flagon in the diocese. This same style of Flagon continued until the end of the seventeenth century, and to some slight extent in the beginning of the following century, when the flattened cover is succeeded by a higher domed cover, which is in several instances surmounted by a knob. An interval of more than fifty years occurs between the date of the Charles I. Flagon at Bangor Cathedral and the next—the one of 1691-2 at Llanbeblig, and another of the same form of the year 1703-4 (PLATE XVIII.), at Llanddeiniolen, given respectively by Robert Wynne, Rector of the latter place, and his wife, Jane Wynne. Of the later silver Flagons with domed cover there are examples at Aber (PLATE XIX.) and Llanllechid, both of the same date—1719-20, and both the gifts of John Jones, then rector of these parishes and Dean of Bangor. Another of 1723-4 is at Dolgelley

Church (PLATE XXI.); a fourth, dated 1793-4, was given to Llanfach-reth, Merioneth, in 1803, by Sir R. Williames-Vaughan, second Baronet, and his wife; and a fifth Flagon, which is a late copy, dated 1773-4, of an early plain Flagon, like that of 1638-9 at Bangor Cathedral, is to be seen at Mallwyd. The silver-gilt Flagon of the year 1777-8, belonging to the second service of sacramental plate in the Cathedral at Bangor, differs from all the other Flagons in that the borders of the cover and base are beaded like the other portions of the service (PLATE XIII.).

Domestic jugs are frequently requisitioned as Flagons in churches, and specimens of these are in use at Llandegfan, where there is one of 1708-9 with a tall, plain, vase-shape body and domed cover; at Beaumaris, where there are two, dated 1771-2 and 1810-11 (PLATE XX.); and a fourth of 1767 at Llanfaes. The three latter have gadroon borders, while the borders of the one at Llandegfan are plain. A silver Jug of another variety, of the year 1738-9, is at Llanelltyd (PLATE XXVII., No. 2).

Ordinary beer tankards are also found doing duty as Flagons, and one of these, which is at Llansadwrn, is fully described later.

Alms Dishes did not come into general use until the seventeenth century, though there is a plain gilt one of 1556 described as such, but more probably a rose-water dish, at S. George's Chapel, Windsor. An early one, of the date 1635, is at Lambeth Palace Chapel. Many of the seventeenth century Alms Dishes are very massive and plain, like the one of 1638-9 at Bangor Cathedral (PLATE XII.). There is a fine Dish, almost as large, made in 1678, amongst the plate of S. David's Cathedral. Two other Alms Dishes, of different sizes, with beaded borders and engraved with the arms of the see, surmounted by a bishop's mitre, belong to the service of silver-gilt sacramental plate (PLATE XIII.) supplied to the Cathedral Church at Bangor in 1777-8, during the episcopate of John Moore, afterwards Archbishop of Canterbury. At Beaumaris there are two with embossed gadroon borders, dated 1810; and at Llandwrog is a large Queen Anne dish of 1703-4. Silver Dishes, which had not been originally intended for ecclesiastical purposes, are at Holyhead, where there is one of 1744-5; and at Aberffraw and Llangadwaladr, which contain two dishes of 1761-2, given by Sir Arthur Owen, third baronet. Two Soup Plates, with fluted borders, which were made at Newcastle in 1778-9, were presented in 1812 to the Churches of Llanfaes and Penmon by the seventh Viscount Bulkeley.

Seven small silver sets for private communion have been found in the diocese of Bangor, and all these were made between 1810-11 and 1819-20. The Chalices and Patens are entirely of silver, and where a receptacle for carrying wine to the sick has been provided, it takes the form of a plain glass bottle with a silver top. The three sets at Llandegfan, Llanfaes, and Penmon in Anglesey, dated 1810-11 and 1812-13, are engraved with the sacred monogram, I.H.S., and were given, like much of the other plate in these churches, by Thomas James Warren Bulkeley, seventh and last Viscount Bulkeley. These three sets have no bottle for the wine, and the Paten at Penmon has been lost. There is a set dated 1808-9 (PLATE XXXIV., No. 3) at Llanfachreth, Merioneth, and a similar set of the following year belongs to the adjoining parish of Llanelltyd. Both these sets are engraved with the name of the rector or vicar, who appears to have held both livings at that time, and also the names of the churchwardens. At Penmachno there is a set of 1814-15 (PLATE XXXIV., No. 1), given by Sir R. Williames-Vaughan, second baronet, of Nannau and Hengwrt; and at Llandegai there is a set (PLATE XXXIV., No. 2), consisting of a small silver Plate in addition to the Chalice, Paten and Glass Bottle, which have the hallmark for 1819-20, though inscribed as the gift of Lady Penrhyn in 1816. A small silver-gilt Chalice, dated 1809-10, of quite another form is at Beaumaris—a reproduction in a much reduced size of the large silver Chalices in that church.

The only pieces of foreign plate in this diocese are the fine German silver-gilt cup at Llanfechell in Anglesey (PLATE VI., No. 1), which has an oviform body, decorated with interlaced strap-work and delicate arabesques in slight relief, the same decoration being repeated on the circular foot. The base of the bowl is embellished with three applied oval medallions of cherub faces surrounded by scrolls, fruit and flowers.

It was wrought in the last quarter of the sixteenth century, about 1585, by Hans Zeiher, of Nuremberg, who was master of the famous Guild of Goldsmiths of that city in 1583, but did not reach this little Anglesey church until a century later, namely, in 1686, as a joint gift of David Lloyd, then rector of the parish, and his wife. The second specimen of plate of foreign origin is the rose-water Dish boldly embossed with a pelican in her piety—the well-known Christian symbol—in the centre, and with vines, foliage, etc., on the wide border, which is probably of Dutch workmanship of about 1685, at Bottwnog (PLATE XV., No. 1). This Dish was doubtless intended as an Alms Dish at the time it was given to this church in 1704 by Dorothy Randolph, daughter of Humphrey Randolph, who was rector there at that date. Rose-water Dishes of similar character were produced in large numbers by Dutch, and especially German, silversmiths, at the end of the seventeenth century. The third example is in the new Church of Brithdir in Merionethshire, namely, a metal-gilt Italian Chalice of no special interest, presented by the foundress.

The new silver plate includes a complete service given to S. Seiriol's, Penmaenmawr, by the late eminent statesman, the Right Honble. W. E. Gladstone.

The diocese still retains a goodly number of old pewter vessels of great variety of form and date. The earliest example is the very fine Charles I. Flagon, in a perfect state of preservation, the gift of William Wynn to Llangoed Church in 1637 (PLATE XVII., No. 1). This Flagon, which bears an unknown pewterer's mark, described on page 39, is closely followed in date by a very similar Flagon, unfortunately in a neglected condition, given to Llangelynin Church, Carnarvonshire, by John Edwards, in the following year. A pewter Flagon, resembling these two, of the early date of 1620, is in the church at Trelleck, Monmouthshire, and another, dated 1642, once in the parish church of Seaford, Sussex, is now in the British Museum. These Flagons are modelled after the contemporary silver Flagons. Considerable variation is noticeable in the form and size of the numerous pewter Flagons, among the more interesting specimens being those at

6

Llanfachraeth and Llanfair-yn-Nghornwy, in Anglesey. The former, which is very tall, with plain sloping body and high domed cover, probably dates from about 1700, and is very like one by the same maker at Llanenddwyn, Merioneth. The Llanfair-yn-Nghornwy Flagon is shorter, with two flat bands encircling the body, and a flat cover, and is engraved with the initials of the original owners and the date 1714. At Llanfechell is a Flagon with flat cover and a short spout, not unlike the Scotch Lavers which date from the latter part of the eighteenth century. Quite a distinct type, more jug-shape than flagon, survives, though in a dilapidated state, at Llanfrothen. It was given, as the inscription denotes, in 1698, by the father of Bishop Humphrey Humphreys, of Bangor, and later of Hereford. Two tall Flagons, exactly similar in form and size, of late seventeenth century date, are at Caerhun; one is plain, while the other is engraved with tulips and other flowers, and on the flat cover there is a stag, in imitation of the embossed work on silver plate of the period of Charles II. This is the only piece of pewter, with any pretensions to decoration, found throughout the diocese.

Other Flagons deserving of more than passing notice are one with a flat cover, presented in 1694 with a pewter plate to Llanbedrog by Love Parry, of Cefnllanfair, who had already provided the church with a massive silver Chalice and Paten-Cover in the previous year; two of different sizes at Towyn; one, dated 1722, at Llanfairfechan; one with globular body and short spout, dated 1728, and engraved with the initials of the vicar and wardens at Abererch; and one of the year 1767 at Llandrygan.

Many of these old Flagons, though intrinsically valueless, by reason of a simple plainness in combination with a pleasing proportion, compel our admiration, and should be carefully treasured. They have in the past been employed not only for communion wine, but also for "Church Ales," for serving hot spiced drinks at funerals, as well as local festivities, in many parishes in Wales even within living memory. The parish register of one parish mentions the quantity of ale drunk at the vestry held "about the militia," namely, a quart a-piece by each person, and the same document refers to the cost of the ale consumed at the summer and autumn vestries, and on these occasions the church Flagon was brought into use. Even the silver Flagons would seem to have been used on similar occasions, for the rector of Llanfechain, in Montgomeryshire, on his appointment to that incumbency in 1851, appears to have raised an objection to the desecration of the sacred vessel in his parish "for the purpose of handing out to each of the attendants on the occasion of funerals for spiced drink, wine or ale." Many other instances of the use of these Flagons for such purposes might be cited.

The enormous size of many of these old Flagons, which has often been remarked upon, is no doubt due to the necessity for providing a large quantity of wine for the celebration of the communion prior to the rise of Nonconformity in Wales, when it may be said that almost the entire adult population of a parish received the communion at the great festival of the Church—Easter Day. At Towyn, where there are two Flagons of large capacity, the average number of monthly communicants was sixty to one hundred, and on Easter Day the number rose to six hundred, as late as the year 1776, when the Church was at a low ebb, and signs of the coming revolt were making themselves manifest in many parishes in Wales.

Occasionally, ordinary beer tankards are met with, and certainly three of these are to be found in this diocese. The one at Dolwyddelan, which has an inscription in Welsh with the name of the donor and the date 1779, has a sloping body with domed cover, and follows in its form the plain silver tankard prevailing about 1725. A similar tankard is at Llanrug, and another, in a battered condition, is at Carngiwch. A quart beer mug, with shaped body, also engraved with a Welsh inscription and the date 1738, is at Capel Curig, where there is a pair of tall pewter candlesticks with beaded edges on circular bases, of about the date 1815—the only candlesticks in silver or pewter in any church in the Bangor diocese.

Pewter Cups, with vase-shape bodies and two handles, are at Llanengan and Penegoes.

Patens, standing on circular feet, like the silver Patens, exist at Llanfechell and Llanwnog, and one with a gadrooned border may be seen at Penegoes.

Pewter Plates, some used as Patens, others as Alms Dishes and Collecting Plates, of every size, are common throughout the diocese, the earliest dated example being a large one of 1671 at Conway, where there is also another Plate, inscribed with the date 1719 and the names of the churchwardens. A Paten and two large Plates or Dishes, engraved with the name of the rector, Ellis Thomas, and the initials of the churchwardens, with the date 1767, are at Llanllyfni; and a large flat Bowl or Dish, dating from perhaps 1700, appears at Caerhun with the two interesting Flagons already described.

The only pewter Font-Bowl or Basin found by the author is at Llanllyfni. These vessels are fairly common in Pembrokeshire, where eight are recorded. Though the attempted suppression of fonts, owing to the supposed superstition attaching to the baptismal rite, by the Cromwellian parliament, ended in failure in a large number of cases, the injunction that basins should be provided in their place was no doubt obeyed in some instances. The Llanllyfni bowl, however, can hardly date from the Commonwealth period, its appearance suggesting a date considerably later, perhaps early in the eighteenth century.

A little piece of pewter, unique of its kind in this diocese, namely, a plain two handled Porringer, is at Llanfrothen. Its maker has been guided in fashioning it by the familiar silver Porringers so extensively used for spiced drinks between 1660 and 1710, and the date of this interesting little vessel cannot be later than 1700; in all probability it may be a few years earlier.

No old pewter vessels of strictly Chalice form have come under notice in the diocese.

Several new pewterers' as well as silversmiths' marks, hitherto unknown, will be found described in the following pages, and these include not only London marks, but also those of provincial pewterers, namely, a Plate at Heneglwys, made at Liverpool; another at Trewalchmai, with the name H. Baldwin, of Liverpool; a Dish, stamped " Birmingham "; and another Plate with the name Yates and Birch, Birmingham, is at Penstrowed. Though pewterers were established at Dublin and other places in Ireland, no pieces of pewter found in this part of Wales can claim an Irish origin, the bulk of the plate having apparently come from the workshops of London pewterers.

Numerous pieces of old Sheffield-plate are scattered about the diocese, and these consist chiefly of Salvers used as Patens or Collecting Plates. There is a complete service of four vessels—Chalice, Paten, Flagon and Dish—given in 1808 to Llanllechid by the Rev. W. W. Coytmor, D.D., of Coytmor in that parish; another service of the same number of vessels, engraved with a baron's coronet and two initials, belong to the church at S. Ann's; and a third at Dwygyfylchi. A Tankard-Flagon, the gift of Viscount Bulkeley in 1817, is at Llangwyllog; a Chalice and Paten of the year 1823 at Cerrigceinwen; a fine Cup, with a Salver, at Llanfaelrhys; and a plain Porringer is at Llangelynin, Carnarvonshire. Soup plates with the date 1821, intended for Patens, are at Treflys and Ynyscynhaiarn.

It will be observed that the dates engraved on much of the silver sacramental plate in the diocese of Bangor, as well as in other parts of England and Wales, cannot always be relied upon as safe guides to the actual date when it was wrought. The valuable German cup at Llanfechell, as previously pointed out, was made in the last quarter of the sixteenth century, whereas the date engraved on it is about a century later, namely 1686. The rare piece of Elizabethan plate, the Tazza, with London date-letter for 1570-1, and the Charles I. Cup of 1638-9, both at Penmynydd, are dated 1707. An Elizabethan Chalice at Rhodwyddgeidio bears the date 1714, though made, or transformed from a medieval Chalice, by a London silversmith in 1574-5. Cups of the reign of Charles I., of the years 1633, 1638, and 1641, at Llanbeblig, Llangybi and Bodewryd, were given by Dr. Peploe, Chancellor of Chester; Thomas Wynne, of Coed Caegwyn; and Edward Wynne, Chancellor of Hereford, respectively, in two cases about a century, and in the other 131 years, later than the date of the hall-mark. The Commonwealth Cup at Carno is dated 1676, and the silver Chalice at Pentraeth, though made about 1685, is inscribed with a date exactly one hundred years after.

Old silver plate, which had in many instances formed part of the domestic utensils of a parishioner, is frequently found in new churches, *e.g.*, at Bryncoedifor there is a charming little Cup of the Commonwealth period (which, with the larger Cup at Carno, are the only two examples in this diocese of the limited quantity of plate wrought at that unsettled time), and also a George I. Paten, engraved with a shield of arms (PLATE XXVII., No. 1); S. David's, Barmouth, contains a fine Chalice of 1633-4, similar to those at Llanwnda and Rhosbeirio, previously described. An old Chalice of about 1690 is in use at Waenfawr, and in the little mission church at Prenteg, near Portmadoc, are a George III. Goblet of 1787-8 and a Salver of 1827-8.

Amongst the notable pieces of sacramental plate recorded in old terriers, which have disappeared from this diocese as recently as the nineteenth century, are three Elizabethan Chalices, one dated 1567 and two others 1574, from Conway, Aberdaron and Bodedern, respectively; a Paten-Cover of 1576 from Llanbedr-y-Cenin; and the two Chalices belonging to the Paten-Covers, both dated 1574, at Llanddona and Llanfwrog.

A Chalice, inscribed—" The gift of Mr. Robert Parry, Cittyson of London, the son of Mr. John Parry of Nevinne 1679," is missing from Nevin, the Paten-Cover which belongs to it being, however, still extant. Beaumaris Church has lost a silver-gilt Chalice, the gift of Anne Sparrow in 1693, and a small Chalice, described in the terrier as " bought in 1752 at the expense of the town." Other plate, of which no trace can be found, includes a Chalice presented by William Griffith, of Cefnamlwch, to Dolbenmaen; a Flagon, dated 1782, a Plate, 1776, and another silver Chalice, in addition to the Elizabethan Chalice mentioned above, said to have been stolen from Conway Church about fifty years ago. A " Salver " of 1687, and a Chalice of 1731, have disappeared from Llanfaglan. Several other silver Chalices, which are only briefly enumerated in the terriers, have been lost.

Not a few pieces of old plate have from time to time been transformed from their original shape into new forms, either to meet changes of fashion, or, where a Chalice or other vessel was in a broken condition, for (perhaps) economical reasons, the intrinsic value of the metal being much greater than it is now. The Chalice at Caerhun (PLATE XXV., No. 1) is an instance where the original Elizabethan vessel has doubtless been re-made, probably about a century later, into another type, and the original date of 1574 retained. A Chalice, which was transferred to Penmon in 1812 from Llandegfan, to which it had been given in 1639 by Thomas Davies, who is described on a tablet in that church as a native of the parish and "servant to yᵉ two most illustrious Princes Henry and Charles both Princes of Wales and now to King Charles yᵉ First,"[1] appears to have suffered transformation in 1812. One of the silver-gilt Chalices at Beaumaris, the gift in 1810 of the seventh Viscount Bulkeley and his wife, reveals traces of hall-marks of an earlier date. The Chalice and Paten, dated 1842-3, at Llanedwen, have been re-fashioned from older pieces of plate, the Paten bearing the London date-letter for 1776-7. A Chalice and Alms-Dish, at Llanidan, re-constructed in 1871-2 from Queen Anne plate of 1701-2, are inscribed with the name of the original donor, Pierce Lloyd of Lligwy and Llanidan. To this list may also be added the Chalice at Llanbeblig, dated 1715, which was re-made in 1851.

While a lack of appreciation for the ancient possessions of our parish churches is not altogether surprising at the time when many of the foregoing sacramental vessels were sent to the silversmith's workshop for re-construction, no words can be too strong in condemnation of such practices in the present day. As recently as 1878 an old silver Chalice, the gift of John Roberts to Maentwrog Church in 1743, was entirely transformed into a "medieval" design; and still more recently, in the year 1888, a Chalice at Towyn suffered a like fate on the ground that the original form of the vessel was "inconvenient"! Where the dilapidated condition of old plate from long usage necessitates more than a mere putting together of a broken fragment in its original position, or the simple repair of cracked parts, the author ventures to urge that these precious relics, many of them hallowed by the most sacred associations throughout long centuries, should be carefully put away in a place of safety in the church and religiously preserved.

[1] Thomas Davies was Constable of Hawarden Castle in 1643.

A regrettable inclination is displayed in some quarters to dispose of Church plate of a domestic origin on the ground that it had never been intended for ecclesiastical purposes, and that consequently its sale could not be regarded as a form of desecration, though one would have thought that the mere fact that a Cup, for example, had been used in the service of the Communion through many generations of parishioners ought to have been sufficient to prove the weakness of such reasoning. The superb Elizabethan Cup and Cover at Llanbadrig, and the valuable Tazza at Penmynydd, are purely secular vessels, but it would be nothing short of sacrilege to offer them for sale.

The Vicar and Churchwardens are the trustees of the sacramental plate as of the other furniture of the Church, but the property is in reality vested in the parishioners, and it cannot be too generally known that a faculty must be obtained before the disposal of plate can take place.

At the Reformation all that was beautiful, if there was the slightest suspicion of superstition connected with it, was ruthlessly destroyed. Later, during the Civil War, vast quantities of the most precious plate, ecclesiastical and secular, as well as other works of art, which can never be replaced, suffered destruction. And in Wales, too, in those days when pluralist and non-resident clergy allowed church fabrics to fall into ruins and when clerical neglect hastened the advent of Nonconformity, much plate disappeared. Now, however, a greater reverence for our ancient possessions is slowly springing up, and this feeling will, it may be hoped, be too powerful for those who propose to sell these valuable relics.

On the James I. Chalice at Llangeinwen, and on the more famous Cup given to Pembroke College, Cambridge, by Dr. Thomas Langton (who became successively Bishop of S. David's, Salisbury and Winchester), is the inscription—" QUI ALIENARIT ANATHEMA SIT." Can one venture to hope that the day will soon come when inscriptions such as this, and the curse that it contains, will be unnecessary?

PLATE II.

CLYNNOG, CARNARVONSHIRE.
MAZER BOWL OF MAPLE WOOD, WITH SILVER-GILT MOUNTS.
DATE : 1480-90.

ANGLESEY

ABERFFRAW—S. BEUNO

THE Chalice here is of plain silver, and of goblet form, 6¾ in. high, and bears the London hall-mark for the year 1866-7.

The Paten is an ordinary silver dish, circular in shape, 9 in. in diameter, the slightly domed centre being engraved with I.H.S., cross, and three nails in glory. On the back this inscription is engraved in script lettering in a circle:—" The gift of Sʳ. Arthur Owen Barᵗ., to the Parish Church of Aberffraw, 1753."

London date-letter for 1761-2. Maker's mark, F·C, with pellet between, in an oblong (Fras. Crump).

An exactly similar dish is in the Church of the adjoining Parish of Llangadwaladr, and was given by the same donor, Sir Arthur Owen, third Baronet (son of Sir Hugh Owen, of Orielton, who married his cousin, Anne Owen, heiress of Bodeon), M.P. for the town and county of Pembroke, married to Emma, daughter of the famous Speaker, Sir William Williams, Bart. Sir Arthur Owen gave in 1753 a silver salver to the Church of Martletwy, and a silver Chalice and Paten-Cover, dated 1711, to the Church of Lamphey, both in Pembrokeshire.

The terriers for the years 1793, 1801, and 1808, contain a list of the plate in existence then, and of this a silver Chalice, a pewter Flagon, and a pewter Paten have disappeared.

AMLWCH—S. ELAETH

CHALICE.—A plain silver Chalice, with deep, inverted, bell-shape bowl, supported by a thick stem with plain knop in the centre, resting on a moulded foot. On one side it is engraved with the arms of the See of Bangor conjoined with those of the donor, Bishop Majendie, *or, on a mount vert a tree between a serpent erect and a dove close.* On the opposite side this Welsh inscription is engraved:—" Y cwppan hwn yw'r testament newydd i yr hwn yr ydys yn ei dywallt drosoch. S. Luc. xxii. 20." And also the sacred letters, I.H.S., cross and three nails. The Chalice is inscribed underneath—

" The Gift of Henry William, Lord Bishop of Bangor,
To the Parish of Amlwch
A.D. 1815."

The donor was Bishop of Chester from 1800 until 1809, when he was translated to the See of Bangor, which he held until 1830.

Marks.—London date-letter for 1717-8. Maker's mark illegible.

Dimensions.—Height, 8 in.; depth of bowl, 4½ in.; diameter of mouth, 3¾ in.

PATEN.—A silver Salver, with shaped and floreated border, plain centre, inscribed—

"OS BWYTTY NEB O'R BARA HWN,
EFE A FYDD BYW YN DRAGYWYDD.   JOAN VI. 51."

And in the centre on an applied shield—

"AMLWCH,
1817."

The three feet have been removed.   Weight marked, 23 ozs. 15 dwts.
Marks.—London date-letter for 1743-4.   Maker's mark, GH, in an oblong (Geo. Hindmarsh).
Diameter, 11 in.

FLAGON.—A plain silver Flagon, with globular body, a vase-shape knob on the cover, the handle springing from vine leaves.   Inscribed—

"St Eleth, Amlwch
To the Glory of God
and in Loving Memory of
the Rev. Richard Roberts
15 years Vicar of this Parish.
Given by his only Daughter
October, 1888."

Marks.—London date-letter for 1888-9.   Maker's mark, TP in an oblong.
Height to top of cover, 10½ in.
The old terriers for 1788 allude to two pewter Flagons, a pewter Dish, and an old silver Chalice, all of which have, unhappily, disappeared.

BEAUMARIS—S. MARY

CHALICE (1).—A silver-gilt Chalice with tapering beaker-shape bowl, the lip reeded, a plain moulding encircling the bowl near the top; the base of bowl moulded. A plain, flat knop, between two collars, in the centre of stem; a moulded foot with gadroon edge. Inscribed—

PLATE III.

LLANBADRIG, ANGLESEY.
ELIZABETHAN SILVER-GILT CUP AND COVER.
DATE : 1573-4.

"The Gift of Thos. James Warren Bulkeley Lord Viscount Bulkeley
and of Eliz{h}. Harriet his Consort
To the Church of St. Mary's at Beaumaris
for the Use and Service of
THE HOLY SACRAMENT
July 2nd 1810."

PATEN-COVER.—The Paten-Cover of this Chalice has a gadroon border, and is engraved with the letters I.H.S., a cross and three nails in glory, and with the same inscription as on the Chalice.

These two pieces show the undecipherable remains of a hall-mark of about a century previous to the date of the gift, thus proving that they have been wrought from older plate.

Dimensions.—Chalice, height, $6\frac{1}{2}$ in.; depth of bowl, $3\frac{1}{2}$ in.; diameter of mouth, $3\frac{3}{4}$ in. Paten-Cover is $3\frac{7}{8}$ in. in diameter.

CHALICE (2).—This is of silver-gilt, and exactly like the other Chalice, and is engraved with the same inscription. It has lost its Paten-Cover.

Marks.—London date-letter for 1809-10. Maker's mark, IC, with pellet between, in an oblong shield.

Dimensions.—The same as the other Chalice.

FLAGON.—A large and massive jug-shape Flagon, of domestic rather than ecclesiastical character; plain, vase-shape body, the edge of lip and spout gadrooned, and a rope moulding running along the lip; the top of scroll handle, with an acanthus leaf on the shoulder, springs from an applied acanthus leaf; a domed, jointed cover, surmounted by a fluted vase-shape knob; a truncated foot with gadroon edge. It is engraved in the centre under the spout with the sacred letters I.H.S., a cross and three nails in glory, and with this inscription—

"The Gift of
Thos. James Warren Bulkeley
Lord Viscount Bulkeley
and of
Eliz{h}. Harriet his Consort
To the Church of
St. Mary's at Beaumaris
for the Use and Service of
THE HOLY SACRAMENT
July 2nd 1810."

B 2

Marks.—London date-letter for 1771-2.   Maker's mark (indistinct) probably Fra^s. Butty and Nicks Dumee.

Dimensions.—Height to top of knob on cover, 12½ in.

FLAGON.—Another silver-gilt Jug, exactly like the other, with the same inscription, the only difference being that this was made in 1810-11, while the other was wrought in 1771-2.

Marks.—London date-letter for 1810-11.   Maker's mark, IC, with pellet between, in an oblong, same as on Chalice No. 2.

PATENS.—Two large silver-gilt Patens, plain centres, with embossed gadroon edges, the same gadroon edge appearing on the truncated feet.   One has IB and AB engraved under the foot. In the centre is engraved the conventional device of the sacred letters, I.H.S., a cross and three nails in glory, surrounded by this inscription—

" The Gift of Thomas James Warren Bulkeley Lord Viscount Bulkeley
and of Elizth. Harriet, his Consort
To the Church of St. Mary's at Beaumaris
for the Use and Service of THE HOLY SACRAMENT
July 2nd, 1810."

Marks.—London date-letter for 1699-1700.   Maker's mark, T.A., in script capitals, in monogram.

Dimensions.—Diameter, 9⅛ in. ; height, 2½ in.

ALMS DISHES.—Two large, circular, silver-gilt Alms or Collecting Dishes, with wide, embossed gadroon border, engraved with the same device and inscription as on the two Patens.   The truncated foot has been removed from each.   There are no marks.   Probable date, 1810—the date of the gift.   Diameter, 10¼ in.

ALMS DISH OR CREDENCE PATEN.—-A large and massive silver-gilt Dish, circular in shape, engraved with Chinese subjects, embossed gadroon border ; plain truncated foot.   In the centre a shield of arms : *a chevron between three bulls' heads cabossed,* surmounted by a viscount's coronet.   Inscribed—

"The Gift of ye R^t. Honble. Visco^t. Bulkeley
to ye Church of Beaumaris An^o. 1734."

Marks.—London date-letter for 1683-4.   Maker's mark, HS, conjoined, in an oval, the S linked to the second stroke of the H.

Dimensions.—Diameter, 13⅝ in. ; height, 3 in.

Weight marked, 32 ozs. 11 dwts.

This is the only piece of plate in the Diocese of Bangor engraved with subjects in the Chinese taste—a style of decoration found on English plate during the last quarter of the seventeenth century. (PLATE XX.)

A large old Pewter Dish, circular, stamped with two marks—an eagle's claw issuing from a ducal coronet, repeated twice, and "LONDON" in a label. Diameter, $15\frac{1}{8}$ in.

An Escallop Shell, intended for Baptismal purposes, carved on the back with the figures of the two Italian Saints, S. Francis of Assisi and S. Anthony of Padua, with their names in Italian—"S. francese, S. Antonio." It is probably Italian work of the nineteenth century, and is said to have been given by the late Rector, the Rev. John Williams Meyrick.

A silver-gilt Spoon, of the ordinary table-spoon type, with reeded edge, one side of the bowl pierced as a strainer. The device, I.H.S., a cross and three nails in glory, engraved on the back, and this inscription—"Beaumaris Church, July 2, 1810," on the front of the handle. 8 in. long. Date, *circa* 1750. Maker's mark, probably Wm. Young.

CHALICE.—A small silver-gilt Chalice for private Communion. It is in all respects, except size, like the two larger ones here, and is inscribed—

" The Gift of Thomas James Warren Bulkeley
Lord Viscount Bulkeley and of Eliz^h. Harriet his
Consort To the Church of S^t. Mary's at Beaumaris
For the Use and Service of
THE HOLY SACRAMENT
July 2nd 1810 "

The Christian symbols, I.H.S., a cross and three nails in glory, are engraved on it.

Marks.—London date-letter for 1809-10. Maker's mark, I·C, with pellet between, in an oblong cartouche.

Dimensions.—Height, $4\frac{1}{8}$ in.; depth of bowl, $2\frac{1}{2}$ in.; diameter of mouth, $2\frac{1}{8}$ in.; diameter of foot, $2\frac{5}{16}$ in.

The terriers between 1763 and 1778 contain references to a " silver Chalice, with a high top, gilt with gold, the gift of Ann Sparrow, Widow, to the Chapel of St. Mary's in Beaumaris 1693," and to a smaller silver Chalice, " used in visiting the sick, marked ' Beaumaris 1752,' bought at the expense of the Town." These are not now in existence. The Sparrows lived at Red Hill, Beaumaris.

The donor of the Alms Dish or Credence Paten at Beaumaris was Richard, fifth Viscount Bulkeley, M.P. for Beaumaris 1734-38, married

Jane, daughter and heiress of Lewis Owen, Esquire, of Peniarth, Merioneth. He died in 1738.

The donors of the other silver plate were Thomas James Warren Bulkeley, seventh Viscount Bulkeley, M.P. for Anglesey 1774-1784, created in 1784 a peer of Great Britain, by the title of Lord Bulkeley of Beaumaris, and his wife, Elizabeth Harriet, only daughter and heiress of Sir George Warren, Knt., of Poynton, Cheshire. With his death in 1822 the title became extinct.

BODEDERN—S. EDEYRN

CHALICE.—A plain silver Chalice, with egg-shape bowl, on stem. It has a domed cover with foot.

Marks.—Chester date-letter for 1887-8.

Dimensions.—Height, 7¼ in.; diameter, 3⅞ in.; height, with cover, 8⅜ in.

PATEN.—A plain silver Paten on truncated stem.

Marks.—London date-letter for 1803-4. Maker's mark, $^{P\,B}_{W\,B}$ in a square (Peter and Wm. Bateman).

Dimensions.—Diameter, 7 in.; height, 2¼ in.

FLAGON.—A plain silver Flagon, the body cylindrical, a moulding encircling lower part, spreading moulded foot, domed cover, pierced thumb-piece, scrolled handle. Inscribed—

"BODEDERN
1809."

Marks.—London date-letter for 1808-9. Maker's mark is the same as on the Paten.

Dimensions.—Height to top of cover, 10 in.; body only, 8½ in.; diameter of mouth, 3½ in.

The terriers from 1776 until 1831 mention "a silver Chalice with the year of our Lord 1574 on the lid," and the earlier terriers allude to a pewter Flagon and a Paten, but all these have disappeared.

BODEWRYD—S. MARY

CHALICE.—A plain silver Chalice with inverted bell-shape bowl, supported by a baluster stem on splayed foot, inscribed—

"The Gift of Doctor Edward Wynne Chancellor of Hereford to the Church of Bodewryd."

PLATE IV.

SILVER-GILT MEDALLION IN
BOWL OF TAZZA.

PENMYNYDD, ANGLESEY.
ELIZABETHAN TAZZA, PARCEL-GILT.
DATE : 1570-1.

On the bowl is a human skull, faintly engraved, and the initials IP, pounced.

Marks.—London date-letter for 1641-2. Maker's mark, CP, with mullet below, in heart-shape shield.

Dimensions.—Height, 6¾ in.; depth of bowl, 3⅜ in.; diameter of mouth, 3¾ in.

The donor was the second son of the Rev. Edward Wynne, M.A., Rector of Llantrisant, and Margaret his wife, eldest daughter of Robert Morgan, Bishop of Bangor. Dr. Edward Wynne was appointed Vicar-General and Official Principal and Chancellor of the Diocese of Hereford by Bishop Humphrey Humphreys on the 19th May, 1707, and held the appointment for some forty-six or forty-seven years.

CHALICE AND PATEN.—A large, plain silver Chalice, with deep beaker-shape bowl, the lip curved, supported by a thick stem, divided by a plain knob, on a moulded foot. Inscribed—

"The Legacy of Ellin Wynne to the Church
of Bodewyrd who died August yᵉ 14. 1703."

The Paten-Cover has a flat depression, with narrow, flat, raised edge, and has a foot. It has an inscription as on Chalice.

Marks.—London date-letter for 1703-4. Maker's mark, Pa, with vase above, pellet below, in shaped shield (Humphrey Payne).

Dimensions.—Chalice, 9¼ in. high; bowl, 5⅝ in. deep; diameter of mouth, 4¼ in. Paten-Cover, 5½ in. in diameter; 1 in. high.

The donor was the sister of Dr. Edward Wynne, who gave the other Chalice.

A pewter Flagon, mentioned in the terrier for the year 1801, has disappeared.

BODWROG—S. TWROG

CHALICE.—A plain silver Chalice, with inverted bell-shape bowl, supported by a stem, with narrow moulding in centre, on a moulded foot. Inscribed—

"W ×O Bodwrog 1773."

Marks.—London date-letter for 1772-3. Maker's mark, TW, with pellet between, in an oblong.

Dimensions.—Height, 6⅝ in.; depth of bowl, 3½ in.; diameter of mouth, 3¼ in.

BRYNGWRAN

Electro-plated set of Chalice, Paten, and small Alms Dish, each inscribed—"Bryngwran Chapel, Anglesey. J. W. Trevor, M.A., Rector, 1842."

CEIRCHIOG

This Church contained in 1817 and 1821, according to the terriers, a small silver Chalice, a pewter Flagon, and a pewter Dish, but these have unfortunately disappeared.

CERRIGCEINWEN—S. CEINWEN

CHALICE.—A large plain Chalice, of old Sheffield plate, the bowl inverted bell shape, on short stem. Inscribed under foot—

" CERIGEINWEN

PARISH

1823."

Height, 7½ in.

PATEN.—A plain old Sheffield-plate Paten on foot, the sacred letters, I.H.S., in glory, engraved in centre. The same inscription as on Chalice engraved on the foot.

Diameter, 9½ in.; height, 3 in.

A pewter Flagon, mentioned in the terriers from 1739 to 1834, has disappeared.

COEDANA—S. ANEF

CHALICE.—A small Elizabethan silver Chalice, with beaker-shape bowl, engraved with the usual plain, double strap-work band, intersecting four times and enclosing the conventional sprays of foliage, a small sprig carried above and below each intersection. Along the lip is an incised line. The stem, which is divided by a flat knop covered with short incised lines or hyphens, has a delicate moulding of small ovolos at the top and bottom, and remains of a similar moulding are to be seen on the edge of the foot. On the shoulder of the foot is a band filled with hyphens. The only mark on this Chalice is the bird's head erased, turned dexter-wise, found on several Chalices in this Diocese. (PLATE XXIV.)

Dimensions.—Height, 5⅝ in.; depth of bowl, 2¾ in.; diameter of mouth, 2⅞ in.

PATEN-COVER.—The Paten-Cover is engraved with a band of hyphens, as on the foot of Chalice, and on the foot is this inscription:

"a n o
1578."

with a small sprig underneath, an incised line running round it. The initial W has been engraved at a much later date. It bears the same maker's mark as on Chalice.

Dimensions.—Diameter, 2⅞ in.; height, 1⅜ in.

CHALICE.—A plain old Sheffield plate Chalice, with deep, inverted bell-shape bowl, on short slender stem.

Height, 6¼ in.

PATEN.—A plain circular Dish of electro-plate.

A pewter Flagon has disappeared from this Church.

GWREDOG—S. MARY

No plate of any description exists in this Church, and no reference to it can be found in the old terriers.

HENEGLWYS—S. LLEVYDIAN

CHALICE.—A plain silver Chalice, with beaker-shape bowl, moulded edge, the stem divided by a plain knop.

Marks.—London date-letter for 1722-3. Maker's mark illegible.

Dimensions.—Height, 7½ in.; depth of bowl, 3¾ in.; diameter of mouth, 3½ in.

PATEN.—A large Paten of old Sheffield plate, plain, with gadroon border on low foot. The Christian emblems, I.H.S., a cross and three nails in glory, engraved in the centre. 10 in. in diameter.

ALMS DISH.—An old pewter Dish, circular, 12 in. in diameter, stamped with—

MADE IN (a device, perhaps)
LIVE . . . . (?) Liverpool.

The Liver between. (?) WROUGHT. A fleur-de-lis in oval cartouche, repeated four times.

The pewter Flagon mentioned in the terrier for the year 1801 is no longer in this Church.

HOLYHEAD—S. CYBI

CHALICE (No. 1).—Large, plain silver Chalice, beaker-shape bowl, on tall stem, divided by a plain knop, on a moulded base, inscribed in two lines, in bold script lettering—"The Legacy of John Owens of Penrhese Esq To the Church of Holyhead who died 13ᵗʰ June 1712."

Marks.—London date-letter for 1713-14. Maker's mark, Pa, vase above, pellet below, in shaped shield—the mark of Humphrey Payne, ent. 1701.

Dimensions.—Height, 10¾ in.; depth of bowl, 5¾ in.; diameter of bowl, 5 in.

PATEN-COVER (No. 1).—Plain, with moulded edge, a crucifix engraved in centre; I.H.S. in glory engraved on foot.

Marks.—The same as on Chalice.

Dimensions.—Diameter, 5⅞ in.; height, 1¼ in.

The donor of this Chalice and Paten-Cover, John Owen, was the son of Thomas Owen, Esquire, of Penrhos, and Margaret his wife, daughter and heiress of Richard Rowland Wynn, Esquire, of Penhesgyn, Llansadwrn.

CHALICE (No. 2).—Tall, plain silver Chalice, with oviform bowl, standing on a tall, slender, baluster-like stem, on splayed foot.

Marks.—London date-letter for 1610-11. Maker's mark, RM, with an illegible device underneath, in plain shield.

Dimensions.—Height 8⅜ in.; depth of bowl, 3¾ in.; diameter of mouth, 3½ in. (PLATE XXIX., No. 2.)

PATEN.—Small, plain silver Paten, with flat rim, the date 1632 engraved on the foot.

Marks.—London date-letter for 1631-2. Maker's mark, RC, with pheon underneath, in heart-shape shield.

Dimensions.—Diameter, 4⅛ in.; rim, ½ in. wide; height, 1 in.

ALMS DISH.—Plain, circular silver Dish, moulded edge, I.H.S., cross and three nails in glory engraved in the centre, and this inscription engraved on the back, in script lettering, in a circle—"The Gift of Mrs. Mary Hughes yᵉ Daughter of Thoˢ. & Jonett Hughes late of Holyhead, to yᵉ Parish Church of Holyhead, A.D. 1745."

Marks.—London date-letter for 1744-5. Maker's mark illegible.

The donor was the daughter of Thomas Hughes, of Plas Llanfigael, and Jonet Davies, of Holyhead, his wife. Jane Hughes, the daughter and heiress of Thomas and Jonet Hughes, married William Morris,

PLATE V.

No. 3.

BRYNCROES, CARNARVONSHIRE.
Elizabethan Silver Chalice and Paten-Cover.
Date : 1574.

No. 2.

CLYNNOG, CARNARVONSHIRE.
Elizabethan Silver Chalice and Paten-Cover.
Date : 1574.

No. 1.

LLANRUG, CARNARVONSHIRE.
Elizabethan Silver Chalice and Paten-Cover.
Date : *circa* 1575.

Comptroller of the Customs at Holyhead, brother to Lewis Morris (Llewelyn ddu o Fon).

FLAGON.—Plain, new silver Flagon, inscribed—" The Gift of the Members of S^t. Cybi's Church Sunday School, March 15th, 1879." London date-letter for 1878-9. Maker's mark, $_W^{HE}$ in trefoil.

HOLYHEAD—S. SEIRIOL

In this Church is a new silver set, consisting of one large and one smaller Chalice, one large and one smaller Paten, and a Flagon, engraved with the sacred symbols, I.H.S., a cross and three nails in glory, the larger Chalice being inscribed—" This Communion Service was presented by Ellin wife of the Hon. Wm. Owen Stanley, M.P., of Penrhos, to the Church of S^t. Seiriol, Holyhead, Octr. 1854."

Marks.—London date-letter for 1852-3, 1854-5. Maker's mark, $_{JB}^{EB\&}$ (E. & J. Barnard).

Dimensions.—Large Chalice, 7¾ in. high; smaller Chalice, 6¾ in. high; larger Paten, 8 in. in diameter; smaller Paten, 6 in.; Flagon, 12¾ in.

LLECHCYNFARWY—S. CYNFARWY

The silver Chalice in this Church affords an interesting and very rare example of a Chalice of the reign of Charles I., with a mixture of characteristics of different periods. The hexagonal stem, with its large wrythen knop with six diamond-shape projections engraved with a floreated design, is typically medieval, and is found on English Chalices from about the middle of the fourteenth century until the dawn of the Reformation, this Diocese of Bangor providing an original and solitary specimen in the Chalice of Llandudwen, in Carnarvonshire. The foot, as will be observed, while it retains its medieval sexfoil form, and the engraved representation of the Crucifixion, with the letters " INRI " above, presents an innovation in the engraved feather-like decoration running along the edges of each angle and along the edge of the foot. The deep, oviform bowl departs from the low, conical or nearly hemispherical pre-Reformation type, and conforms to the familiar shape found with a baluster stem on a plain splayed foot, as on the Chalice, of the year 1610-11, at Holyhead, and at several other places in this Diocese. (PLATE VI., No. 3.)

It is engraved with this inscription—" B : Cap : de Lleaghganferwy, Gu : Bold de Tre-yr-ddole Armiger.

Dat, dicat, dedi^catqz : 1632,"

and a shield of arms : *azure, upon a chevron between three helmets, a crescent* (for cadency).

Crest.—*A helmeted head, the vizor raised.*
Motto.—HEB · DEW · HEB · DYM, DUW a digon.
Dimensions.—Height, 7⅞ in.; depth of bowl, 3 in.; diameter of mouth, 3¼ in.; greatest diameter of foot, 4¾ in.

William Bold, who purchased Tre'r dol, and died without issue in 1652, was the son of Rees Bold, the son of William Bold Owen, the son of Richard Owen Tudor, of Penmynydd. He took the name of Bold from his great-grandmother, Grace, daughter of Sir Henry Bold, of Bold Hall, Lancashire.

The silver Paten is octofoil, and is engraved with the same feather-like decoration as on the Chalice. The letters I.H.S., a cross and three nails in glory, are engraved on the foot. It has no marks. Probable date, nineteenth century.

Dimensions.—Diameter, 5⅝ in.; height, 1⅛ in.

LLECHYLCHED

The Communion plate from this Church has disappeared, and no record of it can be traced.

LLANALLGO—S. GALLGO

CHALICE.—A new silver Chalice, with plain hemispherical bowl, fluted knop on stem, spreading foot, engraved with cross in a circle.
Marks.—London date-letter for 1892-3. Maker's mark, TP, in an oblong cartouche.
Height, 6¾ in.

PATEN.—A plain silver Paten, 5½ in. in diameter, with same marks as on Chalice.

FLAGON.—A pewter Flagon, the body cylindrical, with domed cover surmounted by a cross (recently added), scrolled handle, inscribed—" Llanallgo." It has been electro-plated and gilt inside.
No marks. Height, 8½ in.

ALMS DISH.—A large, circular pewter Dish, which has been plated, inscribed on the back—

"LLANALLGO
E × M
1721."

Marks illegible. Diameter, 12½ in.

These initials probably refer to Elizabeth Mealy, third daughter of the Rev. Richard Parry, M.A., of Perfeddgoed, Bangor, Rector of Llanddeiniolen. Her husband was John Mealy, of S. George's, Middlesex, gent. Her brother, Owen Parry, married Margaret, daughter of the Rev. Hugh Jones, M.A., of Brynhyrdin, Pentraeth, Rector of Llanallgo 1717-35.

ALMS DISH.—A small pewter Alms Dish, plated, 9⅛ in. in diameter.

LLANBABO—S. PABO

An Elizabethan silver Chalice, the bowl engraved with the usual plain, double strap-work, intersecting three times, and enclosing the conventional sprays of foliation, a spray at each intersection. The stem has a plain moulding at the top and bottom, and is divided by a plain depressed knop.

Marks.—London date-letter for 1574. Maker's mark, a capital letter E, with a very small " o," or circle, in front of and attached to the centre bar of this letter, in shaped shield.

Dimensions.—Height, 6 in.; depth of bowl, 3¼ in.; diameter of mouth, 3¼ in.

A plain electro-plate Paten on foot.

LLANBADRIG—S. PADRIG

The Chalice with cover here is Elizabethan, and of the utmost rarity, if not unique. It is of silver gilt, and the bowl and cover together somewhat resemble an elongated egg. At frequent intervals along the lower half of the body are applied vertical bars, fourteen in number; the spaces between are filled with short, incised lines, or hyphens. Springing from each of these bars is an engraved trefoil sprig. Above are several lines of hyphens encircling the body. Suspended from the moulded lip are similar trefoil sprigs. The domed cover has the same applied bars, the spaces filled with hyphens, and a trefoil-like sprig springing from the end of each of the fourteen bars. The cover is surmounted by a fluted pedestal, an ovolo moulding below it, and a tall, slender vase-like knop above. The stem is short, and is fluted in the middle; the foot is truncated, with an engraved line border, the line deviating into an arch four times; the edge of foot has an egg and dart moulding.

Marks on body and cover.—London date-letter for 1573-4. Maker's mark, RH, conjoined, surrounded by dots at irregular intervals, in a plain, circular cartouche.

Dimensions.—Total height to top of knob, $9\frac{11}{16}$ in.; height of body only, $6\frac{1}{4}$ in.; depth of bowl, $3\frac{5}{8}$ in.; diameter of mouth, $2\frac{3}{4}$ in.; diameter of foot, 3 in. (PLATE III.)

Nothing is known of the past history of this fine example of the Elizabethan goldsmiths' art, except that it was found in 1868 by the present Rector of Beaumaris, Rev. T. L. Kyffin, at that time Vicar of Llanbadrig, in a battered condition in an old chest under the altar, where it had apparently lain for many years uncared for. An endeavour has been made in some quarters to elevate this cup into a ciborium, but it is obviously one of the numerous pieces of domestic plate—not ecclesiastical—which graced the splendid sideboards in the houses of the great in the Elizabethan period.

No trace can be found of the old pewter Flagon and the silver Flagon mentioned in the terriers for 1702 and 1776.

LLANBEDRGOCH—S. PETER

CHALICE.—An Elizabethan silver Chalice, engraved with the conventional, plain, double strapwork band, filled with sprays of foliage, and intersecting four times, a small sprig above and below each intersection; a vertical reeded moulding at top and bottom of stem, which is divided in the centre by a plain flattened knob, an egg and dart moulding on edge of foot. The only mark is IL in a shaped shield, as found on other Chalices in this Diocese. Date, *circa* 1575.

Dimensions.—Height, $6\frac{3}{16}$ in.; depth of bowl, 3 in.; diameter of mouth, $2\frac{7}{8}$ in.

PATEN.—A small, plain silver Paten.

Marks.—London date letter for 1904-5. Maker's mark, $J\underset{\text{LTD.}}{\&}W$, in trefoil.

FLAGON.—A small silver Flagon with pear-shape body. Same date-letter and marks as on Paten.

This Church, like many others in this county, is no longer in possession of its pewter Flagon and Dish, included in the terriers from 1788 until 1821.

PLATE VI.

No. 3.

LLECHCYNFARWY, ANGLESEY.

CHARLES I. SILVER CHALICE.

DATE: 1632.

No. 2.

LLANFIHANGEL-YSCEIFIOG, ANGLESEY.

SILVER CUP AND COVER.

DATES: CUP, 1601-2; COVER, 1611-12.

No. 1.

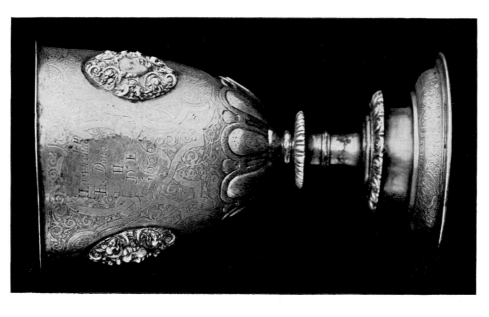

LLANFECHELL, ANGLESEY.

GERMAN SILVER-GILT CHALICE.

DATE: LATE 16TH CENTURY.

LLANBEULAN—S. PEULAN

The Chalice in use in this Church takes the form of a small, domestic drinking mug, of plain silver, on a short moulded foot, with a scrolled handle, on the shoulder of which is engraved in roman capitals, $_{G:M}^{W}$.

Marks.—London date-letter for 1735. Maker's mark, H P, in script capitals, a mullet above and below, in quatrefoil.

Dimensions.—Height, $3\frac{1}{2}$ in.; diameter of mouth, $2\frac{1}{2}$ in.

The Paten is a plain old Sheffield-plate Salver, with beaded edge, on three feet, 6 in. in diameter.

LLANDDANIELFAB—S. DEINIOL

CHALICE.—A plain silver Chalice, with inverted bell-shape bowl, supported by a stem divided by a narrow moulding, on a moulded foot. Marks partially illegible, only R R (Richard Richardson, of Chester) discernible.

Date, *circa* 1750. It is inscribed under the foot—

"LLANDDANIEL FAB."

Dimensions.—Height, $6\frac{3}{8}$ in.; depth of bowl, $3\frac{7}{8}$ in.; diameter of mouth, $3\frac{5}{8}$ in.

PATEN.—A plain silver Paten with moulded edge on a moulded foot, inscribed—"LLANDDANIEL FAB."

London date-letter for 1872-3.

Dimensions.—Diameter, $6\frac{1}{2}$ in.; height, $2\frac{7}{8}$ in.

FLAGON.—An old pewter Flagon, a vase-shaped knob on the broken domed cover. It is stamped with four marks in small shaped shields—(1) HR; (2) a leopard's head above a castellated crown; (3) a bird; (4) three fleurs-de-lis.

Height, $11\frac{1}{2}$ in.

ALMS DISH.—An old pewter Dish, circular, stamped with three talbots' heads erased and "S. DUNCUMB LONDON."

Diameter, $10\frac{3}{4}$ in.

LLANDDEUSANT—S. MARCELLUS

A plain electro-plate Goblet and Plate, both inscribed—"The gift of Humphrey Stanley Jones Esq of Llynon to Llanddeusant Church 1857."

C

LLANDDONA—S. DONA

CHALICE.—A small silver Chalice, with inverted bell-shape bowl, engraved with the sacred symbols, I.H.S., a cross and three nails in glory, supported on a stem with plain moulding in centre, the foot moulded.

Marks.—Chester date-letter for 1769-72. Maker's mark, RR in an oblong shield with scalloped edges (Richard Richardson).

Dimensions.—Height, 6 in.; depth of bowl, $3\frac{1}{8}$ in.; diameter of mouth, $3\frac{1}{8}$ in.

PATEN-COVER.—An Elizabethan silver Paten-Cover, of the usual type, engraved with an intersecting band filled with hyphens. The foot inscribed—

"Ano
1574."

Diameter, $3\frac{3}{8}$ in. The only mark is the bird's head erased, found on several Elizabethan Chalices in this Diocese.

Unfortunately the Chalice to which this belonged has disappeared.

Two electro-plated Chalices, a Paten and Flagon, given by Mrs. Warner, Glan Menai.

An old pewter Flagon and Dish have disappeared from this Church.

LLANDDYFNAN—S. DYFNAN

CHALICE.—A plain goblet with egg-shape bowl, gilt inside, supported by a slender stem on a foot with reeded border. It was given in 1870 by Mrs. Lewis, of Plas Llanddyfnan.

Marks.—London date-letter for 1796-7. Maker's mark, $^{PB}_{AB}$ in a square (Peter and Ann Bateman).

Dimensions.—Height, $6\frac{7}{8}$ in.; depth of bowl, $3\frac{7}{8}$ in.; diameter of mouth, $3\frac{1}{2}$ in.

PATEN.—An old pewter Paten, on a truncated foot, the edge of plate and foot fluted, and a fluted band encircling the centre of foot. It is stamped with several marks, which are almost illegible. One appears to be the name PIERCE, and two of the others are apparently formed of the initials E P in black letter capitals.

Dimensions.—Diameter, $10\frac{1}{2}$ in.; height, 3 in.

FLAGON.—A very tall old pewter Flagon, the body cylindrical, with domed cover (the knob lost), the base splaying out. No marks. Date, *circa* 1700.

Height, $11\frac{1}{2}$ in.

A small circular pewter Dish, 9¼ in. in diameter.   No marks.

A silver Chalice, described in the terrier for 1776 as engraved with this inscription—" Llanddyfnan May 1719," has disappeared.

LLANDEGFAN—S. TEGFAN

CHALICE.—A large silver Chalice with beaker-shape bowl on tall stem, which has a plain depressed knop. The Christian symbols, I.H.S., a cross and nails in glory; and also a shield of arms: *a chevron between three bulls' heads cabossed*, surmounted by a viscount's coronet, are engraved on the bowl, which is inscribed—

" The Guift of the Rᵗ. Honᵇˡ. Rich Lᵈ Viscoᵗ. Bulkeley
to the Church of Beaumaris Anᵒ. 1704.
NB. THIS CHALICE was Transfered from BEAUMARIS CHURCH, COUNTY of ANGLESEY to the CHURCH of LLANDEGFAN by THOˢ. JAMES WARREN BULKELEY LORD VISCᵀ. BULKELEY, on his PRESENTING some NEW COMMUNION PLATE TO the FORMER CHURCH, JUNE 4, 1811."

Marks.—London date-letter for 1706-7.   Maker's mark, an anchor between W A, in shaped shield (Jos. Ward).
Dimensions.—Height, 8½ in.; depth and diameter of bowl, 4¼ in.

PATEN (No. 1).—A large silver Paten, plain, with moulded edge, on truncated foot. The symbols, I.H.S., a cross and nails in glory, engraved in the centre, and inscribed—

" The Gift of
The Right Honᵇˡᵉ. Thomas James Warren Bulkeley
Lord Viscᵗ. Bulkeley
to the Parish Church of LLandegfan
County of Anglesey
JUNE 4, 1811."

Marks.—London date-letter for 1727-8.   Maker's mark, G B, with bird above, in shaped shield (Geo. Boothby).
Dimensions.—Diameter, 10⅝ in.; height, 3¼ in.

PATEN (No. 2).—A smaller plain silver Paten, with flat depression and a flat rim with moulded edge. In the centre is an engraved shield of arms: *a chevron gules between three bulls' heads cabossed*, with decorated mantling, surmounted by a viscount's coronet. On the rim is this inscription—" The Guift of ye R^t. Honble. Rich. L^d. Visco^t. Bulkeley to the Church of Beaumaris An. 1704," and the additional inscription referring to its transference to Llandegfan, as on the Chalice.

On the foot, the conventional device, the letters I.H.S., a cross and nails in glory, are engraved.

Marks.—As on Chalice.

Dimensions.—Diameter, 6¼ in.; height, 1⅝ in.

FLAGON.—A massive, plain, silver Jug, of domestic character, the body globular, with a flat plain moulding encircling it, a short spout, the domed cover surmounted by a vase-shaped knob, double volute thumb-piece, scrolled handle, short moulded foot. I.H.S., cross and three nails are engraved in a floreated mantling formerly filled by a shield of arms. The jug bears the same inscription as the large Paten, No. 1, the only difference being that the name Thomas is abbreviated thus: " Thos."

Marks.—London date-letter for 1708-9. Maker's mark, P Y with rose and crown above (Benj. Pyne).

Height to top of knob, 11¼ in.

There is also a small silver Private Communion set, consisting of a plain Chalice and Paten. The Chalice has a tumbler-shape bowl with moulded edge, supported by a tall truncated stem with ribbed edge. It is engraved with I.H.S., a cross and nails in glory, and this inscription—

" The Gift of
The Right Honble. Thos. Ja^s. Warren Bulkeley, Lord Viscount Bulkeley,
To the Church of LLandegfan, June 4, 1811."

Marks.—London date-letter for 1810-11. Maker's mark illegible.

Dimensions.—Height, 3⅝ in.; depth of bowl, 1¾ in.; diameter of bowl, 2⅛ in.

The Paten has a moulded edge and a foot, and is engraved with the same device as on the Chalice, and with this inscription—" The Gift of The Right Honb^le. Thos. Ja^s. Warren Bulkeley, Lord Visc^t. Bulkeley, to the Parish Church of LLandegfan in the County of Anglesey, June 4, 1811."

No marks.

Diameter, 4¼ in.; height, 1⅛ in.

The earlier silver Chalice, given to this Church by Thomas Davies in 1639, was removed in a transformed condition to Penmon Church in 1812. The donor is described on a tablet in this Church as a

PLATE VII.

No. 3.

LLANDYGWYNNIN, CARNARVONSHIRE.
JAMES I. SILVER CHALICE
AND PATEN-COVER.
DATE : 1610-11.

No. 2.

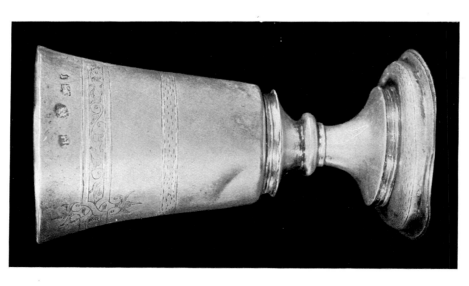

The parish of Boduan

BODFEAN, CARNARVONSHIRE.
JAMES I. SILVER CHALICE AND PATEN-COVER.
DATE : 1623-4.

No. 1.

LLANGWNADL, CARNARVONSHIRE.
ELIZABETHAN SILVER CHALICE.
DATE : 1574-5.

"servant to y^e two most illustrious Princes Henry & Charles both Princes of Wales and now to King Charles y^e first, Messenger in Ordinary of His M^ties Chamber." He was born in this parish, and died in 1649.

The donor of the Chalice and Paten (No. 2) was the third Viscount Bulkeley, M.P. for Anglesey 1695-1704, who married (1st), in 1681, Mary, daughter of Sir Philip Egerton, Knt., of Egerton and Oulton, Cheshire; and (2nd), in 1687, Elizabeth, daughter of Henry White, Henllan, Pembrokeshire, and widow of Thomas Lort. At his death, in 1704, he probably bequeathed a sum of money for the purchase of this plate, which bears the hall mark for 1706-7, though dated 1704.

The donor of the other plate, Thomas James Warren Bulkeley, was the seventh Viscount. He was M.P. for Anglesey 1774-84, and was created a Peer of Great Britain by the title of Lord Bulkeley of Beaumaris in 1784. He married Elizabeth Harriet, only daughter and heiress of Sir George Warren, Knt., of Poynton, Cheshire, when he assumed the additional name of Warren. With his death, in 1822, the title became extinct.

LLANDYFRYDOG—S. TYFRYDOG

An Elizabethan silver Chalice with Paten-Cover. The Chalice is engraved with a double band of strap-work, differing from others in this Diocese in the fact that the strapwork, which encloses the conventional sprays of foliage, is not plain, but is filled with engraved oblique lines. A small single sprig is above and below each of the four intersections. The bowl is deep, and narrow at the bottom, the lip slightly curving out. At the bottom of the stem, which is divided by a plain compressed knop, with a flat collar above and below, is an unusual moulding formed of Xs, while the edge of the foot has an egg and dart moulding, like the Chalice of Llanfair-yn-Neubwll. The Paten-Cover, which has lost its foot, is engraved with a double band of interlaced strap-work, similar to that on the Chalice, but without the sprays of foliage, and the overhanging edge is reeded. The only mark is the bird's head erased, turned sinister-wise, in a shaped shield, of which there are several examples in this Diocese. (PLATE XXX., NO. 1.)

Dimensions of Chalice.—Height, $6\frac{3}{4}$ in.; depth of bowl, $3\frac{5}{8}$ in.; diameter of mouth, $3\frac{5}{8}$ in. The Paten-Cover is $3\frac{1}{2}$ in. in diameter.

A plain silver Paten, engraved in the centre with the letters I.H.S., three nails, and cross in glory, and above, in roman capitals, I O A N. VI. 58. On the border this Scriptural quotation in Welsh is engraved

C 2

in one line—" Y neb sydd yn bwytta'r bara hwn, a fydd byw yn dragy-wydd " (" Whosoever eateth this bread hath eternal life "). The foot is engraved with this inscription in script lettering—

" Rhodd y Parchedig
J. H. Cotton,
i'r Eglwys
Llandyfrydog
1816."

(" The gift of the Rev[d]. J. H. Cotton to the Church of Llandyfrydog, 1816 ").

London date-letter for 1721. Maker's mark illegible.

Diameter, $5\frac{5}{8}$ in.; width of rim, $\frac{5}{8}$ in.; height, $1\frac{3}{4}$ in.

The donor, James Henry Cotton, M.A., was Vicar of Bangor in 1810, and Dean of Bangor from 1830 to 1862. As Dean he held the benefices of Llanfihangel-Ysceifiog with Llanffinan in Anglesey, and Llanllechid and Gyffin in Carnarvonshire.

A large old pewter Dish, 12 in. in diameter, circular, with deep bowl, engraved on the back of the rim, which is $1\frac{1}{8}$ in. wide, in large roman capitals—" LLANDEFERYOD * T.M * H.P * 1711," these initials, no doubt, representing the Churchwardens of that time. There are two small marks, twice repeated, W B in a shaped shield, and a griffin rampant in a shield.

LLANDYSILIO (Menai Bridge)

A new silver set of Chalice, of medieval design, Paten, and a Flagon. London date-letter for 1858-9. Maker's mark, I.K. in an oblong.

LLANDRYGAN—S. TRYGAN

CHALICE AND PATEN-COVER.—The silver Chalice has a short, inverted bell-shape bowl, supported by a thick stem, divided by a plain moulding, and rests on a moulded foot with flat edge. Inscribed—

" LLandrygan
RICE JONES
WILL[M]. OWEN
Chu[r]. Wardens
1740."

The Paten-Cover is plain, with flat depression, and has a foot on which is engraved the date 1740.

Marks.—Chester date-letter for 1739-40. Maker's mark, R R. in an oblong (Richard Richardson).

Dimensions.—Chalice: height, $6\frac{5}{16}$ in.; depth of bowl and diameter of mouth, $3\frac{1}{4}$ in.

Paten-Cover: diameter, $3\frac{3}{4}$ in.; height, 1 in.

FLAGON.—A large old pewter Flagon, the body cylindrical, moulded foot, domed cover surmounted by an acorn, scrolled thumb-piece. Inscribed—

> John Hughes
> Tho⁵. Williams
> Wardens
> 1767."

Height, $10\frac{1}{2}$ in.

A deep, circular pewter Dish, $10\frac{3}{4}$ in. in diameter, stamped with the name BALDWIN, a crowned Tudor rose, twice repeated.

LLANEDWEN—S. EDWEN

CHALICE.—A silver Chalice with short plain bowl, the stem and foot embossed with foliage and floreation. Engraved with the sacred letters I.H.S., a cross and three nails in glory, and this inscription: "Presented by Charles Henry Evans Esqʳᵉ. to Llanedwen Church 1842."

Height, $8\frac{9}{16}$ in.

PATEN.—A silver Paten with plain bowl on a foot embossed in same manner as Chalice, and with the same conventional symbols and inscription engraved on it.

London date-letter for 1776-7. Maker's mark, I.C T.H in a square (John Crouch, Thos. Hannam).

Diameter, $6\frac{1}{2}$ in.; height, $3\frac{3}{4}$ in.

These two pieces of plate have been re-made from other articles, with additional parts. The donor was the eldest son of Hugh Evans, Esq., of Henblas, Trefeilir and Plasgwyn, Llanedwen. He married Henrietta, daughter of John Warren, Dean of Bangor.

FLAGON.—A tall silver Flagon, with plain body, the spout, cover, and the foot embossed with floreation. Engraved with the Christian symbols, I.H.S., a cross and three nails, and inscribed—"Presented by W. B. Hughes, Esq., M.P., at the consecration of Llanedwen new Church, Anglesey, 1856."

London date-letter for 1856-7.   Marks of Chas. T. Fox and Geo. Fox.

Height, 11¼ in.

The donor was the eldest son of Sir W. B. Hughes, Knt., of Plas Coch, Llanedwen.   He was M.P. for the Carnarvon Boroughs for forty years.

There is also an old pewter Flagon, with short cylindrical body, flat cover, scrolled handle.   The cover is stamped with a lion statant in an oval cartouche, repeated four times.   Date, *circa* 1700.   Height, 7¾ in.

And also an old pewter Dish, with wide flat rim, stamped with four marks in small shields : (1) lion statant ; (2) leopard's head ; (3) a rose ; (4) T N.   10⅝ in. diameter.

In the terriers between 1776 and 1811, a silver Chalice, described as the gift of Mrs. Ellen Rowlands, of Plasgwyn, in 1752, is included, but this has since disappeared.

LLANEILIAN—S. ÆLIAN

CHALICE.—A plain silver Chalice, with deep, inverted, bell-shape bowl, supported by a stem, with narrow moulding in centre, on a moulded foot.   Inscribed—

" LLanlilian."

Marks.—London date-letter for 1733-4.   Maker's mark illegible.

Dimensions.—Height, 8⅜ in. ; depth of bowl, 4⅝ in. ; diameter of mouth, 4¼ in.

PATEN.—A small, new, plain silver Paten, with a cross engraved on the edge.   London date-letter for 1890-1.   Maker's mark, $\frac{HE}{W}$ in trefoil.   5⅜ in. in diameter.

FLAGON.—An old pewter Flagon, tall cylindrical body, domed cover with short knob.   On each of the two hollows of the thumb-piece a seeded rose.   The only mark is on the handle—R B or R D above a bird.

Dimensions.—Height to top of cover, 12¼ in. ; height of body, 10⅝ in. ; diameter of mouth, 4¼ in.

ALMS DISH.—An old pewter Dish, circular, stamped between two griffins rampant, $_{LONDON}^{FROM}$, and these four marks in small shields : T B between three mullets and pellets ; a leopard's head erased ; a crowned rose ; and a fleur-de-lys and four mullets.

Diameter, 11 in.

PLATE VIII.

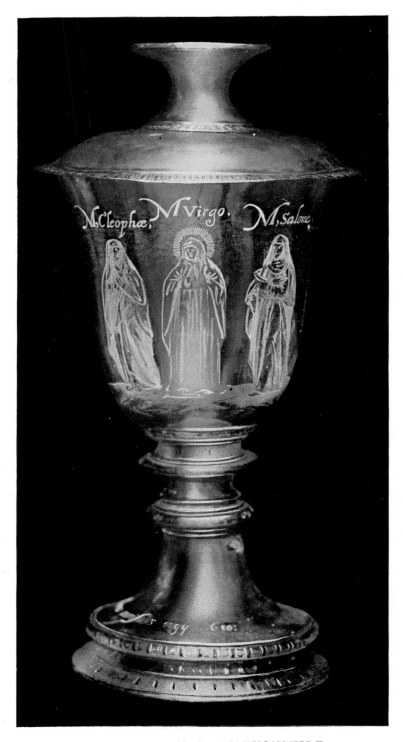

BEDDGELERT, CARNARVONSHIRE.
JAMES I. SILVER CHALICE AND PATEN-COVER.
DATE: 1610.

LLANERCHYMEDD—S. MARY

CHALICE (1).—A large, plain, silver Chalice, with inverted bell-shape bowl, curving out at the lip, on stem with narrow moulding in centre. I.H.S., cross and three nails in glory engraved on the body. Inscribed in script lettering under foot—"The Gift of Mrs. Eliz: Williams to the Church of LLanarchameadd, widow of Jo\ⁿ. W\ᵐˢ. of Chwayn Esqʳ. 1749."

Marks.—Chester date-letter for 1758-9. Maker's mark, R R in oblong (Richard Richardson).

Dimensions.—Height, $8\frac{5}{8}$ in.; depth of bowl, 5 in.; diameter of mouth, 5 in.; diameter of foot, $4\frac{1}{8}$ in.

CHALICE (2).—A very small, plain silver Chalice, with beaker-shape bowl, on a short, thick stem, divided by a plain, narrow moulding, on a moulded foot.

Marks.—Chester date-letter for 1716-17. Maker's mark, Ri in plain shield (the first Richard Richardson).

Dimensions.—Height, $5\frac{1}{4}$ in.; depth of bowl, 3 in.; diameter of mouth, 3 in.; diameter of foot, $3\frac{1}{8}$ in.

PATEN.—A plain, circular, silver salver, with shaped shell edge, standing on three feet, 8 in. in diameter, inscribed in script lettering on the back, "The Gift of Mʳˢ. Williams of Whaeien, Widow, to the Church of Llanarchamead."

Marks.—London date-letter for 1742. Maker's mark, RA, in script capitals, with pellet between, in double-lobed shield (Robt. Abercromby).

PATEN.—Small, new silver Paten, plain, with engraved cross on the border, inscribed on the back—"PRESENTED BY R. THOMAS 1903."

London date-letter for 1902-3. Maker's mark, $_{W}^{H\,E}$ in trefoil. Diameter, $5\frac{1}{4}$ in.

The donor of the large Chalice and Salver, Mrs. Elizabeth Williams, was the daughter of Rowland Whyte, Esq., of The Friars, Beaumaris. She married John Williams, Esq., of Chwaen, Llantrisant, and of Tyfry, Pentraeth. Their great granddaughter, Margaret, married Sir John Williams, of Bodelwyddan, and the present Bishop of Bangor is their grandson.

LLANEUGRAD—S. EUGRAD

A plain electro-plated Chalice, Paten, Flagon, and Alms Dish.

LLANFACHRAETH—S. MACHRAETH

CHALICE.—A plain electro-plated goblet, inscribed under foot—
"John Jones, Rector.
John Jones, Churchwarden.
Llanfachreth 1847."

PATEN.—Plain electro-plate, with I.H.S. engraved in centre.

FLAGON, PEWTER.—Tall, cylindrical body, on short, moulded, splayed foot, 7¼ in. in diameter; a domed, jointed cover, surmounted by a short knob; scrolled handle. There are four marks stamped on it: I & H; a griffin's head erased; three escallop shells on a horizontal bar, and a leopard's head, all in shaped shields.
Dimensions.—Height, 14 in.; diameter of mouth, 3¾ in.
The large pewter Flagon, of similar form, at Llanenddwyn, in Merionethshire, bears the same pewter marks.

PEWTER DISH.—Circular, 12 in. in diameter, with a rim 1½ in. wide, stamped with three marks: S. DUNCOMBC above three talbots' heads erased, LONDON in a scroll, and a Tudor rose crowned.

LLANFAES—S. CATHERINE

CHALICE (1).—A plain silver Chalice with deep beaker-shape bowl, supported by a truncated stem, which has a twisted rope moulding at the top, on a moulded foot with flat edge. The bowl is engraved with the letters I.H.S. and a cross.
Marks.—London date-letter for 1676-7. Maker's mark, T E in monogram, in a shaped shield.
Dimensions.—Height, 5¹³⁄₁₆ in.; depth of bowl, 3¾ in.; diameter of mouth, 3⅜ in.

PATEN-COVER (1).—The plain silver Paten-Cover belonging to this Chalice is 3¾ in. in diameter.

CHALICE (2).—A plain silver Chalice with deep, beaker-shape bowl, inscribed—"The Gift of $^W_{HI}$ of ffryers to the
Church of LLanvaes 1713."
The stem has a plain moulding in centre, and rests on a moulded foot.
Marks.—London date-letter for 1713-14. Maker's mark, Lo with key above, in a shaped shield (Natl. Locke).
Dimensions.—Height, 7⅜ in.; depth of bowl, 4⅜ in.; diameter of mouth, 3½ in.

PATEN-COVER (2).—The Paten-Cover of this Chalice has a moulded edge, and is $4\frac{5}{16}$ in. in diameter, with the same marks.

The donors of this Chalice and Paten-Cover (No. 2) were Henry Whyte, son of Rowland Whyte, Esq., of The Friars, and his wife, Jane, second daughter of John Thelwall, Esq., of Bathafarn Park, Denbighshire. There are tablets to their memory in this Church.

PATENS.—Two plain silver Patens, exactly alike, the edges moulded, on truncated stems. In the centre of each the Christian symbols, I.H.S., a cross and three nails, are engraved, and each is inscribed—" The Gift of Tho⁵. James Warren Bulkeley Lord Viscount Bulkeley to the Parish Church of LLanfaes, County of Anglesea, July 1812."

Marks.—London date-letter for 1726-7. Maker's mark, $\underset{O}{\overset{R}{A.P}}$ in quatrefoil (Hugh Arnett and Ed. Pocock).

Dimensions.—Diameter, 6 in.; height, $2\frac{3}{8}$ in.

FLAGON.—A plain silver Jug, of domestic character, the body globular, gadroon edge on the lip and on the short foot, a vase-shape knob on the domed cover, the handle wickered. The Christian symbols, I.H.S., etc., are engraved on the body, and also the inscription is the same as on the two Patens, except that the last letter in the word Anglesey is y, not a.

Marks.—London date-letter for 1767-8. Maker's mark, $\underset{H}{\overset{W}{O.W}}$
Height, 10 in.

ALMS DISH.—The silver Alms Dish is an ordinary domestic soup-plate, with fluted edge. It is engraved with the Christian symbols, I.H.S., a cross and three nails, and is inscribed—" The Gift of Thomas James Warren Bulkeley Lord Viscount Bulkeley To the Parish Church of LLanfaes, in the County of Anglesey, July 1812."

Marks.—Newcastle date-letter for 1778-9. Maker's mark, W W, with pellet between, in an oblong cartouche (? Wm. Williamson).
Diameter, $9\frac{1}{4}$ in.

Another soup-plate, exactly similar, is at Penmon.

There is also a small, plain silver Chalice for private Communion, similar to that at Llandegfan and Penmon, engraved with I.H.S. and this inscription—" The Gift of Tho⁵. James Warren Bulkeley Lord Viscount Bulkeley, To the Parish Church of LLanfaes July 1812."

Marks.—London date-letter for 1812-13. Makers' mark, $\underset{J P}{\overset{T P}{E R}}$
Dimensions—Height, $3\frac{5}{8}$ in.; diameter of mouth, 2 in.
The Paten has been lost.

LLANFAELOG—S. MAELOG

CHALICE.—The Chalice here is goblet in form, and of plain old Sheffield-plate, with I.H.S., cross and nails engraved in the centre, and inscribed under the foot—" Llanvaelog Church, Anglesey, I. W. TREVOR, M.A., RECTOR, 1849."

PATEN.—A large old Sheffield Paten, similarly inscribed.

FLAGON.—Plain electro-plate, inscribed on foot—" D. D. Canon Robert Williams, M.A., Rector, A.D. 1881."
The small silver Chalice, old pewter Flagon and Dish, mentioned in the terriers between 1808 and 1826, are no longer in this Church.

LLANFAETHLU—S. MAETHLU

CHALICE.—An old Sheffield-plate goblet, plain, with compressed knop in centre of stem : 6¾ in. high.

ALMS DISH.—An old Sheffield-plate dinner plate, with moulded edge ; 9⅜ in. in diameter.

PATEN.—Plain new silver, 5 3/16 in. in diameter, inscribed—D : G :— M : S : Martha Williams. Rectoris . uxor :—ob : Novemb : xxv. 1894."
London date letter for 1895-6. Maker's mark, $_W^{H\,E}$ in trefoil.

FLAGON.—Plain new silver Flagon, 11 in. high, I.H.S. engraved in front, and this inscription engraved on body—" D.G—M.S :—Martha Williams. Rector : uxor : cariss : ob : Novemb : xxv. 1894." On the foot—" D : D : Soror Agnes. Llanvaethlu."
London date-letter for 1891-2. Maker's mark, J S H.
In the old terriers for 1801, 1811, and 1817, reference is made to " a silver Chalice and a handsome embossed small silver Paten with this inscription—' The Gift of Mrs. Mary Hughes now of Garregllwyd To the Church of Llanfaethley in the year 1744,' " and also a pewter Flagon, but neither of these pieces is now in this Church.

LLANFAIRMATHAFARNEITHAF—S. MARY

CHALICE.—Electro-plate.
PATEN.—Electro-plate.

PLATE IX.

No. 3.

LLANFIHANGEL-Y-PENNANT, MERIONETH.
SILVER CHALICE AND PATEN-COVER.
DATE: 1625.

No. 2.

LLANFAIRFECHAN, CARNARVONSHIRE.
CHARLES I. SILVER CHALICE AND PATEN-COVER.
DATE: 1638-9.

No. 1.

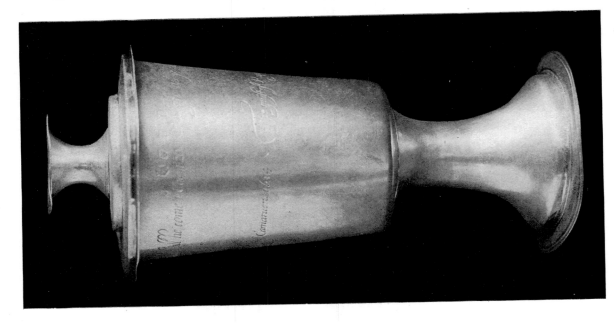

LLANIESTYN, CARNARVONSHIRE.
CHARLES I. SILVER CHALICE AND PATEN-COVER.
DATE: 1634-5.

FLAGON.—A new silver Flagon with long pear=shape body, on hexagon foot, which is inscribed—

"PRESENTED TO LLANFAIR M.E. CHURCH
BY M^{RS}. J. B. WILLIAMS, A VISITOR, AUGUST 1891.
RECTOR, THE REV. F. SINNETT JONES, M.A."

The sacred monogram and the *Agnus Dei*, and this inscription—
"TO THE GLORY OF GOD," are engraved on the flagon.

London date-letter for 1891-2. Maker's mark, $\frac{S\ B}{F\ W}$ in quatrefoil.

A silver Chalice and a pewter Flagon and Dish, mentioned in the terriers between 1808 and 1837, are not, unfortunately, any longer in existence.

LLANFAIRPWLLGWYNGYLL—S. MARY

CHALICE.—A silver Chalice engraved in the centre of the beaker-shape bowl with a band of palm leaves, divided three times by sprigs of foliage, and incised near the lip with three rows of hyphens. It stands on a truncated stem engraved at the edge with hyphens and sprigs of foliage. The bowl bears the London date-letter for 1608-9. The present stem has been added comparatively recently.

Dimensions.—Height, 6¼ in.; depth of bowl, 3⅛ in.; diameter of mouth, 3 5/16 in.

PATEN.—A plain silver Paten, a cross engraved in the centre, on truncated foot, inscribed—"Presented to the Parish Church of Llanfairpwllgwyngyll, by Mr. and Mrs. Clegg, Plas Llanfair, Easter 1905."

London date-letter for 1905-6. Makers' mark, $\frac{J\ \&\ W}{LTD.}$

Diameter, 6½ in.

FLAGON.—Tall, plain silver Flagon, engraved on edge of foot with same inscription as on Paten, except that the date is "Christmas 1892."

Sheffield date-letter for 1892-3. Makers' mark, $\frac{H\ W}{\&\ Co.}$

A small, circular silver Dish, with moulded edge, I.H.S. and a cross engraved in the centre, and this inscription on the back of rim—"Rhodd Richard Briscoe, DD. i Eglys, Llanfairpwllgwyngyll 1853."

London date-letter for 1853-4.

Diameter, 7½ in.

Richard Briscoe was the first son of Richard Briscoe of Llanfairpwllgwyngyll, gent. He was Fellow of Jesus College, Oxford, 1831; Senior Fellow, 1831-66; M.A., 1833; B.D., 1840; D.D., 1845; Vicar of Whitford, Flintshire, 1839-65; Rector of Nutfield, Surrey, 1865 until his death, 1880.

LLANFAIR-Y-CWMMWD—S. MARY

No vessels.

LLANFAIR-YN-NEUBWLL—S. MARY

An Elizabethan silver Chalice, with beaker-shape bowl, on which is engraved a narrow double strap-work band, not interlaced, enclosing sprays of foliage; a plain ribbed moulding at top and bottom of stem, which is divided by a plain, flat knop. The edge of the base has an egg and dart moulding.

Marks.—None. Date, *circa* 1575.

Dimensions.—Height, 7⅛ in.; depth of bowl, 4 in.; diameter of mouth, 3⅝ in.

An old pewter Plate, 8¾ in. diameter, stamped with two marks: LONDON in a scroll, and three leopards' or talbots' heads, erased.

An electro-plated set of Chalice, Paten and Flagon, the Paten inscribed—" To the Glory of God and in loving memory of Owen Lloyd for 40 years Churchwarden of Llanfairyneubwll. This Communion Set was given by his Children, July 31ˢᵗ 1902."

LLANFAIR-YN-NGHORNWY—S. MARY

CHALICE.—Large, plain silver Chalice, with deep beaker-like bowl, with narrow moulded lip, standing on a tall stem, divided by a large plain knop, the base moulded. Inscribed in script lettering in three lines—

" The Gift of Ellen Roberts of
Cayray to LLanvair Church
1713."

The bowl is also engraved with I.H.S., a cross and nails in glory.

Marks.—London date-letter for 1712-13. The Maker's mark, which is almost illegible, is probably W A with anchor between (Jos. Ward).

Dimensions.—Height, 9¾ in.; depth of bowl, 5¼ in.; diameter of bowl, 4⅜ in.

The donor, Ellen Roberts, was the daughter and sole heiress of William Roberts, Esquire, of Caerau and Castellor. She married Thomas Rowlands, Esquire, of Nant, Beddgelert, and their daughter and heiress, Emma, married, first, James, Lord Viscount Bulkeley, and secondly, Sir Hugh Williams, Bart., of Marl, etc.

PATEN.—A plain, circular silver plate, with moulded edge, bearing the London date-letter for 1724-5. Maker's mark illegible. Diameter, $7\frac{5}{8}$ in.

FLAGON.—Pewter, cylindrical in form, surrounded by two plain mouldings, one near the top, the other near the foot; narrow moulded lip; short moulded foot; flat cover, with pierced projecting scrolls in the front; pierced and scrolled thumb-piece; plain handle. I.H.S. and cross, within an ornamental circle, are engraved in front of body. On the cover, the initials and date—$^{AL}_{1714}{}^{*}{}^{B}$ within a circle, are engraved.

Mark, on lid, repeated three times, IF, with fleur-de-lys underneath, in a lozenge.

Date, *circa* 1710.

LLANFECHELL—S. MECHELL

CHALICE.—An interesting silver-gilt cup by a well-known craftsman, one Hans Zeiher, who flourished at the end of the sixteenth century, at the famous centre of the goldsmiths' art in Germany—Nuremberg. The bowl is oval in form, with a surbase of ornamental fluting, and is decorated with interlaced strap-work, scrolls, etc., in flat, low relief. Three bold bosses, oval in form, with cherubs' faces, surrounded by scrolls, fruit, and flowers, are applied on the bowl, at equal intervals. At the top of the stem is a flat, circular, fluted collar, divided from the bowl by two mouldings, one plain, the other of palm or laurel leaves. The stem, which is plain, with a narrow plain moulding encircling it, rests on a shoulder with a very bold egg and tongue moulding. The space between this shoulder and the base is plain, the latter being decorated with strapwork, scrolls, etc., in low relief. Some part of the decoration on the bowl has been removed to contain this inscription—

"LLanvechell
Ex Dono
LL.
D * E
1686."

The donors were David Lloyd, M.A., Rector of Llanfechell, son of John Lloyd of Bwlch-y-fen, and probably Ellen, his second wife, daughter of William Bulkeley of Bryndu. His first wife was Elizabeth, daughter or niece of Robert Lloyd, "y Person Coch."

Marks.—H Z in monogram, and N. for Nuremberg.

Dimensions.—Height, $6\frac{1}{4}$ in.

(PLATE VI., No. 1.)

PATEN-COVER.—A plain, silver-gilt Paten-Cover, with incised edge, on truncated foot. English, date *circa* 1680. Only one mark, D S or O S, with acorn branch below. The silver Chalice belonging to this has disappeared.
Dimensions.—Diameter, 4⅞ in.; height, 1¼ in.

PATEN.—A large old pewter Paten, on truncated foot, stamped with mark—a bird standing on a globe, and the name NICHOLSON.
Dimensions.—Diameter, 11½ in.; height, 3¼ in.

FLAGON.—A tall old pewter Flagon, with cylindrical body, flat cover, scrolled thumb-piece, scroll handle, stamped inside with one mark—an hour-glass with the letter W on one side. Height, 8½ in.

LLANFFINAN—S. FFINAN

An Elizabethan silver Chalice with Paten-Cover, the bowl of the Chalice engraved with a narrow, double, plain strap-work band, interlaced, and enclosing the conventional sprays of engraved foliage. In the centre of the stem, which has a plain moulding at the top and bottom, is the usual plain, compressed knop, with a narrow collar above and below it, and on the outer edge of the foot is an egg and dart moulding. The Paten-Cover is engraved on the shoulder with three rows of hyphens, and the foot is engraved with the date, 1574. Both the Chalice and Paten-Cover bear the maker's mark—a bird's head, erased, turned dexter-wise, in a shaped shield, found on Elizabethan plate in other places in this Diocese. (PLATE XXVI., NO. 3.)
Dimensions.—Chalice, 6 3/16 in. high; depth of bowl, 3⅛ in.; diameter of mouth, 3⅛ in.; diameter of foot, 3⅛ in. Paten-Cover, diameter 3⅛ in.; height, 1 in.

LLANFFLEWIN—S. FFLEWIN

An Elizabethan silver Chalice with Paten-Cover. The Chalice is engraved with the customary double, plain strap-work band, 9/16 in. wide, interlaced three times, enclosing the conventional spray of foliage, a small sprig at each intersection. The stem, which is divided by a knop entirely covered with engraved hyphens, is plainly moulded at the top and bottom. It has been rudely inscribed within recent years—

"Llanfflewin Church."

PLATE X.

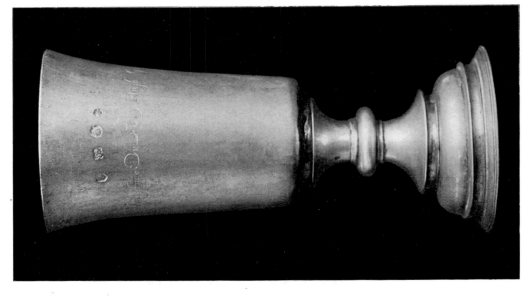

No. 3.

LLANDWROG, CARNARVONSHIRE.
JAMES I. SILVER CHALICE.
DATE: 1619.

No. 2.

PENTIR, CARNARVONSHIRE.
SILVER CHALICE.
DATE: *circa* 1685.

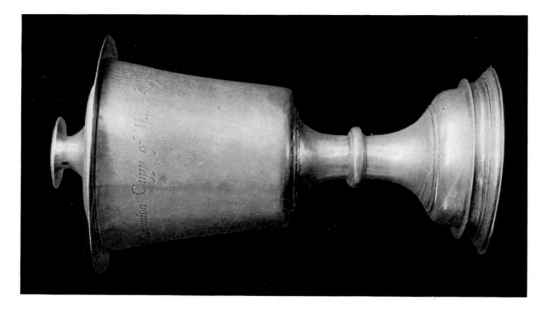

No. 1.

LLANBERIS, CARNARVONSHIRE.
CHARLES I. SILVER CHALICE AND PATEN-COVER.
DATE: 1631.

Marks.—London date-letter for 1574-5. Maker's mark, I P in shaped shield.

Dimensions.—Height, 6⅛ in.; depth of bowl, 3³⁄₁₆ in.; diameter of mouth, 3³⁄₁₆ in.; foot, 3³⁄₁₆ in.

The Paten-Cover is engraved with three rows of hyphens on the shoulder, and on the foot the date 1574 is engraved. It has the same marks as on the Chalice, and its dimensions are: diameter, 3¼ in.; height, 1⅜ in. (PLATE XXXIII., No. 2.)

LLANFIGAEL—S. VIGILIUS or S. BIGAEL

An Elizabethan silver Chalice with Paten-Cover. The bowl of the Chalice is deep and tapering, and is engraved near the top with plain, double-strap band, ½ in. wide, enclosing the conventional spray of foliage, the band intersecting four times, with a large triple-like spray springing above and below each intersection. The stem, which has the usual central knop, in this case quite plain, with a collar above and below it, has a plain moulding at each end. On the bowl, the name of the parish—" LLanfugail "—has been engraved at a much later date.

Marks.—London date-letter for 1574-5. Maker's mark, H C, with a hand holding a hammer, in plain shield (Jackson, 1535-6).

Dimensions.—Height, 6⅜ in.; depth of bowl, 3¾ in.; diameter of mouth, 3⅛ in.; diameter of foot, 3¹⁄₁₆ in.

The Paten-Cover belonging to this chalice has a small, plain foot, on which is engraved the date, 1574, and on the shoulder of the cover are rows of engraved hyphens. The marks are the same as those on the Chalice.

Dimensions.—Diameter, 3³⁄₁₆ in.; height, 1¼ in. (PLATE XXXIII., No. 1.)

PEWTER PLATE.—8½ in. in diameter, the initials $W^{P}K$ engraved on the back. There are two marks stamped on it, repeated twice—a bird on a Tudor rose, with foliations on either side, and BALDWIN in a scroll.

LLANFIHANGEL-DINSYLWY—S. MICHAEL

CHALICE.—A Chalice of old Sheffield-plate, inscribed—" The Gift of Robert Hughes Esqʳ. of Plas yn Llangoed to the Parish of Llanfihangel Tyn Sylwy, 1816."

Height, 7¾ in.

D

PATEN.—Probably plain old Sheffield-plate.

The donor was a son of William Hughes, Esq., nephew and heir to his uncle, Hugh Hughes, who gave the silver Paten to Llangoed Church.

LLANFIHANGEL-TRE'R-BEIRDD—S. MICHAEL

A goblet-shape Chalice of Britannia metal.

A large Paten, with shell and scroll border, on high foot, of the same metal.

An electro-plated set of Chalice, Paten, a Flagon, and Cruet.

The old silver Communion plate was stolen some years ago.

LLANFIHANGEL-YN-NHOWYN—S. MICHAEL

Electro-plated Chalice and Paten, inscribed—"Llanfihangel Church 1877."

A small, old pewter Jug, inverted bell-shape bowl, with small lip, and moulded edge, on a low foot. No marks. Height, $4\frac{1}{4}$ in.

An old pewter dish, circular, flat, $8\frac{3}{4}$ in. in diameter. Marks, three talbot or leopards' heads erased, and LONDON in a scroll.

LLANFIHANGEL-YSCEIFIOG—S. MICHAEL

An interesting Elizabethan silver Chalice, with V-shape bowl, chased with five plain, flat panels containing roses and pomegranates on a scaled background, one of the panels enclosing a plain shield, with the pounced initials—$T\,S$ $R\,(or\,B)$

It stands on a slender, baluster-like stem, chased with acanthus leaves, resting on a splayed foot, with five panels, decorated in a similar manner as those on the bowl. The domed cover, which has similar panels, with the decorative foliage, etc., rather bolder, is surmounted by a steeple, springing from three scrolled terminal figures. The cup itself bears the London date-letter for the year 1601, the maker's mark being illegible, while the cover is stamped with the date-letter for 1611. Maker's mark, R M, with pellet between, in shaped shield.

Dimensions of Chalice.—Height, $8\frac{1}{16}$ in.; depth of bowl, $3\frac{1}{2}$ in.; diameter of mouth, $3\frac{3}{4}$ in.; diameter of foot, $3\frac{7}{8}$ in. The cover is $1\frac{1}{2}$ in. high, and the steeple $4\frac{1}{2}$ in. high. (PLATE VI., No. 2.)

A small, new, silver Paten, the border engraved with panels similar to those on the Chalice. I.H.S. engraved in centre. 6 in. in diameter.

LLANFWROG—S. MWROG

An Elizabethan silver Chalice, with the usual plain, double strap-work band, interlacing four times and enclosing conventional foliage, engraved on the centre of the bowl, and four rows of hyphens engraved near the lip, standing on a stem, with a moulding of vertical reedings above and below. The stem has, unfortunately, been considerably shortened in a recent restoration.

London date-letter for 1561. Maker's mark, the sun in splendour.
Dimensions.—Height, 4⅜ in.; depth of bowl, 2¾ in.

An Elizabethan silver Paten-Cover, engraved with an interlaced strap-work band, enclosing foliage, with reeded edge. On the plain foot, the date, 1574, is engraved. Maker's mark only, a bird's head erased, turned dexter-wise, in shaped shield.

Diameter, 3¼ in.; height, 1⅝ in.

A plain electro-plate Flagon.

An electro-plate Paten.

In 1831 this Church possessed two silver Chalices, a pewter Flagon and a pewter Plate. All have disappeared with the exception of the above Chalice.

LLANGADWALADR—S. CADWALADR

CHALICE.—A tall, plain, silver Chalice, beaker-shape bowl, square-shape lip, the stem divided by a large moulding or knop, on a moulded foot. The letters I.H.S., a cross and three nails in glory, are engraved in large size on centre of bowl, and this inscription is engraved in script underneath the rim of the foot—" The gift of O. P. Meyrick Esqr. to the Parish of Llangadwalader, 1811."
Marks.—London date-letter for 1716. Maker's mark illegible.
Dimensions.—Height, 8½ in.; depth of bowl, 4¾ in.; diameter of mouth, 4½ in.

PATEN.—A plain silver Paten, on a foot with reeded edge, with the engraved letters I.H.S., etc., occupying the centre, and with the same inscription engraved on the rim as on the Chalice.
Marks.—London date-letter for 1810. Maker's mark, I C, with pellet between, in oblong.
Dimensions.—Diameter, 6½ in.; height, 1¾ in.

Owen Putland Meyrick, Esquire, was the son and heir of Owen Meyrick, Esquire, of Bodorgan, and Hester Putland, of London.

FLAGON.—A tall, plain, silver Flagon, with cylindrical body, the edge of lip reeded, a slightly domed cover, pierced thumb-piece, the end of handle terminating in a heart-shape shield; the same letters, I.H.S., etc., engraved in centre; same date-letter and marks as on Paten.

Dimensions.—Height, $9\frac{1}{8}$ in.; height, without cover, $8\frac{1}{4}$ in.; diameter of mouth, $4\frac{1}{2}$ in.; diameter of foot, $3\frac{3}{4}$ in.

ALMS DISH.—Plain, circular silver Dish, exactly like the Dish used as a Paten in the adjoining Parish Church of Aberffraw. Inscribed— "The Gift of S^r. Arthur Owen Bar^t. to the Parish-Church of Llan-Kadwaladr, 1753."

London date-letter for 1761. Maker, Fras. Crump.

LLANGAFFO—S. CAFFO

CHALICE.—This is an interesting eighteenth century reproduction of an Elizabethan Chalice, engraved with the usual plain, double strap-work band, interlacing three times and enclosing the conventional sprays of foliage, a sprig of foliage carried above and below each intersection. At the top of the stem and on the edge of the foot is a delicate ovolo moulding, and the flat knop on the stem has short incised lines or hyphens. It is inscribed—"The Gift of the Rev^d. Thos. Holland of Berw Rect^r. to the Church of LLangeinwen and LLangaffo 1736."

There are no marks.

Dimensions.—Height, $7\frac{1}{2}$ in.; depth of bowl, $4\frac{1}{4}$ in.; diameter of mouth, $3\frac{3}{4}$ in.

The donor, the Rev. Thomas Holland, was the second son of John Holland of Carnarvon and Berw, Gent. He gave a silver Paten to Llangeinwen in 1736.

PATEN-COVER.—The silver Paten-Cover belonging to the Chalice is engraved with a band of hyphens and on the short foot the date 1736. Diameter, $3\frac{7}{8}$ in. No marks.

FLAGON.—A silver Flagon with pear-shape body, engraved with foliage, etc. A fleur-de-lys on the cover. Inscribed—

"PRESENTED TO LLANGAFFO CHURCH CHRISTMAS 1896 BY
A.E.P.
M.A.P. DINAM
M.J.
M.K.J. TREANNA."

Marks.—London date-letter for 1891-2. Maker's mark, $_W^{H\,E}$ in trefoil.

Height, 10 in.

A small plated Salver on three feet.

LLANGEFNI—S. CYNGAR

CHALICE.—A plain silver Chalice, with beaker-shape bowl, on truncated stem. The only mark, which is indistinct, is (?) R L, with fleur-de-lys under, in a plain shield.

Date, *circa* 1690.

Dimensions.—Height, $6\frac{5}{8}$ in.; depth of bowl, $3\frac{3}{4}$ in.; diameter of mouth, $3\frac{3}{4}$ in.

A large and massive silver Service, consisting of a Chalice, Paten and Flagon. The Chalice has an inverted, bell-shape bowl, the lip chased with flowers and scrolls, and the centre of stem similarly chased. The edge of foot has an egg and tongue moulding. Inscribed—" Os oes ar neb syched, deued attaf fi, ac yfed. Ioan. vii. 37." It is also inscribed on the foot—" Purchased by money collected at the Consecration of this Church, 29th. June, 1824.

HENRY WILLIAM MAJENDIE, Bishop.

EVAN WILLIAMS, A.M. Rector.

WILLIAM PRICE POOLE } Church-

RICE ROBERTS } Wardens."

Marks.—London date-letter for 1824-5. Maker's mark, J A, with pellet between, in oblong cartouche.

Dimensions.—Height, $8\frac{5}{16}$ in.; diameter of mouth, 4 in.

The Flagon has fluted edges on base and cover, a part of the body and the domed cover chased with flowers and scrolls, an acanthus leaf on the spout and handle; an egg and tongue moulding above the spreading out base; a scroll thumb-piece. The conventional device, I.H.S., a cross and three nails in glory, is engraved on body, and also this inscription—

"GWAED IESU GRIST

Sydd yn ein glanhau ni oddiwrth bob pechod. Ioan i. 7."

The foot has the same second inscription as on the Chalice.

Marks as on the Chalice.

Height, 12 in.; body only, 10 in.; diameter of mouth, $4\frac{1}{4}$ in.

The Paten is large and has similar chasing, with egg and tongue mouldings. The conventional device, I.H.S., etc., is engraved in the centre, and also this inscription—" Y neb sydd yn bwytta'r BARA hwn, a fydd byw yn dragywydd. Ioan. vi. 51." The second inscription is the same as that on the Chalice.

Marks as on the Chalice.

Diameter, $8\frac{3}{4}$ in.; height, 3 in.

FLAGON.—An old pewter Flagon, slightly tapering cylindrical body, open scroll work on front edge of the flat cover; low moulded foot. On the handle these initials are engraved—$\begin{smallmatrix} F & B's \\ & G \end{smallmatrix}$

No marks.

Height, 9¾ in.; diameter of mouth, 4½ in.

A small, plain, electro-plated Paten.

LLANGEINWEN—S. CEINWEN

CHALICE AND PATEN-COVER.—An interesting Chalice with plain, inverted, bell-shape bowl, supported by a stem with a delicate moulding of ovolos and roses at the top. The knop is entirely covered with ovolos, now nearly worn away. The edge of the foot has a moulding like that at the top of stem, and above it is a delicate moulding of small plain ovolos. The Chalice is inscribed near the lip—

> " Ex dono R. White Lhan-ginwen
> Rectoris regi a sacris qui
> alienarit anathema sit
> 1615."

The Paten-Cover, which has a foot, is quite plain.

Marks.—London date-letter for 1614-15. Maker's mark, F above W, in a shaped shield (Jackson, 1611-12).

Dimensions.—Chalice: height, 8 in.; depth of bowl, 4¼ in.; diameter of mouth, 3¾ in. Paten-Cover: diameter, 4⅜ in.; height, 1⅝ in. (PLATE XXXI., No. 2.)

Robert White, D.D., was a son of Richard White, Esq., of The Friars, Beaumaris. He was Prebendary of Penmynydd and Worcester, Rector of Llangeinwen and Newborough, Archdeacon of Merioneth and Norfolk, and sinecure Rector of Clynnog. He was buried at Llangaffo in 1657.

PATEN.—A plain, silver Paten, with wide, flat rim, on short truncated stem, inscribed—" The Gift of the Rev^d. Thos. Holland of Berw, Rector to the Church of LLangeinwen, 1736."

No marks. (PLATE XXXI., No. 2.)

Dimensions.—Diameter, 7⅜ in.; height, 1⅜ in.

Thomas Holland, second son of John Holland, of Carnarvon and Berw, Gent., was instituted Rector of Llangeinwen in 1708, and died in 1746. He gave the silver Chalice to Llangaffo Church.

PLATE XI.

No. 2.

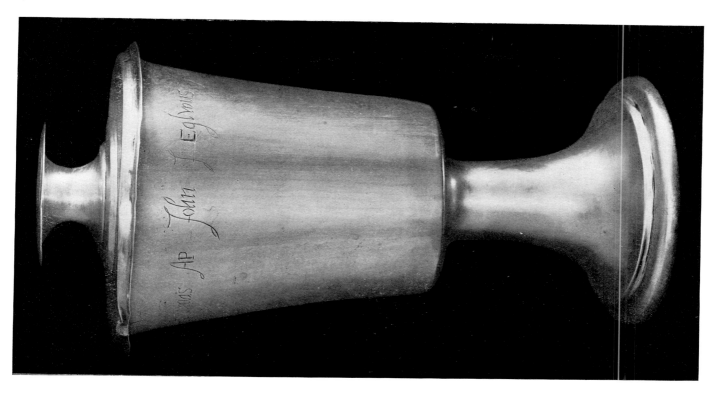

LLANAELHAIARN, CARNARVONSHIRE.

CHARLES I. SILVER CHALICE AND PATEN-COVER.

DATE: 1638.

CLYNNOG, CARNARVONSHIRE.

CHARLES I. SILVER CHALICE AND PATEN-COVER.

DATE : 1636-7.

LLANGOED—S. CAWRDAF

CHALICE.—An Elizabethan silver Chalice with beaker-shape bowl, engraved with plain, double strap-work band, filled with conventional sprays of foliage, a large triple spray carried above and below each of the four intersections. The stem, which is divided in the middle by a plain knop between two narrow, plain collars, has a plain reeded moulding at each end, and stands on a plain moulded foot. This Chalice is stamped with the maker's mark—a bird's head, erased, turned dexter-wise, in a shaped shield, such as is apparently confined to this diocese. (PLATE XXVI., No. 1.)

Dimensions.—Height, $6\frac{3}{8}$ in.; depth of bowl, $3\frac{3}{16}$ in.; diameter of mouth, $2\frac{7}{8}$ in.

PATEN.—A plain, silver Paten, with narrow reeded border, standing on a very short, truncated foot. Inscribed in one line in script lettering on the back—" The Gift of M^r. Hugh Hughes late of LLangoed & Deputy Baron of the Exchecqr in North Wales."

Marks.—London date-letter for 1682-3. Maker's mark, S R with a seeded rose below, in plain shield.

Dimensions.—Diameter, $7\frac{1}{2}$ in.; height, 1 in.

FLAGON.—An interesting old pewter Flagon with tall, cylindrical body, the lip moulded; a low, domed cover, with thumb-piece; a double row of incised lines above the moulded foot. Inscribed in one line, in small roman letters—

" The guift of William Wynn to LLangoyd Church 1637."

The only mark stamped on it appears on the handle, and is an oval enclosing an ewer, an architectural pillar, a rose, and above these the initials E C or E G.

Dimensions.—Height to top of cover, $10\frac{1}{8}$ in.; height of body only, $9\frac{1}{8}$ in.; diameter of mouth, 4 in.

This is the earliest piece of dated pewter in the diocese. (PLATE XVII., No. 1.)

FLAGON.—A plain, electro-plated Flagon.

The donor of the Paten was the eldest son and heir of Roger Hughes, Esq., of Plascoch, and Margaret, his wife, daughter and heiress of Captain Henry Jones of Plas Llangoed. Hugh Hughes was born in 1682, and married Emma, daughter of William Griffith, of Garreglwyd, Esq., January 19th, 1718.

LLANGRISTIOLUS—S. CRISTIOLUS

CHALICE.—A plain silver Chalice, with short beaker-shape bowl rounded at the base, supported by a baluster stem on a splayed foot. A roman capital K stamped under foot.

Marks.—London date-letter for 1638-9. Maker's mark (indistinct), probably D.W. with a mullet below, in heart-shape shield.

Dimensions.—Height, 7⅜ in.; depth of bowl, 3⅝ in.; diameter of mouth, 3⅞ in.

PATEN.—A large, plain silver Paten with embossed gadroon border, supported by a truncated foot. In the centre this inscription, surrounded by foliation, scrolls, etc., and surmounted by a crest—*a Cornish chough*—

" d.d.
H. LM.
1756."

Marks.—None. Date, *circa* 1690.

Dimensions.—Diameter, 10½ in.; height, 2¾ in.

The initials are supposed to represent Henry Morgan, second son of Rev. William Morgan, LL.B., Chancellor of Bangor, and heir of Henblas.

LLANGWYFAN—S. MARY

The Chalice is an ordinary fluted goblet of electro-plate, and the Paten in use is in the form of an ordinary domestic salver, plated, with an engraved ornamentation, 6½ in. in diameter.

The Communion plate belonging to the old Church of Llangwyfan has, unhappily, long since disappeared.

LLANGWYLLOG—S. CWYLLOG

CHALICE.—A small, plain silver Chalice, with inverted bell-shape bowl, supported by a short stem divided by a flattened knop, on a moulded foot. A crest—*a bull's head issuing from a ducal coronet*, with a viscount's coronet above—is engraved on the bowl. The date, 1735, engraved under the foot.

Mark.—WR, conjoined, in an oblong—the mark of the second Wm. Richardson, of Chester, 1720-40.

Dimensions.—Height, 6 in.; depth of bowl, 3¼ in.; diameter of bowl, 3 in.

PATEN.—A plain, circular, electro-plate dish.

FLAGON.—A tall, tankard-like Flagon of old Sheffield-plate, with a spout and a domed cover, a pierced wire thumb-piece, a moulding encircling the body near the foot.   Inscribed in script lettering—

"The Gift of
Thomas James Warren Bulkeley
Lord Viscount Bulkeley
to the Parish Church of Llangwillog,
County of Anglesey
of which He is Lay Improprietor
Septr. 5th, 1817."

LLANIDAN—S. AIDAN

CHALICE.—A small silver Chalice of medieval design, on a sexfoil foot, inscribed underneath—"The Gift of P. LLoyd of LLigwy & LLaniday in ye County of Anglesey Esq to ye Parish of LLanidan."
Marks.—London date-letter for 1871-2.   Maker's mark, JCS, in an oblong.
Height, 5¾ in.
This Chalice and the Alms Dish, which were given probably in 1701, have been re-made.   The donor was the eldest son of Pierce Lloyd, Esq., of Lligwy, Anglesey, and Martha, daughter and heiress of Godfrey Prydderch, of Myfyrian, Llanidan.

PATEN.—A small, plain silver Paten, 5½ in. in diameter, with same marks as on the Chalice.

CRUETS.—Two small glass Cruets with silver handles and mounts. Same marks as on the Chalice and Paten.

ALMS DISH.—A circular silver Alms Dish, with embossed gadroon border.   It is inscribed—"The Gift of Pierce LLoyd of LLigwy & LLanidan in ye County of Anglesey Esq to ye Parish of LLanidan." This is a reconstruction from an old piece—a Paten—one part bearing the London date-letter for 1701-2, with Jos. Ward's mark, the rim having been added in 1871-2.   Diameter, 9¾ in.

Two silver Chalices, a silver Tankard, a silver Salver (Paten), and a large pewter Tankard, are mentioned in the terriers for 1811.   The two Tankards and one of the Chalices have, unfortunately, disappeared.

E

LLANIESTYN—S. IESTYN

A small Elizabethan silver Chalice, with beaker-shape bowl, engraved with a double plain band, enclosing three rows of hyphens, a single row of hyphens carried above, near the lip, and a similar row lower down the bowl. This, as will be observed, is a departure from the conventional sprays of foliage; and another deviation is that the band is carried along without any intersection. The stem, which has suffered damage by an unskilful repairer and has been shortened, has the customary plain compressed knop, and a plain reeded moulding at each end, standing on a plain foot.

The only mark is the bird's head erased, found on other Elizabethan Chalices in this Diocese. (PLATE XXVI., No. 2.)

Dimensions.—Height, $5\frac{1}{2}$ in.; depth of bowl, $2\frac{7}{8}$ in.; diameter of mouth, $2\frac{11}{16}$ in.

In this Church are a Chalice and Paten of old Sheffield-plate, engraved with the letters I.H.S. and a cross in glory, both inscribed— "Llaniestyn, Anglesey 1836."

Height of Chalice, $6\frac{7}{8}$ in.; depth of bowl, $4\frac{3}{8}$ in.; diameter of mouth, $3\frac{7}{8}$ in.; of foot, 3 in. The Paten is $7\frac{1}{2}$ in. in diameter, and $1\frac{1}{2}$ in. high.

LLANRHWYDRUS—S. RHWYDRUS

There is no plate of any description in this Church, though reference is made in the old terriers for 1811 and 1814 to a "silver cup and platter."

LLANRHYDDLAD—S. RHYDDLAD

CHALICE.—A large, plain silver Chalice, with beaker-shape bowl, standing on a truncated stem, the edge of foot incised with three lines.

Marks.—London date-letter for 1660-1, 1662-3, or 1664-5. Maker's mark, TD above a mullet between two annulets, in shaped shield.

Dimensions.—Height, $6\frac{7}{8}$ in.; depth of bowl, $4\frac{3}{16}$ in.; diameter of mouth, $4\frac{1}{2}$ in.; foot, $4\frac{7}{16}$ in.

Mention is made in the old terriers for the years 1722, 1817, 1821, and 1831, of a pewter Flagon and Plate, but these are no longer in this Church.

There is at Llanrhyddlad an old silver Paten Cover, which probably belongs to the old Chalice, and is perhaps of the same date.

PLATE XII.

BANGOR CATHEDRAL.

CHARLES I. SILVER-GILT SERVICE OF COMMUNION PLATE.

DATES: { TWO CHALICES AND PATEN-COVERS, 1637-8.
{ FLAGON AND ALMS DISH, 1638-9.

LLANSADWRN—S. SADWRN

CHALICE AND PATEN-COVER.—An interesting silver Chalice, with deep beaker-shape bowl, encircled in the centre by a double engraved band—the band filled with a single row of incised lines or hyphens—enclosing delicately engraved sprays of foliations, among them the emblems of the three kingdoms—the rose, thistle and shamrock; and above the band: "LLan * Sadurn." The bowl stands on a truncated stem with moulded foot. The Paten-Cover of this Chalice is quite plain, and is engraved on the foot with the same inscription as on the Chalice, with this difference, that the "u" in Sadurn is substituted by a "w." Both are stamped with two marks: TG, in script capitals, in a shaped shield, and "stā." in an oblong shield with cut-off corners; the first representing the mark of Timothy Gardener, silversmith, of Chester, *circa* 1690, and the second an abbreviation of the word Sterling, or Starling, used by the Chester goldsmiths at the end of the seventeenth century. This maker's mark, it is interesting to observe, is now brought to light for the first time. (PLATE XVII., No. 2.)

Dimensions.—Chalice: height, 8 in.; depth of bowl, $4\frac{7}{8}$ in.; diameter of bowl, 4 in. Paten-Cover: diameter, $4\frac{1}{2}$ in.; height, $2\frac{1}{4}$ in.

PATEN.—A large plain silver Paten with moulded edge, standing on a foot, which is inscribed—

> " The gift of
> Mᵣ. Eliz: Wynne of
> Penheskin Wid: to
> the Parish Church of
> LLansadurn.
> 1714."

Marks.—London date-letter for *1714*-15. Maker's mark, Lo, with key above, a pellet below, in shaped shield (Natl. Locke).

Dimensions.—Diameter, $8\frac{1}{2}$ in.; height, $1\frac{1}{2}$ in.

The donor, Elizabeth Wynne, was the widow of Richard Wynne, Esq., of Penhesgyn, now a farmhouse $1\frac{1}{2}$ miles south-west of Llansadwrn Church. She was a daughter of Dr. William Wynne, of Garthewyn-uchaf, Llanfair-tal-haiarn, and of Ty-gwyn in Llanllechid—a younger son of Melay. She died in 1714, and was buried in the chancel of Llansadwrn Church, where a marble tablet is erected to her memory.

Extract from Elizabeth Wynne's Will:—" I do hereby give and dispose to yᵉ use of yᵉ Church of Llansadwrn, £5 . 4 . 5 to buy a Communion Cup and Table Cloth for yᵉ Altar."

FLAGON.—A plain silver quart Tankard, domestic in character, with globular body, engraved with a band like that on Chalice, a moulding encircling lower part of body; short moulded foot; a domed cover, with open scrolled thumb-piece; the scrolled handle terminating in a plain shield. In 1881 a spout was added, and at this time the band was no doubt engraved on the body. It is inscribed—" The Gift of Brownlow W. Wynne of Garthewin in the County of Denbigh Esquire to the Parish of LLan-Sadwrn 1881."

Marks.—London date-letter for 1766-7. Maker's mark, W·S, with pellet between, in an oval (Wm. Shaw).

Brownlow Wynne Wynne, who presented this Tankard or Flagon at the restoration of the Church in 1881, was a representative of the Wynnes of Penhesgyn. He died 1st May, 1882.

LLANTRISANT

An Elizabethan silver Chalice, the bowl engraved near the top with the customary plain strap-work, filled in with sprays of conventional foliage. This Chalice has been considerably restored within recent years, and the only original parts are probably the bowl and the edge of the foot, the stem being entirely new. It bears no marks of any description. Probable date, 1575.

Dimensions.—Height, $6\frac{3}{4}$ in.; length of bowl, $3\frac{1}{2}$ in.; diameter of mouth, $3\frac{1}{2}$ in.

A small, plain, new silver Paten.

The whereabouts of the old pewter Flagon and Paten, described in the terriers between 1801 and 1831, cannot be ascertained.

LLANWENLLWYFO—S. GWENLLWYFO

CHALICE (No. 1).—A large, plain silver Chalice, with deep beaker-shape bowl, curved lip, supported by a short stem, divided by a plain rounded moulding, resting on a moulded foot.

Marks.—London date-letter for 1711-12. Maker, probably Natl. Locke.

Dimensions.—Height, $8\frac{1}{2}$ in.; depth of bowl, $5\frac{3}{8}$ in.; diameter of mouth, $4\frac{1}{4}$ in.

PATEN (No. 1).—An old pewter Paten, with moulded edge, on a moulded foot, inscribed—

"Eglwys lLanwenllyfo 1749."

No marks.

Dimensions.—Diameter, 9 in.; height, 2¼ in.

CHALICE (No. 2).—A small, plain silver Chalice, with inverted bell-shape bowl on a tall stem. I.H.S. in glory engraved on bowl, and this inscription on the foot—

"LLANWENLLWYFO CHURCH
MAY 20th, 1866."

Marks.—London date-letter for 1854-5. Maker's mark, R·H, with pellet between, in an oblong cartouche (R. Hennell).

Height, 6¼ in.

PATEN (No. 2).—A plain silver Paten with moulded edge on foot. I.H.S. in glory engraved in the centre, and the same inscription as on the Chalice on the foot.

Marks.—London date-letter for 1861-2.

Diameter, 6½ in.; height, 2¾ in.

FLAGON.—A plain silver Flagon, the body cylindrical, with domed cover. I.H.S. in glory engraved under the spout, and this inscription on the foot:—" This Flagon with Chalice and Paten presented to Llanwenllwyfo Church by the Hon: Gwen Gertrude Hughes of Llysdulas on the occasion of her coming of age. May 20. 1866."

Marks.—London date-letter for 1863-4. Maker's mark, AM, in oblong cartouche.

Height, 8 in.

LLANYNGHENEDL—S. ENGHENEDL

Silver Chalice and Paten-Cover, plain. The bowl of the Chalice resembles an inverted bell, standing on a stem, divided by a flat moulded knop, on a moulded foot. It is inscribed in script lettering—

" Thos. Vincett, Vicar of LLanyngenedle
Griffith Edward ⎫
Owen Hughes ⎬ Chur. Wardens 1724."

Marks.—Chester date-letter for 1724-5. Maker's mark, Ri, with crescent above, in square shield—the mark of the first William Richardson (1697-1727).

Dimensions.—Height, 7⅝ in.; depth of bowl, 3⅝ in.; diameter of mouth, 3¼ in.

The Paten-Cover of this Chalice is flat, with a narrow edge, and has a plain foot. Diameter, $3\frac{5}{8}$ in.; height, 1 in. The maker's mark and leopard's head only are stamped on it.

Thomas Vincent, M.A., was Rector of Llanfachraeth with Llanynghenedl and Llanfigael from 1713 to 1738, and there is a tablet to his memory in Llanfachraeth Church.

NEWBOROUGH—S. PEDR A CHAPEL MAIR

CHALICE.—A plain silver Chalice, with beaker-shape bowl, narrow at the base, supported by a truncated stem with moulding in centre, resting on a moulded foot. The only mark is RR addorsed, with an illegible device underneath in a shaped shield, twice repeated.
Date, *circa* 1710.
Dimensions.—Height, $6\frac{5}{8}$ in.; depth of bowl, $3\frac{3}{4}$ in.; diameter of mouth, $3\frac{5}{8}$ in.

PATEN.—A plain silver Paten, the edge moulded, on a truncated stem. Inscribed on the back:—"In Usum Ecclesiæ Parochialis S^{ti}. Petri de Newborough hanc Scutellam. Gul. Williams Ejusdem Rector D.D.D. 1744."
Marks.—London date-letter for 1719-20. Maker's mark illegible.
Dimensions.—Diameter, $8\frac{3}{8}$ in.; height, $2\frac{1}{8}$ in.

William Williams, Rector of Newborough 1722-1746, was the second son of Thomas Williams, Esq., of Quirt, Llangeinwen.

The old pewter Flagon and pewter Salver mentioned in the terriers between 1722 and 1820 have disappeared.

PENMON—S. SEIRIOL

CHALICE.—A plain silver Chalice with beaker-shape bowl, a rim added to the lip, a plain flattened knop on the stem, the foot moulded. The Christian symbols, I.H.S., a cross and three nails, are engraved on the bowl, which has this double inscription—

" The free gift of Thomas Davies to LLandegvan Parish in the County of Anglesey Anno Domine 1639.

" NB. This Chalice was Transfered from the Parish Church of LLANDEGVAN to the Parish Church of Penmon By Thomas James Warren Bulkeley LORD VISCOUNT BULKELEY on his Gift of other Sacramental Plate TO THE FORMER CHURCH JUNE 1812."

Marks obliterated.

Dimensions.—Height, 7⅝ in.; depth of bowl, 3⅞ in.; diameter of mouth, 4 in.

The original character of this Chalice suffered complete transformation at the date when it was transferred here. (*See note under Llandegfan as to Thomas Davies.*)

PATEN.—A plain silver Paten with flat rim, which is inscribed— " The Guift of yᵉ Rᵗ. Honᵇˡᵉ. Rich. Lᵈ. Viscoᵗ. Bulkeley to the Church of Beaumaris Anᵒ. 1704." In the centre of the flat depression a shield of arms : *a chevron gules between three bulls' heads cabossed*, with mantling, and surmounted by a viscount's coronet, and this inscription, are engraved:—" NB. This Paten was Transfered From the Church of Beaumaris to the Parish Church of Penmon By Thoˢ. James Warren Bulkeley Lᵈ. Visᶜᵗ. Bulkeley On his Gift of other Sacramental Plate to the former Church. JUNE 1812."

On the foot is the conventional device, I.H.S., etc.

Marks.—London date-letter for 1706-7. Maker's mark, WA, with anchor between, in shaped shield (Jos. Ward).

Dimensions.—Diameter, 6¼ in.; height, 1⅝ in.

This is exactly like the Paten at Llandegfan.

ALMS DISH.—This is a silver soup-plate, with fluted edge, and is exactly similar to that at Llanfaes, and is inscribed—" The Gift of Thomas James Warren Bulkeley Lord Viscount Bulkeley To the Parish Church of Penmon in the County of Anglesey, June 1812." I.H.S., etc., in centre.

Marks.—Newcastle date-letter for 1778-9. Maker's mark, W·W, with pellet between in plain oblong (? Wm. Williamson).

Diameter, 9¼ in.

A very small, plain silver Chalice and Paten, for private Communion, both engraved with sacred letters I.H.S., etc., and with this inscription—" The gift of Thoˢ. James Warren Bulkeley Lord Viscount Bulkeley To the Parish Church of Penmon, June 1812."

Marks.—London date-letter for 1812-13. Makers' mark, _{E R} ^{T P} _{J P}

Dimensions.—Height, 3⅝ in.; diameter of mouth, 2 in.

PENMYNYDD—S. GREDIFAEL

An interesting and valuable Elizabethan silver Tazza, which, though originally intended for sweetmeats, has been used here as a Chalice. It has a plain shallow bowl, with a gilt embossed bust of a Roman warrior, on a matted surface, enclosed in a wreath of laurels, 2³⁄₁₆ in. in diameter, in the centre of the bowl inside. The stem is plain, and is divided by a plain compressed knop between two small collars, and at the top and bottom is a vertical reeded moulding. The foot, which is gilt, is rounded, and is embossed with four grotesque human masks in plain strap-work cartouches, scrolled, and separated by clusters of various fruits, embossed. Dividing this decorated part of the foot from the extreme edge, which has an egg and dart moulding, is a vertical reeded moulding, as on the stem. The initials and date, OP 1573, are deeply engraved under the edge of the foot, and on the same edge are these initials, IG. EMR ROT, rudely engraved.

On the bowl is this inscription in one line in script lettering—" The Gifft of Coningesby Williams Esquire to the Church of Pen Mynidd Feb^r. y^e. 1707." (PLATE IV.)

Marks.—London date-letter for 1570-1. Maker's mark, SL in a shaped shield.

Dimensions.—Height, 4$\frac{3}{8}$ in.; depth of bowl, $\frac{7}{8}$ in.; diameter of bowl, 6$\frac{1}{4}$ in.; diameter of foot, 3$\frac{3}{4}$ in.

A plain silver Chalice, with plain bell-shape bowl, supported by a baluster foot on a splayed foot, the edge of foot incised with three lines. Inscribed—

" The Gifft of Coningesby Williams Esquire
To the Church of Pen Mynidd Feb^r 26th. 1707."

The initials $^*_*{}^B_I{}^*_*{}^M_*$ are pounced on the bowl near the lip.

Marks.—London date-letter for 1638-9. Maker's mark, RC, with three pellets and mullets above and below, in a shaped shield.

Dimensions.—Height, 7$\frac{3}{8}$ in.; depth of bowl, 3$\frac{5}{8}$ in.; diameter of mouth, 4 in. (PLATE XIV., No. 3.)

A tall pewter Goblet, a moulding encircling centre of body, supported on a slender stem. It is stamped with four marks, (1) a lion; (2) illegible; (3) a buckle; (4) HJ in an oblong. Date, *circa* 1780. Height, 8$\frac{1}{2}$ in.

A plain, new silver Paten, 6 in. in diameter, inscribed—" The Gift of H. D. O., Vicar, to Penmynydd Church 1897."

The donor of this Paten is the present Vicar, the Rev. H. Davies Owen, M.A.

The donor of the Elizabethan Tazza and Charles I. Chalice, Coningsby Williams, was the son and heir of Glanygors, Llanfihangel-Ysceifiog. He married Margaret, daughter and heiress of Richard Owen Tudor of Penmynydd, and was buried in Penmynydd Church in 1707. The Tazza is believed to have formed part of the domestic plate of the ancient house of Penmynydd.

PLATE XIII.

BANGOR CATHEDRAL.

SILVER-GILT SERVICE OF COMMUNION PLATE.

DATE: 1777-8.

PENRHOSLLIGWY—S. MICHAEL

CHALICE.—A large silver Chalice, engraved with various embellishments and the sacred letters I.H.S., the foot ornately engraved and the edge beaded. The knop on stem is also beaded. Inscribed on foot—

"Presented to the Church of Penrhos
Lligwy, by HON. F. IRBY, April, 1860."

London date-letter for 1859-60. Maker's mark, GA, in quatrefoil (Geo. Angell).
Height, 8⅝ in.

PATEN.—A silver Paten on foot, I.H.S. in glory engraved in the centre, and arabesques and crosses on the rim, the edge of foot beaded. Engraved with same inscription as on the Chalice.
Marks as on the Chalice.
Diameter, 7¾ in.; height, 3 in.

The terriers between 1811 and 1837 contain a reference to a silver Chalice, a pewter Flagon and Plate, but no trace of these can be found.

PENTRAETH—S. MARY

CHALICE.—A plain silver Chalice with deep, beaker-shape bowl, supported by a short truncated stem. Inscribed—

"PENTRAETH
T W ×
W E × Wardens, 1785."

Marks.—NB conjoined, and "Sterl:" in an irregular cartouche—the mark of Nathaniel Bullen, of Chester, *circa* 1685, as on the Chalice at Llanfihangel Bachellaeth, Carnarvonshire.
Dimensions.—Height, 6⅝ in.; depth of bowl, 4¼ in.; diameter of mouth, 3⅞ in.

PATEN.—A small new silver Paten, plain, 5 in. in diameter.
London date-letter for 1874-5. Maker's mark, TP, in an oblong.

FLAGON.—Electro-plate.

The old Flagon, Dish and Plate, of pewter, mentioned in the terriers between 1776 and 1837, have unfortunately disappeared.

F

RHODWYDDGEIDIO—S. CEIDIO

An unusually small Elizabethan silver Chalice, with beaker-shape bowl, and with the customary plain, double strap-work band, ½ in. wide, intersecting three times, enclosing the conventional sprays of foliage, a single sprig above and below each intersection, engraved round the centre of the body. The stem, which is divided by a plain knop, and the foot, are plain. The cup is roughly inscribed, partially in roman capitals, and partially in small roman letters—

" This Cup Belongs to Rhodygeidio Chapel
T W
W P   Wardens
1714."

The unusual smallness of this interesting Chalice, which is, un-fortunately, in a battered condition, suggests that it was probably hammered out of the pre-Reformation Chalice when the injunction went forth that all Massing Chalices were to be turned into " decent Communion Cups." (PLATE XXX., No. 2.)

Marks.—London date-letter for 1574. Maker's mark, a capital roman " E " with a very small letter " o " or circle attached in front of the central horizontal stroke, exactly corresponding to the mark on the Chalice at Llanbabo.

Dimensions.—Height, 5 in.; depth of bowl, 2⅞ in.; diameter of bowl, 2⅞ in.

An old Sheffield-plate Salver, plain centre, with gadrooned border, standing on three foliated and scrolled feet—6⅞ in. in diameter—inscribed—

" Ceidio
D D
H.W.I.
1838."

These initials stand for Hugh Wynne Jones, of Treiorwerth, Rector of Llantrisant, Llechcynfarwy, Llanllibio, and Rhodwyddgeidio from 1819 to 1849.

RHOSBEIRIO—S. PEIRIO

CHALICE.—A plain silver Chalice, with beaker-shape bowl, standing on a truncated stem, with a collar at the top, immediately under the bowl, the edge of foot moulded and with four incised lines near the border. Inscribed near the mouth, in large and small pounced lettering—

"Ex dono $\left\{\begin{array}{l}\text{Ludovici Edwards. gen:}\\\text{Catherinæ Griffith uxoris eius}\end{array}\right\}$ 1630."

Marks.—London date-letter for 1630-1. Maker's mark, an escallop shell, in a shaped shield (Jackson, 1628-29).

Dimensions.—Height, $6\frac{3}{4}$ in.; depth of bowl, $3\frac{1}{2}$ in.; diameter of mouth, $3\frac{3}{4}$ in. (PLATE XXVIII., No. 2.)

PATEN.—A small, plain, circular silver Salver, with beaded border, standing on three beaded feet, inscribed at the back, RLC.

Marks.—London date-letter for 1784-5. Maker's mark, $\begin{smallmatrix}T P\\A H\end{smallmatrix}$ in shaped shield, probably T. B. Pratt and Arthur Humphreys.

The donors of the Chalice were Lewis Edwards, of Rhosbeirio, son of Edward ap Howell of the same place, and his wife, Catherine Griffith, was a daughter of Sir or Revd. William Griffith, Rector of Llanfaethlu, 1544, who was the son of Edmund Griffith, of Talybont, Llangeinwen, Constable of Carnarvon Castle.

The initials on the Salver-Paten may be those of Richard Lloyd, of Rhosbeirio, eldest son of Francis Lloyd, of Rhosbeirio, and of Catherine, his wife, daughter of William Wynne, of Wern, Carnarvonshire.

RHOSCOLYN—S. GWENFAEN

An Elizabethan silver Chalice, with beaker-like bowl, engraved near the top with the customary plain strap-work band, $\frac{7}{16}$ in. wide, intersecting four times, and filled in with the conventional sprays of foliage, a triple form of spray at each intersection, an incised line surrounding the lip of the Chalice. The stem has a plain moulding at the top and bottom, and is divided by the usual plain knop, with a plain collar above and below it, the edge of the base having an ovolo moulding.

Marks.—London date-letter for 1574. Maker's mark, a hand grasping a hammer, between H.C., in plain shield, as on the Chalice in the neighbouring Church of Llanfigael.

Dimensions.—Height, $7\frac{1}{8}$ in.: depth of bowl, 4 in.; diameter of mouth, $3\frac{5}{8}$ in.; diameter of base, $3\frac{5}{8}$ in. (PLATE XXV., No. 2.)

A small, plain, silver dish, sexfoil in form, moulded edge, the centre engraved with I.H.S. and a cross in glory. Inscribed on the back in script—" Presented by G. L. Hampton Lewis, Bodior, to Rhoscolyn Church, 1877."

London date-letter for 1849-50.   Diameter, 7 in.

A Flagon and a Plate, both of pewter, mentioned in terriers between 1776 and 1811, have disappeared.

RHOSYBOL—CHRIST

A plain silver Chalice, with inverted cone-shape bowl on slender stem with splayed foot.   London date-letter for 1898-9.   Maker's mark, $\frac{H\ E}{W}$ in trefoil.

Height, $5\frac{7}{8}$ in.; diameter of bowl, $3\frac{5}{8}$ in.

A plain silver Paten, $5\frac{5}{8}$ in. in diameter.   Same marks as on Chalice.

A glass Flagon with silver handle and mounts.   Same marks as on Chalice and Paten.

TALYLLYN—S. MARY

CHALICE.—This silver Chalice has a plain beaker-shape bowl, the lip slightly curving outwards, on stem, moulded base.

Marks.—London date-letter for 1713-4.

Dimensions.—Height, $7\frac{1}{2}$ in.; depth of bowl, 4 in.; diameter of mouth, $3\frac{3}{4}$ in.

PATEN-COVER.—This silver Paten-Cover has a moulded edge, and has a small foot.   It bears the same marks, and its dimensions are: $4\frac{3}{8}$ in. in diameter, and 1 in. high.

FLAGON.—This silver flagon is plain and cylindrical in form, slightly tapering, a moulding surrounding lower part of body; a domed cover with a pierced thumb-piece; plain spout; the handle terminating in a heart-shape shield.   It is inscribed underneath, " The gift of Clara Meyrick, 1826, for Talyllyn Chapel."

Marks.—London date-letter for 1826-7.   Maker's mark, G·B, with pellet between, in quatrefoil.

Clara Meyrick was the daughter of Owen Putland Meyrick, Esq., of Bodorgan, and Clara, daughter of Richard Garth, Esq., of Morden, Surrey.   She married Augustus Elliott Fuller, Esq., of Ashdown, Sussex, 1801.

TREFDRAETH—S. BEUNO

CHALICE.—A plain, V-shape silver Chalice, on tall baluster-like stem on a splayed foot, the initials ER rudely engraved under the foot at a later date.

Marks.—London date-letter for 1610-1. Maker's mark appears to be like TYW, or TW, in monogram, in shaped shield, a similar mark appearing on the Chalice at Llaniestyn in Carnarvonshire.

Dimensions.—Height, 7$\frac{9}{16}$ in.; depth of bowl, 3$\frac{1}{2}$ in.; diameter of mouth, 3$\frac{1}{2}$ in.

PATEN.—Large, plain silver Paten on foot, with moulded edges. The centre is occupied by an engraved oval shield of arms with scrolled and foliated mantling: *Two foxes counter-salient, the dexter surmounted of the sinister impaling a chevron ermine between three Cornish choughs, each holding in its beak an ermine spot*: and this inscription in script—" The Gift of Jane Lewis of Marrian widow to the Parish Church of Tredraeth 1751."

Marks.—London date-letter for 1719. Maker's mark, F·A, with pellet between and an illegible device above, in shaped shield.

Dimensions.—Diameter, 10 in.; height, 2$\frac{3}{4}$ in.

Jane Lewis was the second daughter of Roger Hughes, Esq., of Plascoch. Her first husband was Owen Williams, Esq., of Marian, Trefdraeth, and her second husband Hugh Lewis, Esq., of Cemlyn.

A small, plain silver domestic Salver, 6$\frac{1}{2}$ in. in diameter, with a shaped shell edge, standing on three feet. In the centre are engraved *upon a lozenge two foxes counter-salient the dexter surmounted of the sinister;* and on the back, in roman capitals, this name, " ELIZ : LEWIS," is engraved, while below it is this inscription, in script lettering—" The Gift of Chas. Evans Esqr. 1837."

Marks.—London date-letter for 1743. Maker's mark, R·A, in script in double-lobed shield, probably Robt. Abercromby.

Elizabeth Lewis, the daughter and heiress of Hugh Lewis, Esq., of Pontnewydd, was the wife of Charles Evans, Esq., of Trefeilir and Henblas.

An electro-plated Flagon.

The old terriers contain a reference to an old silver Chalice, inscribed 1574, and a pewter Flagon and Dish, now, unhappily, no longer here.

TREGAIAN—S. CAIAN

CHALICE.—A plain silver Chalice with beaker-shape bowl with curved lip, supported by a short thick stem, divided by a plain moulding, resting on a moulded foot. Inscribed—

" Tregayan
1714."

Marks.—London date-letter for 1714-15. Maker's mark, Lo, with key above and pellet below, in shaped shield (Natl. Locke).
Dimensions.—Height, 6½ in.; depth of bowl, 3¾ in.; diameter of mouth, 3¼ in.

PATEN.—A small plated Salver with pierced border on three feet.

PATEN-COVER.—A small silver Paten-Cover, with the sacred symbols, I.H.S., and cross in glory, engraved on the foot. There are two makers' marks, very indistinct, RL and AT. This may belong to the old Chalice at Llangefni.
Diameter, 4¾ in.; height, ⅝ in.
The disappearance of an old pewter Flagon and a Plate from this Church has to be chronicled with regret.

TREWALCHMAI—S. MORHAIARN

CHALICE.—A plain silver Chalice, with inverted bell-shape bowl, supported by a stem divided in the centre by a plain, narrow moulding, and resting on a moulded foot.
Marks.—Chester date-letter for 1758-9. Maker's mark, RR, in an oblong cartouche (Richd. Richardson).
Dimensions.—Height, 7¼ in.; depth of bowl, 3⅞ in.; diameter of mouth and foot, 3¾ in.

PATEN.—A plain electro-plate dish, circular, with I.H.S. engraved in centre.

FLAGON.—Plain electro-plate.

ALMS DISHES.—Two small old pewter plates, 9⅛ in. diameter, one engraved on the back ₁ ᴵₓ ᴬ and stamped with the maker's mark, H. BALDWIN LIVERPOOL; the other with three talbots' heads erased, and S. DUNCUMB LONDON.

The pewter Flagon mentioned in the terriers for 1793, and again as late as 1837, cannot be traced.

PLATE XIV.

No. 3.

PENMYNYDD, ANGLESEY.
CHARLES I. SILVER CHALICE.
DATE : 1638-9.

No. 2.

LLANGYBI, CARNARVONSHIRE.
CHARLES I. SILVER CHALICE.
DUBLIN DATE LETTER : 1638-9.

No. 1.

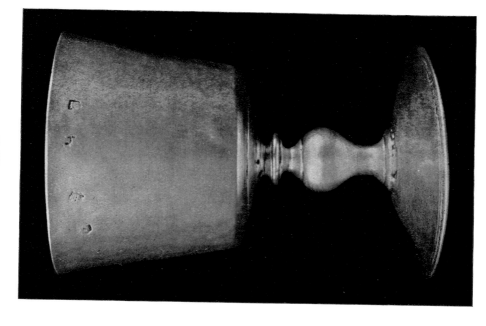

HARLECH, MERIONETHSHIRE.
SILVER CHALICE.
DATE : 1664-5.

CARNARVONSHIRE

ABER—S. BODFAN

CHALICE.—An Elizabethan silver Chalice, with beaker-shape bowl, engraved near the lip with a double matted band, $\frac{9}{16}$ in. wide, intersecting four times, and enclosing the conventional sprays of foliage, a small sprig carried above and below each intersection. The moulding at the top and bottom of the stem, which is divided by a plain compressed knop between two collars, consists of a delicate and, so far as this Diocese is concerned, unique moulding of small diamond-shape decorations. On the rounded shoulder of the foot are three rows of incised hyphens, and on the edge of the foot is an ovolo moulding. The date of this Chalice is *circa* 1575.

Maker's mark, a bird's head, erased, turned dexter-wise, in a shaped shield, as on the Chalice, dated 1574, at Clynnog.

Dimensions.—Height, $6\frac{3}{4}$ in.; depth of bowl, $3\frac{5}{8}$ in.; diameter of bowl, $3\frac{3}{8}$ in.; diameter of foot, $3\frac{13}{16}$ in.

CHALICE.—A large, silver Chalice, with plain beaker-shape bowl, rounded at the base; with very narrow moulded edge to the lip; a wide, plain rounded knop or moulding in the centre of the stem; on a moulded foot. The centre of the bowl is occupied with the engraved letters I.H.S., a cross, and three nails in a halo, and by this inscription in three lines—

> " The Gift of Iohn Iones, D.D.
>   to the Church of Aber in
>   Carnar : shire Anno 1712."

Marks—London date-letter for 1712-13. Maker's mark, WA, with anchor between, in shaped shield (Jos. Ward).

Dimensions.—Height, 9 in.; depth of bowl, $5\frac{1}{8}$ in.; diameter of mouth and foot, $4\frac{1}{4}$ in.

PATEN-COVER.—The silver Paten-Cover belonging to this second Chalice has a flat border with moulded edge, and the moulded foot is entirely covered with the engraved letters, I.H.S., a cross and three nails in a halo. The same inscription is engraved on the rim of the cover.

Marks.—Same as on the Chalice.

Dimensions.—Diameter, $6\frac{3}{8}$ in.; width of rim, $\frac{7}{8}$ in.; height, $1\frac{1}{2}$ in.; diameter of foot, $2\frac{7}{8}$ in.

The donor of this Chalice and Paten-Cover, and the silver Flagon, John Jones, D.D., was of Plasgwyn, Pentraeth, Anglesey, and was Dean of Bangor from 1689 until 1727. He gave a similar Chalice and Paten-

G

Cover to Gyffin and Llanllechid Churches, and a massive silver Flagon to the latter Church.

PATEN.—A plain, silver Paten, with wide flat rim, standing on a very short truncated foot. This inscription is pounced on the rim in faint lettering—

"The Guift of Mr. Richard Fletcher to Abber Church, 1677."

No marks. Probable date, 1675.
Dimensions—Diameter, $7\frac{1}{8}$ in.; width of rim, $1\frac{3}{8}$ in.; height, $1\frac{1}{4}$ in.; diameter of foot, $3\frac{11}{16}$ in.
The donor was the second son of Thomas Fletcher, of Treborth, Bangor. He was canon of Bangor, 1667-72.

FLAGON.—A tall silver Flagon, with plain cylindrical body, a moulding running round the lower part; narrow moulded lip; a domed cover, surmounted by a short, vase-shape knop; a scrolled thumb-piece, the handle terminating in a plain shield; standing on a wide, spreading moulded foot. Inscribed in one line—
"The Gift of John Jones D.D. to the Church of Aber: A.D. 1719."

Marks—London date-letter for 1719-20. Maker's mark, F·A with pellet between, an illegible device above (probably Wm. Fawdery).
Dimensions.—Total height, $11\frac{3}{8}$ in.; height of body, $8\frac{7}{8}$ in.; diameter of mouth, 4 in.; diameter of foot, $6\frac{5}{8}$ in.

PATEN.—A large, plain silver Paten, with narrow moulded edge, standing on a truncated foot with moulded border. Inscribed on the back—

"The gift of HUGH DAVIES, Rector to the Parish of ABER 1794."

Marks—London date-letter for 1793-4. Maker's mark illegible.
Dimensions.—Diameter, $8\frac{3}{4}$ in.; height, $2\frac{1}{8}$ in.; diameter of foot, $3\frac{3}{8}$ in.
The donor of this Paten was a well-known Welsh naturalist, author of a work on the botany of Anglesey; a friend and companion of Pennant on some of his tours in Wales and the Isle of Man; born in 1739 at Llandyfrydog, Anglesey, of which place his father, Lewis Davies, was Rector; educated at Beaumaris Grammar School and Jesus College, Oxford, subsequently taking holy orders and becoming an usher at his old school. In 1778 he was appointed to the living of Beaumaris, where he remained nine years, removing in 1787 to Aber.

A pewter Flagon and a Bason, mentioned in the terriers for 1817 and 1826, are missing.

(PLATE XIX.)

PLATE XV.

No. 1.

BOTTWNOG, CARNARVONSHIRE.

Dutch Silver Dish.

Date : *circa* 1685.

No. 2.

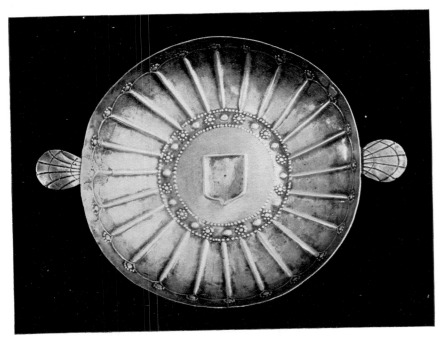

LLANDUDWEN, CARNARVONSHIRE.

Charles I. Silver Saucer Dish.

Date : 1636-7.

ABERDARON—S. HYWYN

CHALICE.—A plain, V-shape silver goblet, with an engraved shield, the edge of foot reeded. No inscription.

Marks.—London date-letter for 1815. Maker's mark, $^{PB}_{AB}$ in square-shape shield.

Dimensions.—Height, 6 in.; diameter of mouth, $3\frac{1}{4}$ in.

PATEN.—An old Sheffield-plate Salver, plain centre, with gadroon border, 8 in. in diameter.

The terriers for 1796 and 1808 refer to a silver Communion Cup, marked " Ann 1574," which, however, has disappeared. It may be conjectured that as this is not mentioned in the terrier for 1826, the Vicar and Churchwardens, finding it in a dilapidated condition, replaced it by the present Chalice. The Benefice was held in 1574 by Richard Johns.

ABERERCH—S. CAWRDAF

CHALICE.—Plain silver Chalice, with beaker-shape bowl, on which is engraved, in shaded roman capitals, " SANCTÆ COVORDᴬ DE· ABERERTHE, enclosed within a double band of strap-work, intersecting three times, the strapwork band being filled with a single row of hyphens. There are no marks. The stem is entirely new, and the foot has been formed from the old Paten-Cover, which is engraved with the date 1611.

Dimensions.—Height of Chalice, $5\frac{1}{2}$ in.; depth of bowl, $3\frac{1}{2}$ in.; diameter of bowl at mouth, $3\frac{3}{4}$ in.

FLAGON.—A small new silver Flagon, the body globular in form, a cross on the cover.

London date-letter for 1900. Maker's mark, GL in monogram. Height, $8\frac{1}{4}$ in.

FLAGON.—An old pewter Flagon, with a globular body, a short spout, and a domed cover, with scrolled thumb-piece. Inscribed—

" Abererch   W.
O. H. Vʳ.   R. W * I. H.
                1728."

Height, $9\frac{1}{4}$ in.

The initials represent the name of the then Vicar, Owen Humphreys, and the Churchwardens, Richard Williams and John Hughes.

PATEN.—A large old Sheffield-plate Paten, plain, with gadroon edge, standing on a foot fluted near the junction to the body, 10 in. in diameter.

BANGOR CATHEDRAL—S. DEINIOL

A Communion service of massive silver-gilt, consisting of two Chalices with their Paten-Covers, a tall Flagon, and a large Alms-Dish, all quite plain. (PLATE XII.)

CHALICES.—The two Chalices, which are identically alike, are tall, with beaker-shape bowls, standing on stems divided by a small, plain compressed knop, on moulded feet. Under the foot of one of the Chalices is a wyvern, with a coronet on neck, standing on a cap of maintenance, and the initials N.B. very roughly engraved, and not contemporary with the date of the Chalice. The date, 1638, is also engraved thereon.

Marks.—London date-letter for 1637-8. Maker's mark, RW, a mullet or rose below, in shaped shield.

Dimensions.—Height, $9\frac{1}{2}$ in.; depth of bowl, $5\frac{1}{8}$ in.; diameter of bowl, 5 in.

PATEN-COVERS.—The two Paten-Covers have a large depression, with a flat rim, $\frac{5}{8}$ in. wide, the edge of the foot moulded.

Marks.—The same as on the Chalices.

Dimensions.—Diameter, $6\frac{3}{8}$ in.; height, $1\frac{3}{8}$ in.; diameter of foot, 3 in.

FLAGON.—A tall Flagon, with cylindrical body, slightly tapering. A concave moulding surrounds the lower part of the body where the foot begins to splay out; on the edge of the foot are three incised lines. The lip has a wide, flat moulding. Around the narrow part of the low, slightly-rounded cover is a concave collar; the thumb-piece has two triangular or shield-shape piercings, with a flat bar across the top, the handle terminating in a plain tongue-shape shield.

Marks.—London date-letter for 1638-9. Maker's mark, IM, with a bear below, in plain shield (Jackson, 1630-1).

Dimensions.—Height to top of cover, 11 in.; body only, $9\frac{1}{4}$ in.; diameter of mouth, $4\frac{1}{8}$ in.; foot, $6\frac{1}{4}$ in.

ALMS-DISH.—A large plain Alms-Dish, with a wide flat rim, $2\frac{1}{2}$ in. in width, in the centre of the dish a slightly-domed circle, $4\frac{5}{8}$ in. in diameter.

Marks.—The same as on the Flagon.

Dimensions.—$18\frac{3}{8}$ in. in diameter.

The Cathedral appears to have been provided with this massive service of plate shortly after the consecration of William Roberts as Bishop of Bangor in 1637, and the provision of Sacramental vessels, worthy of the Cathedral Church, is in keeping with the character of a prelate who did so much in his day to rescue the ornaments of the Church from destruction. The Bishop received his education at Queens' College, Cambridge, and in 1629 was appointed Sub-Dean of Wells. He was a friend of Archbishop Laud, and a noted loyalist, and is said to have received his appointment as Bishop on the recommendation of Laud in recognition of his saving Church goods of the value of £1,000 from destruction.

No written records or description of the numerous Chalices and costly ornaments in silver, vestments, etc., necessary for the ornate services of pre-Reformation times, removed from the Cathedral and other Churches in the Diocese of Bangor by the Royal Commissioners of Edward VI., can be found at the Public Record Office. And, further, nothing can be discovered as to the plate in use in the Cathedral from the Reformation until the date when this service was provided.

The Cathedral is also in possession of another equally massive service of plain silver-gilt, consisting of two Chalices, two Patens, a Flagon, a large and a smaller Alms-Dish (PLATE XIII.):—

CHALICES.—The two Chalices have beaker-shape bowls, with very narrow moulding on the lips, which are curved outwards, standing on truncated stems, with a beaded moulding on the edges.

Marks.—London date-letter for 1777-8. Maker's mark, JD, in black letters, in a shaped shield (J. Denzilow).

Dimensions—Height, $9\frac{1}{4}$ in.; depth of bowl, $5\frac{1}{2}$ in.; diameter of mouth, $4\frac{3}{4}$ in.

PATENS.—The two Patens have a large depression in the centre, with a plain flat border, the edge beaded. The edge of the foot moulded.

Marks—The same as on the Chalices.

Dimensions.—Diameter, $7\frac{1}{8}$ in.; height, $2\frac{1}{4}$ in.; width of border, $\frac{5}{8}$ in.

FLAGON.—A tall plain Flagon, with cylindrical body, narrow moulded lip, a narrow moulding carried along the lower part of the body where the foot begins to splay, the edge of foot beaded; the cover is domed and moulded, surmounted by the remains of a broken knop; the thumb-piece is double-scrolled, arched by scrolls and shell. On the shoulder of the scrolled handle is a short applied moulding; the handle termination is scrolled and moulded.

Marks.—The same as on the Chalices and Patens.

Dimensions.—Height to top of cover, $13\frac{1}{4}$ in.; height of body, $10\frac{1}{2}$ in.; diameter of mouth, $4\frac{3}{8}$ in.; diameter of foot, $7\frac{1}{4}$ in.

ALMS-DISHES.—A large and a smaller Alms-Dish, identically alike in every detail except size. Both have flat borders with beaded edges, and the centre of each is slightly domed.

Marks.—The same as on the Chalices, Patens and Flagon.

Dimensions.—Large Alms-Dish is 18 in. in diameter, the rim 2⅛ in. wide; the smaller Dish is 11 in. in diameter, and the rim ⅞ in. wide.

Each piece in this service is delicately engraved with the arms of the See of Bangor: *gules, a bend or guttee de poix* (argent armoye azure, *Procession Roll*, 1512) *between two pierced mullets argent*, the shield contained in an oval, surmounted by a Bishop's mitre, from which are suspended festoons, ribbons and scrolls.

This service of plate was provided during the Episcopate (1775-83) of John Moore, who had held, previous to his appointment to the Bishopric of Bangor, the Deanery of Canterbury, and who subsequently became Archbishop of Canterbury.

A new Communion set has recently been added to the Cathedral plate, and this comprises two silver Chalices of medieval form, the bowls engraved with an inscription in black letters:—" Calicem salutaris accipiam et nomen Domini invocabo." The stems are hexagonal, divided by the usual large knop, and the bases sexfoil.

Marks.—London date-letter for 1873-4. Makers, J. E. W. and J. Barnard.

Two small, plain Patens, 6 in. in diameter. London date-letter for 1886-7. Maker's mark, J $_J^W$ in trefoil.

BANGOR—S. JAMES

CHALICES.—Two tall silver-gilt Chalices, with plain, short, inverted bell-shape bowls, tall hexagonal stems, on sexfoil feet. Engraved with the Christian symbols, I.H.S., a cross and nails in glory, and inscribed—" Altari Ecclesiæ S. Jacobi de Bangor. In memoriam J. H. Cotton, Decani Bangorˢ."

Height, 8¾ in.

PATENS.—Two silver-gilt Patens, with nine-lobed border, supported by hexagonal stems on sexfoil feet, engraved with same symbols, and inscribed—" Church of S. James, Bangor. In memory of James Henry Cotton, Dean. Obiit. 1862."

Diameter, 7⅝ in.; height, 3 in.

FLAGON.—A tall silver-gilt Flagon, with plain cylindrical body, a

moulding, with a scalloping below, encircles the lower part; the domed cover and the foot are octofoil; a trefoil thumb-piece. Inscribed— "J. H. Cotton Decani Bangor⁵. Altari Ecclesiæ S. Jacobi de Bangor."
Height, 11 in.

ALMS-DISH.—Plain silver-gilt dish, circular sunk centre, nine-lobed border. The Christian symbols as on the Chalice, engraved in centre, and with same inscription as on the Patens.
Diameter, 12⅜ in.
Marks on each piece.—London date-letter for 1864-5. Maker's mark, GF, in shaped shield.

BANGOR—S. MARY

CHALICE.—A silver Chalice of medieval design, the bowl gilt inside and inscribed in black letters—" Calicem salutaris accipiam et nomen Domini invocabo." The stem hexagonal, and divided by a large knop, the foot sexfoil.
Marks.—London date-letter for 1863-4. Makers' mark, EB & JB (E. and J. Barnard).
Height, 8 in.

PATEN.—Silver Paten, sexfoil centre, inscribed on the edge in black letters—" Agnus Dei qui tollis peccata mundi da nobis tuam pacem."
Marks.—London date-letter for 1864-5. Same maker as Chalice.
Diameter, 7 in.

FLAGON.—Tall silver Flagon, the body globular and inscribed— " Pascha nostrum immolatus est Christus." The foot sexfoil, the handle scrolled.
Marks.—Same as on Chalice.
Height, 11⅜ in.

BEDDGELERT—S. MARY

A highly interesting, and perhaps unique, silver Chalice with Paten-Cover. The bowl is in the form of an inverted bell, and is delicately engraved with three standing figures of the three Marys—Mary the Virgin, with halo round her head, in the centre; Mary Cleophas on the left side and Mary Salome on the right side, looking towards the Blessed Virgin. Above each figure is engraved the name, M. Cleophæ.

M. Virgo. M. Salome. The engraving of the figures is contemporary with the date of the Chalice, 1610. The two compressed knops on the stem are decorated with a moulding of ovolos and roses, and the same style of moulding separates the higher knop from the bowl. On the three edges of the foot are two forms of mouldings, an ovolo, and a rose and alternate ovolo. The foot is inscribed—

"Donum Iohannis Williams aurificis regis. 1610."

The Paten-Cover takes the form of a tazza, with an ovolo moulding on the edge, and has a curved foot, engraved with a gilt shield of arms quarterly, 1 *and* 4, . . . *three eagles displayed,* 2 *and* 3, *a chevron gu. between three fleurs-de-lis, held by an eagle displayed.* The edges of the foot have a moulding of ovolo alternate with a mullet.

Marks.—London date-letter for 1610. Maker's mark, RS, with a rose below, in a plain shield.

Dimensions of Chalice: height, 9 in.; depth of bowl, $4\frac{1}{2}$ in.; diameter, $4\frac{3}{4}$ in. Paten-Cover: diameter, $5\frac{7}{16}$ in.; height, $2\frac{1}{4}$ in.

The donor, Sir John Williams, who was born at Hafod Llwyfog, in this parish, was goldsmith to James I., and resided at Minster Court in the Isle of Thanet. In 1623 a certificate was granted to him by the Earl of Suffolk and Sir Henry Cary that there was no evidence that he had sold deceitful plate to the King. (PLATE VIII.)

FLAGON.—This is a plain silver Flagon having an upright cylindrical body, with the edges moulded in the same style as those on the Chalice; a cross surmounts the domed cover, and the spout is short. On the body is an engraved representation of the Crucifixion. The base is inscribed—"Presented to Beddgelert Church by James B. Elkington, December 25th 1891."

Marks.—Birmingham date-letter for 1891-2.

Height, $9\frac{3}{4}$ in.

There is also in this Church an old pewter Paten, standing on three ball and claw feet, stamped with several marks—a bird's claw and leg, and LONDON in a label, and four other small marks in separate shields, one of them ID, the others illegible, $9\frac{5}{8}$ in. in diameter; and a tall old pewter Flagon with cylindrical body, domed cover and splayed foot.

BETTWS GARMON—S. GARMON

A plain electro-plated Chalice and Paten, given in 1878 by the Rev. John Parry, M.A., Wolverhampton.

The pewter plate previously in use here has disappeared.

PLATE XVI.

No. 1.

No. 2.

No. 3.

LLANFIHANGEL-BACHELLAETH.

SILVER CHALICE.

CHESTER MARK : *circa* 1693.

LLANBEDROG.

SILVER CHALICE AND PATEN-COVER.

DATE : 1693.

LLANGIAN.

SILVER CHALICE AND PATEN-COVER.

CHESTER MARK : *circa* 1692-4.

BETTWS-Y-COED

CHALICE (No. 1).—A plain silver Chalice with inverted bell-shape bowl, the lip slightly moulded, gilt inside, supported by a plain stem, moulded in the centre, and resting on a moulded base. Inscribed—

"Ex Dono Ducis Ancastriensis A: D: 1731."

Marks.—Chester date-letter for 1730-1. Maker's mark, RR addorsed, in a shaped shield (Richd. Richardson).

Dimensions.—Height, $6\frac{7}{8}$ in.; depth of bowl, $3\frac{5}{8}$ in.; diameter of mouth, $3\frac{1}{4}$ in.; diameter of foot, $3\frac{5}{8}$ in.

The donor was Peregrine, second Duke of Ancaster.

CHALICE (No. 2).—A silver-gilt Chalice, with plain bowl enclosed in a surbase of foliage in vandyke fashion. On the chased knop on the stem are six blue enamel discs, a cross on one, and IESUS on the others. The foot is quatrefoil, and is set with carbuncles and diamonds in a floreated design. It is inscribed—" To the Glory of God and the dearly-loved memory of Edward Scott Gifford, given by his sister, Harriet Jane Gifford, May, 1872."

Marks.—London date-letter for 1872-3. Maker's mark, J H & Cº.

Dimensions.—Height, $8\frac{3}{8}$ in.; depth of bowl, 3 in.; diameter of bowl, $3\frac{3}{4}$ in.; diameter of foot, $5\frac{5}{8}$ in.

PATEN (No. 1).—A plain silver-gilt Paten, a floreated cross engraved in the centre, $6\frac{1}{2}$ in. in diameter. Same marks as on Chalice No. 2.

PATEN (No. 2).—A small, plain silver-gilt Paten, 5 in. in diameter. *Marks.*—London date-letter for 1874-5.

FLAGON.—A ruby glass Flagon, with plain silver-gilt foot, handle and mounts, the edge with twisted rope moulding.

BODFEAN—S. BUAN

CHALICE.—A silver Chalice with beaker-shape bowl, engraved with the customary plain double strap-work band, intersecting three times and enclosing the usual sprays of foliage, a large spray carried above and below each intersection. Above this band runs this inscription—" The parish of Boduean. Drinke yee all of itt. Math: 26: ver: 27."

The stem is divided by a plain rounded knop between two collars, and has an incised line at the top and bottom. The foot is rounded and the edge moulded.

H

Marks.—London date-letter for 1623-4. Maker's mark, $\frac{S}{W}$, in a shaped shield.

Dimensions.—Height, 7¼ in.; depth of bowl, 3½ in.; diameter of mouth and foot, 3½ in.

PATEN.—This silver Paten has a wide flat rim, with three incised lines near the edge. On the foot is engraved the date, 1623.

Marks.—The same as on Chalice.

Dimensions.—Diameter, 4¹¹⁄₁₆ in.; height, 1 in.

This is an interesting and unusually late example of a Chalice of the end of the reign of James I., with all the characteristics of an Elizabethan Chalice, while the Paten differs from the Paten-Covers found on the earlier Chalices in that it has a wide, flat rim, and does not fit over the lip of the bowl. (PLATE VII., No. 2.)

CHALICE.—A large silver Chalice of goblet-form with oviform bowl, slightly narrowing at the mouth, the bowl decorated with vertical graduated flutings, standing on a tall stem, divided by a plain globular knop, below which the stem and the foot are fluted in like manner to the bowl. This inscription is engraved on the bowl, in script lettering in one line—

"The Gift of Sʳ. John Wynn Barᵗ. to the Church of Bodvean Anno 1772."

Marks.—London date-letter for 1772-3. Maker's mark, O·J, with pellet between, in an oblong—the mark of Orlando Jackson, entered 1759 (Jackson, 1770-1).

Dimensions.—Height, 8⁹⁄₁₆ in.; depth of bowl, 4¼ in.; diameter of mouth, 4¼ in.; diameter of foot, 3½ in.

This Chalice is in its original leather case.

ALMS DISH.—A large, circular, silver dish, 14 in. in diameter, with a wide border, 2¾ in. wide, chased and boldly embossed with foliage of acanthus form, in six large, long oval panels, divided by an embossed foliated design. On the plain centre are engraved the letters I.H.S., a cross and three nails in glory, and below, in roman capitals—

"THE GIFT OF Sᴿ. JOHN WYNN BARᵀ.
1769."

This Dish was originally quite plain, and stood on a truncated foot, which has been removed. The ornamental border was no doubt added at the date of the gift, 1769, and three small feet substituted for the large foot. The original part bears the London date-letter for the year 1669.

The donor of the later Chalice and this Dish was Sir John Wynn, Bart., only son of Sir Thomas Wynn, Bart., of Bodvean. His wife was Jane, only surviving daughter of John Wynn, of Melay. He was Custos Rotulorum for the County of Carnarvon, elected Member of Parliament in 1739 for that county, in 1741 for the Borough of Denbigh, in 1754 a second time for the county of Carnarvon, and in 1761 for the borough of Carnarvon. He died in 1773, aged 72 years.

BOTTWNOG—S. BEUNO

CHALICE AND PATEN-COVER.—An unusually perfect and highly interesting Elizabethan silver Chalice, of very small size, with a short beaker-shape bowl, rounded at the base, engraved with the customary double, plain strap-work band, intersecting four times, and filled with conventional sprays of foliage, a sprig of foliage carried above and below each intersection, an incised line running along the edge near the lip. The flattened knop, between two small collars in the centre of the stem, is covered with incised lines or hyphens, and at the top and bottom of the stem there is a delicate moulding of a series of ovals, divided by pellets. On the shoulder of the rounded base there are three rows of engraved hyphens, while on the edge of the foot there is an ovolo moulding. The Paten-Cover belonging to this Chalice has a reeded edge where it overlaps the Chalice, and on the top is an engraved band filled with two rows of hyphens. On the foot the date, 1575, with ANO above, and a sprig below, within a circle, are engraved. The interior of the bowl of this fine example of an Elizabethan Chalice shows signs of some original gilding, and there can be little doubt that this piece has been fashioned out of a pre-Reformation Massing Chalice, and it has another interest for Welshmen in that its date is contemporaneous with the time when this benefice was held by a distinguished native of the parish—Henry Rowlands, D.D., Rector from 1572 to 1581, founder of Bottwnog Grammar School, Dean of Bangor from 1593 to 1598, and Bishop of Bangor from 1598 until his death in 1616.

The only mark on the Chalice and Paten-Cover is IL in a shaped shield, exactly like the mark on the Elizabethan Chalices in the neighbouring Churches of Bryncroes and Tydweiliog. In all probability this was the mark of a provincial craftsman, and as Chester was doubtless the nearest centre where an important guild of Goldsmiths was flourishing at that time, it is not unlikely that the silversmith who re-fashioned this piece was John Lynglay of that city. Its dimensions are: Chalice, $4\frac{7}{8}$ in. high; depth of bowl, $2\frac{5}{16}$ in.; diameter of mouth, $2\frac{3}{4}$ in.; diameter of foot, $2\frac{3}{4}$ in. Paten-Cover is 3 in. in diameter. (PLATE XXX., No. 3.)

In this Church is a silver Alms Dish of foreign origin, probably Dutch, oval in shape, with a wide border of flowers and foliage in bold relief, and the Christian symbol, a pelican in her piety, repoussé, in the centre. The name, perhaps that of the original owner, and date— LORENS FRIS Ao. 1693. are engraved on the back, while in front this inscription is engraved:—" Given in Memory of Humphrey Randolph who Dyed Rector of this place in 1704 & of Sarah His Wife Daughter of Hugh Jenkins Rector of Rhue by their Da: Dorothy Randolph."

Date, *circa* 1685. It is $11\frac{7}{16}$ in. long, and $9\frac{7}{8}$ in. wide. (PLATE XV., No. 1.)

The terriers for 1784, and from 1808 until 1834, contain references to a Flagon, presumably pewter, which, however, has disappeared.

BRYNCROES—S. MARY

A tall, Elizabethan silver Chalice, with Paten-Cover. The Chalice has a beaker-shape bowl, slightly curved at the lip, an incised line running along the edge of the lip, engraved in the centre with the usual double plain band, intersecting four times, and filled with the conventional sprays of foliage, shaded, a small spray carried above and below each intersection. The stem is divided in the centre by a plain compressed knop, and has a vertical reeded moulding at the junctions with the bowl and the foot. An egg and dart moulding is along the edge of the foot. On the Paten-Cover is an engraved double plain band, filled with two rows of incised lines or hyphens, a small spray of foliage springing from above and below each of the four intersections of the band. The foot is engraved with this inscription—

" Ano

1574

XD."

enclosed in an incised circle with four vandykes at intervals.

The only mark on this Chalice and Paten-Cover is IL, in a shaped shield, as on the Elizabethan Chalices in the neighbouring Churches of Tydweiliog and Bottwnog.

Dimensions.—Chalice, $6\frac{15}{16}$ in. high; depth of bowl, $3\frac{5}{16}$ in.; diameter of mouth, $3\frac{1}{16}$ in.; diameter of foot, 3 in.

PATEN-COVER, $3\frac{3}{8}$ in. in diameter. (PLATE V., No. 3.)

CAERHUN—S. MARY

CHALICE.—A plain silver Chalice, with beaker-shape bowl, slightly curved at the lip, inscribed in a label with scrolled ends—

"+ CAERHVN
A°· 1574."

At the junction of the bowl with the stem is a plain collar or moulding. The foot is truncated, with flat edge, slightly moulded. The only mark, which is almost worn away, resembles a small capital letter M, repeated thrice, near the lip. The rim of foot underneath is engraved with this Welsh inscription—" ADNEWYDDWYD GAN Y MILWRIAD HUGH S. GOUGH, C.M.G. A BEATRICE EI WRAIG, 1893." (" Restored by General Hugh S. Gough, C.M.G., and Beatrice, his wife, 1893.")

Dimensions.—Height, $5\frac{7}{8}$ in.; depth of bowl, $3\frac{1}{2}$ in.; diameter of mouth, $3\frac{3}{4}$ in.; diameter of foot, $3\frac{7}{8}$ in.

Although this interesting Chalice bears an Elizabethan date, the author is of the opinion that it has been re-made at a later period, and from its general form and severe plainness, and complete departure from all Elizabethan style, it is attributed to the end of the seventeenth century, *circa* 1685, when Chalices of this type are found in abundance. The maker's mark, were it only known, would definitely settle this point. This Chalice was in all probability wrought by a provincial craftsman, perhaps at Chester. (PLATE XXV., No. 1.)

PATEN.—A plain, new silver Paten, inscribed on back—"+ RHODD HUGH S. GOUGH A BEATRICE EI WRAIG I EGLWYS S. MAIR CAERHUN 1893." (" The gift of Hugh S. Gough, and Beatrice, his wife, to the Church of S. Mary, Caerhun, 1893.")

London date-letter for 1893-4. Maker's mark, M.B A.T in a square. Diameter, 6 in.

CREDENCE PATEN.—A plain plated Paten, by same donors.

ALMS BASON.—A large deep, circular, pewter Dish, stamped with four marks in shields: (1) a buckle; (2) T·F; (3) a lion statant; (4) a leopard's head.

Dimensions.—Diameter, $12\frac{3}{8}$ in.; width of rim, $1\frac{1}{8}$ in.; depth, $1\frac{1}{2}$ in. Date, *circa* 1680.

FLAGONS.—Two very large interesting old pewter Flagons, with flat covers, scroll thumb-pieces, standing on wide spreading bases, a moulding encircling lower part of the bodies. One is engraved in front with large tulips and other flowers, and on the cover is a roughly-engraved stag.

This is the only instance in this diocese of a piece of pewter with decoration. The other Flagon, though identical in form and size, is quite plain. There are no marks.

Dimensions.—Height to top of cover, 10⅜ in.; body only, 9¾ in.; diameter of mouth, 4½ in.; diameter of base, 7⅞ in.

The terriers for 1780 and 1784 include, in addition to the above Chalice and pewter vessels, a "small pewter Chalice and a pewter Plate for the Communion." These have since disappeared.

CAPEL CURIG—S. CURIG A'I FAM JULITA

A new silver Chalice and Paten, gilt, inscribed—

"In memory of T. T. Carter for 35 years Sup. Gen. Confraternity of the Blessed Sacrament, R.I.P. Oct 28 1901."

An old pewter Mug, holding about a quart, the body rounded and narrowing at the neck, scrolled handle. Inscribed in Welsh in a rude manner, probably locally—"Rhodd : OT · O : BENGCREJ Att : J CCPEL : GiRRiG 1738" ("The Gift of O.T. of Pen-y · to Capel Curig"). No Marks.

Height, 6⅛ in.

A small pewter Plate, with initials E : R: Mark, London. Diameter, 8⁷⁄₁₆ in.

A pair of tall pewter Candlesticks with baluster stems on circular feet, the edges beaded, 10⅛ in. high. Date, *circa* 1815.

CARNARVON—CHRIST CHURCH

Chalice.—A silver Chalice, on tall stem with knop in centre, the sacred symbols, I.H.S., a cross and nails in glory, engraved on the bowl.

Marks.—London date-letter for 1865-6. Maker's mark, RG, in script capitals, crowned (Robt. Garrard).

Dimensions.—Height, 7⁵⁄₁₆ in.; diameter of bowl, 3⅛ in.

Paten.—An old silver Paten, with narrow moulded edge, on foot, which is engraved, $\begin{smallmatrix} M \ I \\ 1715 \end{smallmatrix}$

Marks.—London date-letter for 1720-1. Maker's mark, BO, with bird above, in shaped shield (Geo. Boothby).

Dimensions.—Diameter, 6⅛ in.; height, 1¼ in.

The initials on this Paten, which came from Llanbeblig, are perhaps

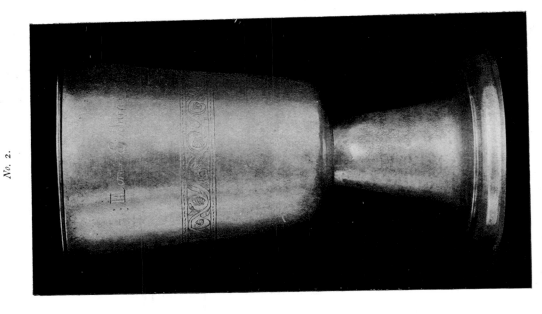

No. 2.

LLANSADWRN, ANGLESEY.
SILVER CHALICE AND PATEN-COVER.
CHESTER MARK : *circa* 1690.

PLATE XVII.

No. 1.

LLANGOED, ANGLESEY.
CHARLES I. PEWTER FLAGON.
DATED 1637.

those of Margaret Jones, Spinster, who gave the Chalice to Llanbeblig, and the money for its purchase may have been bequeathed at her death.

FLAGON.—A small, plain silver Flagon, 9¾ in. high. Same marks as on Chalice.

CARNGIWCH—S. BEUNO IN CARNGIWCH

A highly interesting and rare miniature silver Cup, only 3⅜ in. high, with fluted tapering body, the mouth octofoil, on short, fluted, vase-shaped stem, resting on an eight-lobed foot. The only mark is IM, in an oval. Its probable date is *circa* 1690. (PLATE XXXIV., No. 4.)
Dimensions.—Height, 3⅜ in.; depth of bowl, 2⅛ in.; diameter of mouth, 1 15/16 in.; diameter of foot, 2⅛ in.
A small pewter Tankard with domed cover, in damaged condition.
A pewter Goblet, 6¼ in. high, *circa* 1825.
A circular pewter Dish, stamped with two marks: × crowned, and BIRMINGHAM in a scroll, 9¼ in. in diameter. *Circa* 1825.

CEIDIO—S. CEIDO

CHALICE.—A plain silver Chalice with an inverted bell-shape bowl, on a baluster stem, resting on a splayed foot. It is engraved with a shield of arms—a stag statant impaling three eagles displayed, within a wreath of laurels, and is inscribed—

" Benedictione Dei res parua crescit."

Marks.—London date-letter for 1638-9. Maker's mark, WC, with heart below, in a shaped shield (Jackson, 1637-8).
Height, 6 in.

PATEN.—A plain silver Paten with moulded edge, on foot.
Marks.—London date-letter for 1723-4. Maker's mark, TT, with crown and rose above, in a shaped shield (Thos. Tearle).
Diameter, 6¾ in.; height, 2¼ in.

CLYNNOG—S. BEUNO

A fifteenth century Mazer Bowl of the highest interest and importance, of dark maple wood, mounted with silver-gilt band engraved with this inscription in black letters—

𝔍𝔥𝔊 *nazarenus rex iudeorum fili dei miserere mei.*

("Jesus of Nazareth, King of the Jews, Son of God, have mercy upon me.")

Each word is divided by small leaves, sprays, trefoil or quatrefoil. The band containing the inscription is $\frac{3}{8}$ in. wide, and the entire band outside $1\frac{1}{4}$ in. in depth. In the centre of the bowl inside is a plainly-moulded boss of silver-gilt, $1\frac{5}{8}$ in. in diameter, enclosing a silver print engraved with flowers originally enamelled.

Date, *circa* 1480-90.

Dimensions.—Diameter, $5\frac{1}{4}$ in.; depth, $2\frac{3}{16}$ in.

This valuable specimen is believed to have formed part of the treasure of the monastic house at Clynnog, and is the only known piece of plate which escaped destruction at its dissolution. It has since been in use here as an Alms Dish. (PLATE II.)

CHALICE AND PATEN-COVER (No. 1).—This is an Elizabethan silver Chalice, of the date 1574, with beaker-shape bowl, engraved with the usual plain, double strap-work band, filled with conventional sprays of foliage. The band intersects twice, and at the other two points it meets in a semi-circle without interlacing. The customary spray of foliage is carried above and below each of the divisions of the band. Lower down the bowl are three rows of engraved hyphens, broadening out at intervals into seven graduated rows in the form of a lozenge. The stem has a plain compressed knop between two collars, and a reeded moulding at the top and bottom. On the rounded shoulder of the foot are three rows of hyphens, and on the edge is a delicate egg and dart moulding. The Paten-Cover has a double strap-work band, like that on the bowl, but filled with three rows of hyphens, a small sprig springing from each of the four divisions, and on the edge is a single row of hyphens. On the foot the date, 1574, is engraved within a circle.

Mark.—A bird's head, erased, turned dexter-wise, in a shaped shield, as on the Elizabethan Chalice at Aber and several other places in this Diocese.

Dimensions—Height of Chalice, $6\frac{1}{2}$ in.; depth of bowl, $3\frac{1}{4}$ in.; diameter of mouth, 3 in.; diameter of foot, $3\frac{1}{4}$ in. Paten-Cover: diameter, $3\frac{3}{8}$ in.; height, 1 in. (PLATE V., No. 2.)

CHALICE AND PATEN-COVER (No. 2).—A very tall and capacious plain silver Chalice, with beaker-shape bowl, slightly curved at the lip, standing on a truncated stem with moulded edge. It is inscribed near the top in one line in roman lettering—

"Calix Ecclesiæ de Clynnocke Ex dono Olivi LLoyd LLD. rectoris ibm."

Marks.—London date-letter for 1636-7. Maker's mark, RM, with rose below, in a shaped shield, as on the large Chalice of similar form in the neighbouring Church of Llanaelhaiarn.

Dimensions.—Height, $9\frac{7}{16}$ in.; depth of bowl, $5\frac{1}{2}$ in.; diameter of mouth, $4\frac{7}{8}$ in.; diameter of foot, 5 in.

The Paten-Cover of this Chalice has two circular depressions, the smaller one measuring $2\frac{3}{4}$ in. in diameter. The narrow flat rim has an incised line, which is repeated on the large foot, which is 3 in. in diameter, and is inscribed along the edge—"Operculum calicis ecclesiæ de Clynocke ex dono Ioannis Griffith clerici Vicar ibm."

Marks.—Same as on Chalice.

Dimensions.—Diameter, 6 in.; height, $1\frac{3}{4}$ in.

Oliver Lloyd, the donor of the Chalice, was a native of Montgomeryshire, and was educated at S. Mary Hall, Oxford, Fellow of All Souls', B.C.L. 1597, D.C.L. 1602, Rector of Clynnog 1615, Chancellor of Hereford, Canon of Windsor, 1615, Dean of Hereford from 1617 until his death in 1625.

It is supposed that as the Chalice is dated 1636-7, Oliver Lloyd left a sum of money for its purchase—a frequent custom in Church and College plate. (PLATE XI., No. 1.)

CONWAY—S. MARY B. V. AND ALL SAINTS

CHALICE (No. 1).—A silver Chalice with inverted bell-shape bowl, supported by an engraved hexagonal stem, divided by a spirally-fluted knop, with eight circular projections engraved with quatrefoils, and resting on an octofoil foot, engraved with foliage, etc. The bowl is engraved with a band filled with this inscription in black letters— "Calicem salutaris accipiam et nomen Domini invocabo"; and the foot underneath is inscribed—"The Gift of Dame Iane Silence Erskine to the Church of Conway, September MDCCCXLIX."

Marks.—Birmingham date-letter for 1849-50.

Height, $7\frac{5}{8}$ in.

I

CHALICE (No. 2).—A silver Chalice of medieval design, hexagonal stem divided by a large knop, sexfoil foot with I.H.S. engraved on one lobe. The bowl has a Latin inscription similar to that on Chalice No. 1. Inscribed under foot—" Presented to the Parish Church of Conway, by the Rev. D. Grimaldi Davis, M.A., for five years Curate of this Parish 1885."

Marks.—London date-letter for 1884-5. Maker's mark, jSH.

Height, 7⅝ in.

PATEN.—A silver-gilt Paten, the *Agnus Dei* engraved in the centre, and this inscription in black letters on the rim—" Agnus Dei qui tollis peccata mundi Miserere nobis." It bears on the back an inscription denoting the gift, as on Chalice No. 1.

Marks.—As on Chalice No. 1.

Diameter, 5¾ in.

FLAGON.—A tall cylindrical-shape silver Flagon, covered with a flat decoration of vines on a matted surface. Given by Dame Iane Silence Erskine.

Marks as on Chalice and Paten.

Height, 10 in.

FLAGON.—An old pewter Flagon, with cylindrical body, short spout, domed cover, scrolled handle. Inscribed on the back (partially erased)—

" Richard Munks
Churchwarden
of Blakrod
1719
DR."

And on the front—

" John Bember
Henry Hughes
Wardens of Conway
1719."

No marks.

Dimensions.—11¼ in. high to top of cover; 9¼ in. to top of lip; diameter of mouth, 4¾ in.; foot, 7 in.

A large pewter Dish, circular, inscribed—

" Aberconway
1671."

Stamped with one mark in a circular cartouche, F M, with a head or sheaf of corn between.

Diameter, 10⅝ in.

Another pewter Dish, larger, with moulded edge, stamped with one mark, in a circular cartouche, T H, with a crowned rose between.

Diameter, 13⅞ in.

The old silver communion plate, including the Elizabethan Chalice and Paten-Cover, described as follows in the old parish terriers, are said to have been stolen about the year 1837—"One silver Chalice and Paten, marked 1567; a new silver Flagon marked 1782 and Plate 1776, the gift of Mrs. Coytmore; and another silver Chalice."

CRICCIETH—S. CATHERINE

CHALICE.—A plain silver Chalice, with inverted bell-shape bowl, supported by a tall stem divided by a narrow moulding, and resting on a moulded foot. On the bowl the sacred symbols, I.H.S., a cross and three nails in glory, are engraved, and under the edge of the foot this inscription is engraved—"Dono Dedit Johannes Jones de Brynhir, A.M. Coll. Jes. Oxon. Hujus Ecclesiæ Rector 1770."

Marks.—Chester date-letter for 1768-9. Maker's mark, RR, in scalloped edge, oblong shield (the third Rd. Richardson).

Dimensions.—Height, 6¾ in.; depth and diameter of bowl, 3⅝ in.; diameter of foot, 3 9/16 in.

PATEN-COVER.—The Paten-Cover belonging to the above Chalice has a flat depression, with a narrow flat edge, and a plain foot.

Marks.—Same as on Chalice.

Dimensions.—Diameter, 4¼ in.; height, 1¼ in.

PATEN.—A plain silver Salver with shaped scroll and shell border on three feet, 8 in. in diameter.

Marks.—London date-letter for 1759-60. Maker's mark, I·C, with pellet between, in an oblong.

An old pewter Flagon mentioned in the old terriers has disappeared.

CRICCIETH—S. DEINIOL

CHALICE.—A small silver Chalice, with plain bowl, stem divided by large knop. On the foot are six engraved circles filled with ornamental crosses, I.H.S., quatrefoils, etc. Inscribed—"THE GIFT OF C.A.J. TO S. DEINIOL'S CHURCH, CRICCIETH, 1891."

Marks.—London date-letter for 1890-1. Maker's mark, $\frac{H\,E}{W}$ in trefoil.

Height, 6⅝ in.

PATEN.—A small silver Paten, plain, 5¼ in. diameter, same inscription and marks as on Chalice.

FLAGON.—A small silver Flagon with globular body, with an engraved band of foliage, divided by three circles containing I.H.S. and cross, a double cross on cover, scrolled handle, same marks as on Chalice.
Height, 10¼ in.

DOLBENMAEN—S. MARY

Electro-plate Chalice.
A plain silver Paten on foot, inscribed—" Presented to Dolbenmaen Church by Griffith Williams Cefn Cochuchaf, in memory of his parents. Rector, W. Evan Jones. Whitsunday 1897."
London date-letter for 1897-8. Maker's mark, $^{H}_{W}{}^{E}$ in trefoil.
In the old parish terriers, between 1786 and 1837, " a silver Goblet, the gift of William Griffith, Esq., of Lleyn, and one pewter Plate and Trencher," are mentioned, but have, with the Chalice and Cover in the adjoining parish of Penmorfa, disappeared. The donor was of Cefnamlwch.

DOLWYDDELAN—S. GWYDDELAN

CHALICE (No. 1).—An Elizabethan silver Chalice, with plain beaker-shape bowl, with an engraved band filled with this inscription in large Lombardic capitals—

"✠ THE CVPPE OF DOLWYDDELAN."

Each word is divided by a quatrefoil. A vertical reeded moulding at top of stem. This interesting Chalice, which was evidently wrought by the same silversmith as the one at Llanbedr-y-Cenin, and may be assigned to the same date, 1576, is in a sadly mutilated condition, A roughly made rim has been attached to the lip by brass pins, partially concealing the inscription; the bowl has been repaired with lead, and the foot consists entirely of brass and lead!

CHALICE (No. 2).—A new silver Chalice, the base of bowl decorated with engraved roses, the knop on stem scaled, the plain circular foot moulded.
Marks.—London date-letter for 1869-70.

PLATE XVIII.

LLANDDEINIOLEN, CARNARVONSHIRE.

ELIZABETHAN SILVER CHALICE
AND PATEN-COVER.
DATE: 1599-1600.

SILVER FLAGON.
DATE: 1704-5.

SILVER PATEN.
DATE: 1703-4.

PATEN.—A silver Paten, the sacred letters, I.H.S., engraved four times on the rim, and a Pelican in her piety engraved in the centre. Same marks as on Chalice No. 2.

FLAGON.—A glass Flagon with silver handle, foot and mounts. Same marks as on Chalice and Paten.

There are also three pieces of old pewter—a quart tankard with cylindrical body, slightly tapering, a domed cover, scrolled thumb-piece, and scroll handle. This Welsh inscription roughly engraved under base—

"R Hodd Ellis Jones i Eglwys Dolwyddelan."
(" The gift of Ellis Jones to the Church of Dolwyddelan.")

And these initials, DT. The date, 1779, is engraved on the handle.

A large, deep, circular Dish, marked G BA·D · · · in a label (? G. Baldwin), 12 in. in diameter; and a circular plate, $8\frac{3}{4}$ in. in diameter, marked LONDON, the other marks illegible.

DWYGYFYLCHI—S. GWYNAN

A Communion set of old Sheffield plate, consisting of a Chalice, with fluted bowl, gilt inside; a Paten, with moulded shaped edge, on a foot; a Flagon, with tall cylindrical body, a cross on the cover; and an Alms Dish, with moulded shaped edge. Each piece is engraved with the Christian symbols, I.H.S., a cross and three nails in glory, and is inscribed—" Presented to the Parish Church of Dwygyfylchi by Elizabeth, Lady Smith of Pendyffryn, 1844."

In the terrier for 1801 are included " a silver Chalice of the value of about £3 10s., a pewter Tankard and two Dishes of the value of about ten shillings," which have disappeared.

EDERN—S. EDEYRN

CHALICE.—A plain silver Chalice, with deep beaker-shape bowl on trumpet-shape stem. No marks. Date, *circa* 1685.
Height, $5\frac{7}{8}$ in.; depth of bowl, $3\frac{3}{4}$ in.; diameter of mouth, $3\frac{1}{2}$ in.

PATEN-COVER, with foot. No marks. Date, *circa* 1685. Diameter, $4\frac{3}{8}$ in. Height, $\frac{3}{4}$ in.

PATEN.—A modern electro-plate Salver.

GLANADDA—S. DAVID

A silver Chalice, 8¼ in. high; silver Paten, 6¹³⁄₁₆ in. in diameter; and a silver Flagon, with London date-letter for 1882-3, 1887-8 and 1886-7, respectively, all with same maker's mark, T.P. in an oblong. These were given in memory of Dean Edwards.

GLANOGWEN—CHRIST

Two silver Chalices of medieval design, with sexfoil feet.
Marks on one: London date-letter for 1854-5; the other has date-letter for 1856-7; both with same makers' mark, $\begin{smallmatrix} E & B \\ & \& \\ J & B \end{smallmatrix}$ in quatrefoil (E. & J. Barnard).
Two silver Patens with sexfoil centre. London date-letter for 1856-7. Same makers' mark as Chalices.
Silver Flagon, globular body, on sexfoil foot. London date-letter for 1855-6. Same makers as Chalices and Patens.

GYFFIN—S. BENEDICT

CHALICE.—A large, plain silver Chalice, with beaker-shape bowl, the lip slightly moulded, supported by a stem which has a plain depressed knop, and resting on a moulded foot. Inscribed—

" The Gift of Jo: Jones D.D. & Dean
of Bangor to the Church of Gyffin
in Carnarvonshire, 1721."

Marks.—London date-letter for 1721-2.
Dimensions.—Height, 9 in.; depth of bowl, 4⅝ in.; diameter of mouth, 4⅜ in.

PATEN-COVER.—The Silver Paten-Cover belonging to the Chalice has a moulded edge, and has the usual form of foot.
Marks.—Same as on Chalice.
Dimensions.—Diameter, 5⅛ in.; height, 1½ in.
The donor of this Chalice and Paten-Cover gave plate to the Churches of Aber and Llanllechid.
An old pewter Plate, stamped with two roses crowned, and " HARD METAL," 8¾ in. in diameter.

LLANAELHAIARN—S. AELHAIARN

CHALICE.—A large, tall, plain silver Chalice, with beaker-shape bowl, the lip slightly curving out, standing on a truncated stem with moulded foot. The bowl is inscribed with this Welsh inscription in irregular script lettering—

"Rhodd Thomas Ap John Y Eglwus Ailhaiarn."

(" The Gift of Thomas ap John to the Church of Ailhaiarn.")

Marks.—London date-letter for 1638-9. Maker's mark, probably RM, with rose below, in shaped shield.

Dimensions.—Height, $8\frac{9}{16}$ in.; depth of bowl, $5\frac{1}{8}$ in.; diameter of mouth, $4\frac{3}{8}$ in.; diameter of foot, $4\frac{1}{4}$ in.

PATEN-COVER.—The silver Paten-Cover belonging to the above Chalice has a narrow flat edge, $\frac{1}{8}$ in. wide, and double sunk centre, as in the Paten-Cover at Clynnog, the smaller depression being $2\frac{3}{8}$ in. in diameter. On the foot, the edge of which is incised with a single line, the date, 1638, is engraved.

Marks.—Same as on Chalice.

Dimensions.—Diameter, 5 in.; height, $1\frac{1}{2}$ in.

This Chalice and Paten-Cover are very similar to, and by the same maker as, those in the adjoining parish of Clynnog. (PLATE XI., No. 2.)

PATEN OR ALMS DISH.—A small silver dish, circular, flat, with a narrow flat edge, incised with a single line. Though bearing no marks of any description, its date would appear to be about 1695.

Dimensions.—Diameter, 7 in.; width of edge, $\frac{5}{8}$ in.

LLANARMON—S. GARMON

CHALICE.—A plain silver Chalice with inverted bell-shape bowl, supported by a baluster stem on a splayed foot.

Marks.—London date-letter for 1632-3. Maker's mark, RG, with two annulets above, and a pheon between two annulets below, in a shaped shield.

Height, $7\frac{3}{8}$ in.

PATEN.—A large plain old Sheffield-plate Paten on foot, like the one at Llangybi.

FLAGON.—A new silver Flagon with plain cylindrical body and flat cover, given in 1906 by Colonel O. Lloyd J. Evans.

In this Church is one of the Celtic bronze hand-bells, 6¼ in. high.

Two pewter Flagons and a Dish have gone from this Church.

LLANBEBLIG—S. PEBLIG

CHALICE (No. 1).—A plain silver Chalice with inverted bell-shape bowl, supported by a baluster stem on a splayed foot. On the bowl is this inscription—

"Sacrum Ecclesiæ de LLANBEBLIG,"

and the sacred symbols, I.H.S., a cross and three nails in glory. The foot is inscribed underneath—

"The Gift of Doc^r. Saml. Peploe
Chancellor of the Diocese of Chester 1769."

Marks.—London date-letter for 1633-4. Maker's mark, RM, with rose under, in shaped shield.

Dimensions.—Height, 6¾ in.; depth of bowl, 3½ in.; diameter of mouth, 3⅝ in.

The donor, who was the son of Dr. Samuèl Peploe, Bishop of Chester, 1726-52, was Chancellor of the Diocese of Chester from 1748 until his death in 1781, and Rector of Tattenhall, Cheshire, where he gave a silver Chalice and Paten. The living of Llanbeblig and the Chapel of S. Mary's, Carnarvon, were bestowed by Richard II. on the nuns of S. Mary's in Chester in consideration of their poverty, and at the dissolution of the religious houses became attached to the See of Chester, and the Bishop of Chester has been from that time to the present day patron of Llanbeblig, hence the possible reason for Dr. Peploe's gift.

CHALICES (Nos. 2 and 3).—Two plain silver Chalices, with inverted bell-shape bowls, plain knops in centre of the stems, one inscribed—

"DONUM
MARGARETÆ IONES SPINSTER
IN USUM
ECCLESIÆ LLAN-BEBLICK
1715."

The other—

"LLAN-BEBLICK
1851."

PLATE XIX.

ABER, CARNARVONSHIRE.

ELIZABETHAN
SILVER CHALICE.
DATE: *circa* 1575.

SILVER PATEN.
DATE: 1677.

SILVER FLAGON.
DATE: 1719.

SILVER PATEN.
DATE: 1794.

SILVER CHALICE
AND PATEN-COVER.
DATE: 1712.

Marks.—London date-letter for 1851-2. Makers' mark, J S A S in a square (J. & A. Savory).

Dimensions.—Height, 7 in.; diameter of bowl, 3½ in.

The older Chalice, given by Margaret Jones, was re-made in 1851-2.

PATEN (No. 1).—A large, plain silver Paten, with moulded edge, supported by a truncated and moulded stem. It is inscribed on the back—"In Usum Ecclesiæ Parochialis dn LLanpeblig hanc Scutellam Dna Maria Williams vic ux D.D.D. 1743."

Marks.—London date-letter for 1743-4. Maker's mark, HP, with pellet between, rose below, in shaped shield.

Dimensions.—Diameter, 10¾ in.; height, 3 in.

PATEN (No. 2).—A small silver Paten—probably a Paten-Cover without its companion Chalice—with a flat depression with narrow, flat edge, on a foot.

Marks.—Chester date-letter for 1767-8. Maker's mark RR, in a scalloped edge oblong cartouche (Rd. Richardson).

Dimensions.—Diameter, 4⅜ in.; height, 1¼ in.

FLAGON.—A large plain silver Flagon, with tall cylindrical body, a moulding encircling it near the base, scrolled handle, terminating in an hexagonal shield (recently added); the thumb-piece with two V-shaped piercings; the flat cover, with moulded edge, engraved with the sacred device, I.H.S., a cross and three nails in glory, at the time of the gift, 1710. The body inscribed—

"DONUM DEI DEO
IN USUM
ECCLESIÆ CARNARVON."

and—

"Rob: Wynn
dedit
1710."

Marks.—London date-letter for 1691-2. Maker's mark, IY, with horse between, in an oval cartouche (Jackson, 1684-5).

Dimensions.—Height to top of cover, 12 in.; body only, 9¾ in.; diameter of mouth, 4¾ in.

This Flagon is very similar to the one at Llanddeiniolen, given by Jane, wife of this same Robert Wynne, Rector of that place, who was the sixth son of John Wynn, of Bodewryd, in Anglesey.

K

PATEN (No. 3).—A plain silver Paten on truncated stem.

Marks.—London date-letter for 1751-2. Maker's mark, JB, with pellet between, in a rectangular shield (John Berthellot).

Dimensions.—Diameter, 8⅜ in.; height, 2⅜ in.

Some of this plate has been in use at S. Mary's Chapel, Carnarvon.

LLANBEDROG—S. PEDROG

CHALICE WITH PATEN-COVER.—The Chalice is plain, with a beaker-shape bowl, standing on a tall, slender, truncated stem with moulded foot. Inscribed in script in one line—"The Gift of Love Parry of Cefnllanfair Esq to yᵉ Parish Church of Llanbedrog 1693." The Paten-Cover is plain with a moulded edge, on a foot. (PLATE XVI., No. 2.)

Marks, on both: London date-letter for 1693-4. Maker's mark, AN, with rose underneath, in shaped shield (Ant. Nelme).

Dimensions of Chalice.—Height, 7 7/16 in.; depth of bowl, 3¾ in.; diameter of mouth, 3¾ in.; diameter of foot, 4 in. The Paten-Cover is 5 3/16 in. in diameter, and 1 in. high.

FLAGON.—A pewter Flagon, with upright cylindrical body, flat cover, scrolled thumb-piece, a heart forming part of it; wide spreading base, with four incised lines round lower part. No marks. Height to top of cover, 8½ in.

ALMS DISH.—A large, circular, pewter Dish with flat border. It is stamped with three marks: LONDON in a scroll; three leopards' or talbots' heads erased; a Tudor rose with palm branches (partially obliterated). 12 in. in diameter.

Benefactions to the Church of Llanbedrog after the year 1691:—

"John Williams, Rector, gave a handsome altar cloth of Linen. Love Parry of Cefnllanfair gave A.D. 1694:

a Railing about the Alter
a new Pulpit and Reading seat.
a silver chalice—a Pewter Flagon & Plate.
a Folio Bible & Common Prayer Book
a Chest for the Church Utensils
a Lock for the church door—and
a Vellum Register Book.

Mrs. Ellin Parry, wife of the above Love Parry, gave a new Holland altar cloth, 1694."

The date of the Chalice and Paten-Cover is determined by the hall-mark as well as the inscription, and it may be assumed that the pewter Flagon and Dish are those which are mentioned in the preceding list, and that, therefore, there date is 1694, or a year or two earlier.

LLANBEDR-Y-CENIN—S. PETER

CHALICE.—An Elizabethan silver Chalice with beaker-shape bowl, engraved with a band $\frac{1}{4}$ in. wide, which is filled with this inscription in plain Lombardic capitals, preceded by a cross, on a matted surface—

" ✠ THE CVPPE OF LLANBEDER."

A quatrefoil divides the second from the third, and the third from the fourth, word. At the top of the stem, which is divided by a compressed knop between two collars (the knop recently punched with dots), of the usual type, is a vertical reeded moulding. The bottom of the foot was originally moulded in the same manner, but this moulding has gone. There are no signs of hall marks or maker's mark. The original Paten-Cover, described in the terrier for 1780 as bearing the date 1576, has unfortunately disappeared. From this note the date of the Chalice itself is definitely fixed as of 1576. A Chalice with similar characteristics, and no doubt the work of the same craftsman, is at Dolwyddelan.
Dimensions.—Height, $5\frac{7}{8}$ in.; depth of bowl, $3\frac{1}{8}$ in.; diameter of mouth, $2\frac{7}{8}$ in.; diameter of foot, 3 in. (PLATE XXV., No. 3.)

PATEN.—A small, circular, silver dish, with moulded edge, engraved with the letters I.H.S., a cross and three nails in glory, and inscribed on the back in script lettering—

" Eglwys
Llanbedr-y-Cennin
Ei ddo Duw
i Dduw."

London date-letter for 1842-3. Maker's mark, $_{G\,S}^{G\,R}$ in quatrefoil. 7 in. in diameter.

ALMS DISH.—A silver dish, exactly like the Paten, but $\frac{7}{8}$ths of an inch greater diameter, inscribed on the back—

"In Usum Ecclesiæ de Llanbedr-y-Cennin
Nuper restituæ
I. Hamer, A.M. Rectore
A.D. MDCCCXLIII
Præcipue
Curâ et Labore
Ioannis Evans, A.B.
Presbytere."

Same marks as on Paten.

John Hamer, son of James Hamer, of Llanfihangel Helygen, Radnorshire, matriculated at All Souls', Oxford, in 1802, and was Vicar of Bangor and Rector of Llanbedr-y-Cenin until his death in 1858.

FLAGON.—A large old pewter Flagon, cylindrical body, flat domed cover, with double volute thumb-piece, on spreading moulded base (much damaged). The only mark is inside, TF, with a spray above and below, in a lozenge.

Dimensions.—Height, $7\frac{3}{4}$ in.; body only, 7 in.; diameter of mouth, 4 in.; foot, $6\frac{1}{8}$ in.

LLANBERIS—S. PERIS

CHALICE.—A plain silver Chalice, with beaker-shape bowl, top and bottom of stem plainly moulded; a flat compressed knop between two small collars, in the centre of stem; a high, rounded and moulded foot. Inscribed—

"The Communion Cupp of LLanberys 1631."

Marks.—London date-letter for 1631-2. Maker's mark, an anchor between the letters DG, in a plain shield (Jackson, 1629-30).

Dimensions.—Height, 7 in.; depth of bowl, $3\frac{1}{2}$ in.; diameter of mouth, $3\frac{7}{8}$ in.; diameter of foot, $3\frac{5}{8}$ in.

PATEN-COVER.—The Paten-Cover of this Chalice has a flat rim, $\frac{11}{16}$ths of an inch wide, on which is inscribed—

"LLanberys,"

and on the foot the date, 1631, is engraved.

Marks.—The same as on Chalice.

Dimensions.—Diameter, $4\frac{5}{8}$ in. (PLATE X., No. 1.)

PLATE XX.

BEAUMARIS.

TWO SILVER-GILT DISHES.
DATE: PROBABLY 1810.

SILVER CREDENCE PATEN
OR ALMS DISH.
DATE: 1683-4.

TWO SILVER-GILT PATENS.
DATE: 1691-2.

SILVER-GILT CHALICE
AND PATEN-COVER.
RE-MADE IN 181C.

SILVER-GILT
JUG.
DATE: 1771-2.

SILVER-GILT
SPOON.
DATE: circa 1750.

SILVER-GILT
JUG.
DATE: 1810-11.

SILVER-GILT
CHALICE.
DATE: 1810.

FLAGON.—A small old pewter Flagon, *circa* 1685, with cylindrical body, and a flat cover, on which is a mark, a lion rampant, repeated four times—in very bad condition.

ALMS DISH.—A circular pewter Dish, with flat rim; stamped with four marks: (1) L.B., in black letters; (2) illegible; (3) a lion rampant; (4) a bird on a seeded rose, with " HARD METEL " above, twice repeated. Diameter, 12½ in.

In 1898 a new silver communion set was given to the Church. It consists of a plain Chalice, of medieval form, with sexfoil foot; a small plain Paten, both bearing the London date-letter for 1898-9; and a small silver-mounted glass Flagon, hall-marked 1894-5, and a small Cruet.

LLANBERIS—S. PADARN

The Communion Service in this Church is of electro-plate.

LLANDEGAI—S. TEGAI

CHALICE.—A very large, plain silver Chalice, with deep, beaker-shape bowl, engraved with the sacred symbols, I.H.S., a cross and three nails in glory, and inscribed—

" The Gift of the Rᵗ. Honbˡᵉ yᵉ Lord Edward Russell to yᵉ Church of Llandegai   Richᵈ Williams   ⎱ Church-wardens."
                                                      Thomas Morgan   ⎰

The stem, which rests on a moulded foot, is divided by a flattened knop.

Marks.—London date-letter for 1714-15. Maker's mark, Ne, in a shaped shield (Anthony Nelme).

Dimensions.—Height, 10⅝ in.; depth of bowl, 5½ in.; diameter of mouth and foot, 4⅝ in. (PLATE XXIII., No. 1.)

PATEN.—A plain silver Paten, with a slightly moulded edge, on a foot, and engraved with symbols and inscription as on Chalice.
Marks as on Chalice.
Diameter, 5¾ in.; height, 1½ in.

PATEN.—A larger silver Paten, slightly moulded edge, supported by a truncated stem with moulded edge. The same symbols and inscription as on Chalice and smaller Paten are engraved, but on this the word " the " is substituted for " ye."

Marks as on Chalice and smaller Paten.

Diameter, 9½ in. ; height, 3¾ in.

The donor of the Chalice and two Patens, Lord Edward Russell, was the second son of the first Duke of Bedford, and married Frances, daughter and heiress of Sir Robert Williams, Bart., of Penrhyn. Lord Edward was a brother of the celebrated William, Lord Russell.

FLAGON.—A tall, plain silver Flagon, with cylindrical body, small spout, slightly domed cover, scrolled handle, moulded foot. It is engraved with the Christian symbols as on Chalice, etc., and is inscribed under edge of foot—" Presented by the Lady Penrhyn to the Church of Llandegai 1871."

Marks.—London date-letter for 1871-2.

Height, 10¾ in.

A small silver set for private Communion, consisting of a Chalice with egg-shape bowl, moulded lip, 3⅛ in. high ; a Paten on foot ; and a small circular Dish with moulded edge, all engraved with the Christian symbols, I.H.S., a cross and three nails in glory, and inscribed—

" The Gift of the
RIGHT HON^{BLE} LADY PENRYN
1816."

There is also a small glass bottle with silver top.

Marks.—London date-letter for 1819-20. Maker's mark, $_{IED}^{SR}$

Dimensions.—Chalice, 3⅛ in. high ; Paten and Dish, 2$\frac{7}{16}$ in. diameter ; Bottle, 3¾ in. high. (PLATE XXXIV., No. 2.)

The parish terrier for 1834 refers to a pewter Flagon and Dish, " the gift of Mr. Richard Williams Gent. in the year of Our Lord 1713," probably the Churchwarden whose name is inscribed on the silver Chalice and Patens, but the whereabouts of these cannot, unfortunately, be traced.

LLANDINORWIC

Two silver Chalices of medieval design, with hexagonal stems divided by the usual knop, on sexfoil feet, engraved with " IHC." 7½ in. high. A silver Paten, engraved with the *Agnus Dei*, and inscribed— " O Lamb of God that takest away the sins of the world. Have mercy upon us." 8¼ in. in diameter. A silver Flagon of globular form, inscribed—" Glory be to God on high." 12 in. high. A silver Alms

Dish, with I.H.S. embossed in the centre, and inscribed—" All things come of the Lord, and of Thine own have we given Thee."   12 in. in diameter.

Marks.—London date-letter for 1862-3.   Maker's mark on Chalices and Paten $\frac{IK}{RS}$; on Flagon and Alms Dish, I·K. (John Keith).

This silver service is believed to have been given by the late Thomas Assheton Smith, Esq.

LLANDDEINIOLEN—S. DEINIOL

CHALICE.—An Elizabethan silver Chalice, with plain beaker-shape bowl, engraved near the lip with a band, $\frac{3}{8}$ in. wide, which is filled with this inscription on a fine matted surface, in Lombardic capitals, and preceded by a cross—

"✠ THE CUPPE OF LLANDENIOLEN."

Each word is divided by a quatrefoil.   The stem, which is entirely plain, is divided by a plain knop between two collars, and rests on a plain rounded foot.

Marks.—London date-letter for 1599-1600.   Maker's mark, IH, with a bear passant below, in a circle (Jackson, 1597-8).

Dimensions.—Height, $6\frac{5}{16}$ in. ; depth of bowl, $3\frac{1}{8}$ in. ; diameter of mouth, $3\frac{3}{4}$ in. ; diameter of foot, $3\frac{5}{8}$ in.

PATEN-COVER.—The silver Paten-Cover of this Chalice is engraved with a band of arabesques, and on the bottom of the foot is an engraved Tudor rose.

Dimensions.—Diameter, 4 in. ; height, $1\frac{1}{2}$ in.   (PLATE XVIII.)

FLAGON.—A tall, plain silver Flagon, with cylindrical body ; moulded lip ; the foot moulded and splaying out from a moulding ; flat, moulded cover, with scrolled thumb-piece ; scrolled handle, terminating in a heart-shape shield.   In front is a shield of arms, with delicately engraved scrolled and floreated mantling, *on a bend three leopards' faces impaling two bars gu. and in chief three cinquefoils.*   And, below, this inscription in script lettering—

" The Gift of Mʳˢ. Jane Wynne
(the Wife of Robert Wynne Clarke)
to the Church of LLanddeniolen.
Anno Domini 1704."

Marks.—London date-letter for 1704-5. Maker's mark, Pa. with vase above, pellet below, in shaped shield—the mark of Humphrey Payne.

Dimensions.—Height to top of cover, 10⅜ in.; body only, 9⅝ in.; diameter of mouth, 4⅜ in.; diameter of foot, 6⅞ in.

PATEN.—A large, plain silver Paten, with embossed gadroon border, standing on a truncated foot with similar border. In the centre is the same shield of arms as on Flagon, and above it this inscription in script lettering—

"The gift of M^rs. Jane Wynne Wife of Robert Wynne Cle^r.
To the Church of LLan DDeniolen. A.D. 1704."

Marks.—London date-letter for 1703-4. Maker's mark, same as on Flagon.

Robert Wynn, M.A. of Jesus College, Cambridge, the sixth son of John Wynn, of Bodewryd, in Anglesey, married Jane, the third daughter and co-heiress of Wm. Denton, of Skillington, Lincolnshire, Esq., the other co-heiress being Elizabeth, the wife of Dr. H. Brooks, "an eminent and learned Physician of London." He was instituted to this living on the 20th May, 1679, and was buried at Llanddeiniolen on the 18th October, 1720.

The similar silver Flagon, dated 1691, at Llanbeblig, was given by Robert Wynn in 1710.

LLANDUDNO—S. TUDNO

A plain silver Chalice with V-shape bowl, on a tall baluster stem resting on a splayed foot, with delicate ovolo moulding on the edge. (PLATE XXIX., No. 3.)

Marks.—London date-letter for 1607. Maker's mark, SO, a pellet above, and a rose between two pellets below, in shaped shield (Jackson, 1608-9).

Dimensions.—Height, 7 7/16 in.; depth of bowl, 3½ in.; diameter of mouth, 3⅜ in.; diameter of foot, 3⅛ in.

A similar Chalice, but without the ovolo moulding on the foot, is to be seen at two other Churches in this Diocese—Trefdraeth and Llanllyfni.

The old pewter Tankard and Plate mentioned in the terriers from 1806 to 1834 cannot be traced.

CHALICE.—A tall silver Chalice, plain inverted bell-shape bowl, 7⅞ in. high.

PLATE XXI.

DOLGELLEY.

CHARLES II. SILVER CHALICE
AND PATEN-COVER.
DATE: 1683.

SILVER FLAGON.
DATE: 1723-4.

SILVER PATEN.
DATE: 1709-10.

PATEN.—A plain silver Paten on foot, 7 in. in diameter and $1\frac{7}{8}$ in. high.

FLAGON.—A tall plain silver Flagon, with cylindrical body, $13\frac{1}{2}$ in. high.
These three pieces are inscribed—

"A thank offering, Presented to S^t. Tudno's Church, Llandudno, by W. F. Chapman Esq. Oct. 11th, 1858."

The Flagon and Paten bear London date-letter for 1846-7; the mark on Chalice is indistinct. All made by the firm of Barnard.

PATEN.—A plain silver Paten, inscribed—
"S^t. Tudno's Church 1894 per Frances Dalton."

Sheffield date-letter for 1893-4.
Diameter, 7 in.
In the Bodafon Mission Room are a silver Chalice, $6\frac{1}{2}$ in. high, inscribed—"The gift of E. & M. A. Turner 1905." Sheffield date-letter for 1904-5. A silver Paten, with I.H.S. in centre, inscribed—"The gift of Richard Conway 1885"; and another silver Paten, inscribed—"The gift of William Laycock 1890." London date-letter for 1890-1.

LLANDUDNO—HOLY TRINITY

CHALICE.—A silver-gilt Chalice, inscribed on the bowl, which has a surbase of engraved foliage—"calicem salutaris accipiam et nomen Domini invocabo," in black letters. The knop on the stem is plain, and has six oval projections, on which are crosses in relief. The foot is sexfoil, and one lobe is engraved with I.H.S., and another with the *Agnus Dei*. Inscribed—

"SACRED TO GOD & TO HOLY TRINITY CHURCH LLANDUDNO 1882."

PATEN.—A silver-gilt Paten, I.H.S. engraved within a circle in the centre. On the rim, which has an engraved zig-zag border with fleurs-de-lis, are six applied oval medallions with symbols of the Crucifixion in relief.

FLAGON.—A silver-gilt Flagon, with globular body, on sexfoil foot.
Marks on each, London date-letter for 1879-80. Maker's mark, FE, in double-lobed shield.
L

LLANDUDNO—S. GEORGE

A silver Communion service of plain Chalice; small plain Paten on truncated foot; a plain Flagon engraved with Christian symbols, I.H.S., a cross and nails in glory; and a small circular Dish. The Flagon is inscribed—

"Presented by
Lady Charlotte Margaret Mostyn Champneys,
of Gloddaeth, To the Parishioners of Llandudno,
for the use of S^t. George's Church 1840."

Marks on each.—London date-letter for 1840-1. Maker's mark, GG, in an oblong.

LLANDUDWEN—S. TUDWEN

In this Church is the only example in the Diocese of Bangor of a pre-Reformation silver Chalice which has survived destruction at the Reformation. The bowl is plain hemispherical, and is supported by an hexagonal stem, divided by a large ornate knop, pierced and gilt, with six diamond-shape projections chased with rosettes. The foot is curved hexagonal with a moulded edge and at the points are small applied semi-circular, pierced discs, one of which is missing. One of the compartments is filled with an engraved representation of the Crucifixion, with the arms drawn back over the Saviour's head, on a foliated background, which is gilt. There are no marks. (PLATE I.)

Dimensions.—Height, $5\frac{1}{4}$ in.; depth of bowl, $1\frac{3}{4}$ in.; diameter of bowl, $3\frac{3}{4}$ in.; extreme width of foot, including the projections, $4\frac{1}{2}$ in.; width of foot at narrowest point, $2\frac{7}{8}$ in.; diameter of knop, $1\frac{3}{16}$ in.

The date of this Chalice is *circa* 1500.

This, and the almost identical one at Llanelian, in Denbighshire, are the only two pre-Reformation silver Chalices of English work in the whole of Wales which have escaped the ravages committed in Parish Churches and Chantries by the Commissioners of Edward VI. and the injunctions of Archbishop Parker that all Massing Chalices should be turned into "decent communion cups." The only pre-Reformation silver Paten to be found in Wales is that at Llanmaes in Glamorganshire—dated 1535.

PATEN.—The Paten used in this Church is a silver Saucer-Dish, circular in shape, with a plain square-shape shield in the centre, pounced with the initials $_T^P{}_A$, and surrounded by a double dotted circle enclosing a row of rosettes and plain bosses, all, including the shield, being punched out. Flutings radiate from the centre and terminate in a punched rosette, divided by a thin arched line. The two small handles are incised with lines to resemble escallop shells. (PLATE XV., No. 2.)

Marks—London date-letter for 1636-7. Maker's mark, probably RS, with a mullet between two pellets above.

Dimensions.—Diameter, exclusive of handles, $5\frac{7}{8}$ in.; depth, $1\frac{1}{8}$ in.

LLANDWROG—S. TWROG

CHALICE.—A plain, silver Chalice, with very deep beaker-shape bowl, curved outwards at the lip, standing on a short stem, divided by a plain compressed knop between two collars, resting on a domed and moulded foot. Inscribed, in one line—

"Hugh Gwynne and William Glyn Gent. Church wardens Anno Dni 1619."

Marks.—London date-letter for 1619-20. Maker's mark, RS, with an illegible device above and below, in a shaped shield.

Dimensions.—Height, $7\frac{7}{8}$ in.; depth of bowl, $4\frac{3}{4}$ in.; diameter of mouth, $3\frac{3}{8}$ in.; diameter of foot, $3\frac{1}{2}$ in. (PLATE X., No. 3.)

Hugh Gwynne was perhaps of Pengwern, Llanwnda, who was living in 1624.

William Glynne, of Plasnewydd, Llandwrog, was the son of William Glynne ap Richard of Glynllifon.

CHALICE.—A large plain Chalice, with unusually capacious beaker-like bowl, standing on a very short, small, baluster stem on a moulded foot.

Marks.—London date-letter for 1699-1700. Maker's mark, LE, crowned, in shaped shield (George Lewis).

Dimensions.—Height, $9\frac{1}{8}$ in.; depth of bowl, $4\frac{7}{8}$ in.; diameter of mouth, $4\frac{3}{8}$ in.; diameter of foot, $4\frac{5}{8}$ in.

PATEN-COVER.—The plain silver Paten-Cover belonging to the second Chalice has a narrow moulded edge, with a short foot, and bears the same marks. Date letter, 1699-1700. Diameter, $5\frac{3}{8}$ in.

ALMS DISH OR PATEN.—A large circular silver Dish, plain, with narrow flat rim, the edge moulded. A lozenge, with double-headed eagle displayed, engraved on the border. Weight marked, 22 oz. 14 dwt.

London date-letter for 1703-4. No maker's mark.

Diameter, $11\frac{1}{8}$ in.

FLAGON.—A large, tall silver Flagon, with cylindrical body, and a domed cover, surmounted by a cross. The letters I.H.S., a cross and three nails in glory engraved on the body.

London date-letter for 1856. Makers' mark, $^{C}_{G}{}^{T}_{F}{}^{F}$ in shaped shield (Chas. T. Fox and Geo. Fox).

Height to top of cross, 12⅜ in.

FLAGON.—An old pewter Flagon, in a dilapidated condition, the spout and cover missing. No marks.

LLANDYGWYNNIN—S. GWYNNIN

CHALICE.—A silver Chalice, with deep, beaker-shape bowl, a narrow band of laurel leaves, ¼ in. wide, engraved around its centre, supported by a very slender stem, which is divided in the centre by a wide moulding, resting on a plain, moulded foot.

Marks.—London date-letter for 1610-11. Maker's mark, TWY, or TYW, in monogram, in shaped shield.

Dimensions.—Height, 5⅝ in.; depth of bowl, 3⅛ in.; diameter of mouth, 2¾ in.; diameter of foot, 2${}_{16}^{7}$ in.

PATEN-COVER.—The silver Paten-Cover belonging to this Chalice overlaps the edge, and is engraved with a band filled with three rows of hyphens. The foot is plain.

Marks.—Maker's mark only, as on Chalice.

Dimensions.—Diameter, 3 in.; height, 1 in. (PLATE VII., No. 3.)

PATEN.—A plain, domestic Salver, of old Sheffield-plate, with gadroon edge, standing on three feet, decorated with acanthus leaves; 8 in. in diameter.

LLANENGAN—S. ENGAN

CHALICE (No. 1).—A plated Chalice, inscribed—" Llanengan Church, Presented by Mrs. Jones of the Rectory. June 6ᵗʰ 1861."

CHALICE (No. 2).—A silver Chalice, inscribed—" Llanengan Parish Church—a Thank offering from Mrs. Harry Morgan, Abersoch, July 1905."

Sheffield date-letter for 1905-6. Maker's mark, W. & H. on a flag. Height, 9 in.

PATEN.—A circular silver Dinner-plate, with moulded edge, 10 in. in diameter.

PLATE XXII.

No. 1.

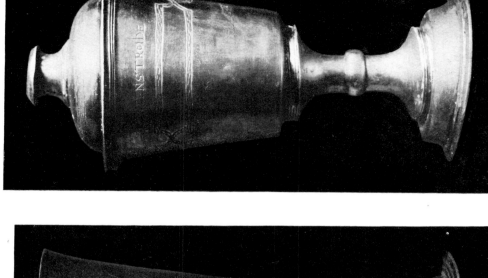

No. 2.

No. 3.

DAROWEN, MONTGOMERYSHIRE.
ELIZABETHAN SILVER CHALICE.
DATE: *circa* 1575.

LLANBRYNMAIR, MONTGOMERYSHIRE.
ELIZABETHAN SILVER CHALICE.
DATE: 1595-5.

PENSTROWED, MONTGOMERYSHIRE.
ELIZABETHAN SILVER CHALICE AND
PATEN-COVER.
DATE: 1576

London date-letter for 1812-13.
A pewter Cup with two handles, 7¾ in. high. Date, *circa* 1725.
The silver Communion Cup mentioned in the parish terriers between 1804 and 1817 is missing.

LLANFAELRHYS—S. MOEL RHYS

CHALICE.—An old Sheffield-plate Chalice, with plain, beaker-shape bowl, a narrow gadroon and shell moulding at the junction of the bowl with the stem. The knop in the centre of the stem is decorated with projecting escallop shells, flutings and beadings, and the edge of the foot decorated with bold escallops, fruit and flowers in relief.
Height, 6½ in.; diameter of mouth, 4 in.
Date, *circa* 1810.

PATEN.—An old Sheffield-plate Salver, plain centre, with a shaped shell and foliated border, alternating with a triple device consisting of a spade, a fork, and an escallop shell. 9 in. in diameter.

LLANFAGLAN—S. BAGLAN

CHALICE.—A large, massive, silver Loving-cup, with two harp-shape handles, the lower ends of which are joined to the plain moulding encircling the body; the upper part above the moulding is chased with foliage, scrolls and scales, and the lower part with foliage and scrolls of a different character. The foot is low, plain, and moulded. Inscribed—

Presented for the Service of the Church
in the Parish of Llanfaglan
By Mʀˢ. SUSANNAH JONES
Widow of the late Richard Jones Esqʳᵉ of Cefnycoed.
June 1841."

Marks.—Dublin date-letter for 1723-4. Maker's mark, TS crowned (Thos. Sutton).
Dimensions.—Height, 6⅜ in.; diameter of mouth, 5⅜ in. Weight marked, 24 oz. 19 dwts.

PATEN.—A plain silver Salver with shaped shell border, on three feet, inscribed with same inscription as on the Cup.
Marks.—London date-letter for 1752-3. Maker's mark, WP, conjoined, in a heart (Wm. Peaston).
Diameter, 11½ in.

These two pieces of domestic plate replace the " silver Chalice and square silver Salver, inscribed—' The Gift of Ellen Lewis of Plas Llanfaglan, Dec. 25, 1731,' and the round silver Salver, inscribed—' Llanfaglan 1687,' and a pewter Flagon," stolen from this Church.

Ellen Lewis was the second daughter of Hugh Lewis of Plas Llanfaglan. She married James Vincent.

LLANFAIRFECHAN—S. MARY

CHALICE.—A silver Chalice with beaker-shape bowl, gilt inside and curved at the lip, supported by a truncated stem on a moulded base. Inscribed—

"LLanvair Vechan."

Marks.—London date-letter for 1638-9. Maker's mark, MW conjoined, annulets and pellets above and below.

Dimensions.—Height, 6⅜ in.; depth of bowl, 4 in.; diameter of mouth, 3⅜ in.; diameter of foot, 4 in.

PATEN.—Silver Paten, with wide flat rim, ⅞ in. wide, incised with lines near the edge, a flat depression, on a foot engraved with date, 1639, within an incised line circle.

Marks.—As on Chalice.

Dimensions.—Diameter, 4⅞ in.; height, 1¼ in.; diameter of foot, 2¼ in.

This is an interesting example of a Chalice with a separate Paten, which was not intended to fit closely on to the mouth of Chalice. (PLATE IX., No. 2.)

CHALICE.—A tall silver Chalice with plain bowl; a circular knop, chased with trefoils and diamond-shape projections, is on the hexagonal stem. The foot is sexfoil with beaded edge, a spray of foliage engraved at each angle and a cross in a circle engraved on one lobe.

Marks.—London date-letter for 1840-1. Maker's mark, $\frac{EC}{W}$ in trefoil.

Height, 8 in.

PATEN.—A silver Paten, a cross engraved in the centre, and acanthus foliage on the rim.

London date-letter for 1875-6. Maker's mark, $\frac{HE}{W}$ in trefoil.

Diameter, 6 in.

FLAGON.—A glass Flagon, engraved with symbols of the four Evangelists, with silver top.

There is also an old pewter Flagon with tall cylindrical body, encircled by two incised lines; domed cover; scroll thumb-piece; spout; scrolled handle; moulded spreading base. Inscribed—

"LLan Fair Fechan
1722."

Stamped with one mark inside, CB.

Height, exclusive of cover, 8¾ in.; with cover, 10⅛ in.

A pewter Plate, engraved on the rim with initials TOT. Stamped with three marks—(1) a bird on a globe, with the name Nicholson underneath; (2) LONDON; (3) a Tudor rose crowned.

Diameter, 10⅞ in.

LLANFAIRFECHAN—CHRIST CHURCH

Two silver Chalices of medieval form, 8 in. high, one with London date-letter for 1838-9, the other 1839-40; two silver Patens, 6 in. in diameter, London date-letter for 1840-1; a glass Flagon with silver mounts; and a glass Cruet.

LLANFAIRISGAER—S. MARY

A silver set, consisting of a Chalice of medieval design, with plain bowl, sexfoil foot, 9 in. high; a Paten, with inscription in black letters— "O Lamb of God that takest away the sins of the world, have mercy upon us," 7 in. in diameter; and a Flagon with globular body, inscribed— "Glory be to God on high," 12 in. high.

Marks.—London date-letter for 1860-1. Maker's mark, I·K in an oblong (John Keith).

The old silver Chalice and Paten, and pewter Flagon, referred to in the terriers between 1801 and 1834, have disappeared.

LLANFIHANGEL-BACHELLAETH—S. MICHAEL

A plain silver Chalice with beaker-shape bowl, resting on a very short truncated stem on a rounded foot with flat edge. The letters WL are rudely engraved on the foot. The only marks stamped on it are NB, conjoined, in a shaped shield, and the word "sterling," abbreviated thus—"sterl:" These are the marks of a well-known Chester

Silversmith, Nathaniel Bullen, who flourished from about 1668 to 1712. The date of this Chalice is probably about 1693. The same two marks appear on a similar Chalice at Pentraeth, in Anglesey. In the terrier for 1811 this Chalice was described as having a Paten-Cover, now, however, no longer in existence. (PLATE XVI., No. 1.)

Dimensions.—Height, 6½ in.; depth of bowl, 4$\frac{5}{16}$ in.; diameter of mouth and of foot, 3$\frac{9}{16}$ in.

LLANFIHANGEL-Y-PENNANT—S. MICHAEL

CHALICE.—A plain silver Chalice with bell-shape bowl on tall stem. Inscribed—

"IG
e } Wardens 1736."
EW

London date-letter for 1736-7.
Height, 8 in.

PATEN.—A plain silver Paten, engraved in the centre with the Christian symbols, I.H.S., a cross and nails in glory, and inscribed— "The legacy of Catherine Meyricke, Widow, daughter of Ellis Brynker Esq. to the Church of S^t. Michael in Pennant."
London date-letter for 1724-5.
Diameter, 7¾ in.

LLANGELYNIN—S. CELYNIN

The plate here consists of an old Sheffield-plate Porringer, with plain bell-shape bowl; an old Sheffield-plate Cup, on tall stem; a small, plain electro-plated Alms-Dish; and an electro-plated Paten and large Flagon. These two latter pieces given by Thomas Williams, of Glyn.

There is also an interesting old pewter Flagon, unfortunately damaged, with tall cylindrical tapering body. It has a slightly domed cover surmounted by a knob. The base and lip are moulded. On the thumb-piece is a little floral ornament in low relief. It is inscribed—

"Given by JOHN EDWARDS. AN: DO: 1638."

The initials IE or IF have been roughly carved at a later date on the front.

No. 3.

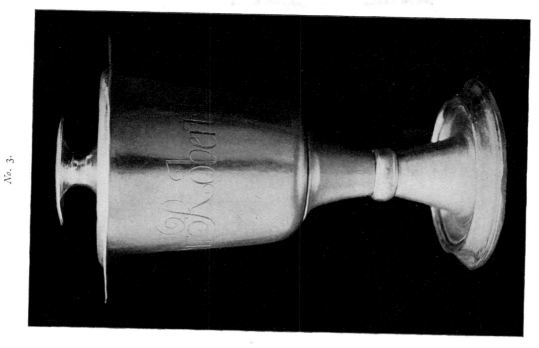

PENMORFA, CARNARVONSHIRE.

WILLIAM III. SILVER CHALICE AND PATEN-COVER.

DATE : 1697-8.

PLATE XXIII.

No. 2.

PENMACHNO, CARNARVONSHIRE.

QUEEN ANNE SILVER CHALICE AND PATEN-COVER.

DATE : 1712-13.

No. 1.

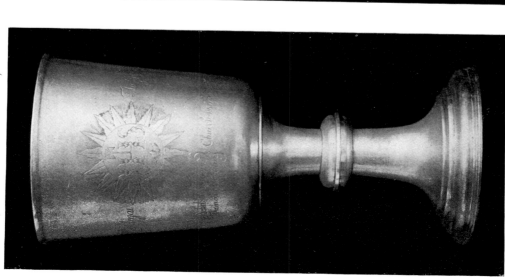

LLANDEGAI, CARNARVONSHIRE.

GEORGE I. SILVER CHALICE.

DATE : 1714-15.

Dimensions.—Height, to top of cover, 11 in.
No marks.

An old pewter Plate, 10¾ in. in diameter, inscribed—

"I : W
W : D } WARDENS."
1731

It is stamped with several marks—an X crowned, ^{FROM}LONDON, and four small marks in separate shields—(1) three lions' heads; (2) a man's head?; (3) a talbot's head; (4) ID.

LLANGIAN—S. GIAN

A plain silver Chalice with Paten-Cover. The Chalice has a deep beaker-like bowl, on a very short truncated stem, encircled by three incised lines, resting on a moulded foot. The Paten-Cover has a flat edge and a short spreading foot. The three marks stamped are the initials PP in a plain shield, the word STER/LING in a shield, and a letter, probably a C, in a plain shield. The first represents the mark of Puleston Partington or Peter Pemberton, two silversmiths who flourished at Chester between 1673 and 1706; the second is the STERLING mark used by Chester goldsmiths in the seventeenth century, the earliest instance of the use of this mark probably being an Alms-Dish, dated 1683, in the Church of S. John the Baptist, Chester; and the third mark is believed to represent the date-letter for 1692-4. (PLATE XVI., No. 3.)

Dimensions.—Chalice, height, 5 13/16 in.; depth of bowl, 3 11/16 in.; diameter of mouth and of foot, 3½ in. Paten-Cover is 4 7/16 in. in diameter, and ¾ in. high.

There is also in this Church an old Sheffield-plate Dinner-plate and a silver-mounted glass Cruet.

The Churches of Llanbedrog, Llangian, and Llanfihangel-Bachellaeth appear to have been provided with newer and larger silver Chalices during the time (1688-1709) these livings were held by the Rev. John Williams, M.A., of Jesus College, Cambridge, youngest son of Alfred Williams, of Pentir, near Bangor, and of Margaret Robyns, daughter of John Robyns, of Castellmai.

LLANGWNADL—S. GWYNHOYDL

An Elizabethan silver Chalice with a beaker-shape bowl, curving outwards considerably, engraved near the top with the customary plain, double strap-work band, interlacing three times, filled with conventional

M

sprays of foliage, a triple sprig carried above and below each intersection Below this is a single band, filled with four rows of incised hyphens, a similar band, containing three rows, appearing on the rounded shoulder of the foot. The top and bottom of the stem, which has a plain compressed knop near the top, are plainly moulded, as is also the edge of the foot or base. The bowl of this Chalice is deeper than usual, and another characteristic is the shortness of the stem, with the knop near the top rather than in the centre. (PLATE VII., No. I.)

Marks.—London date-letter for 1574-5. Maker's mark, HS in monogram, in shaped shield (? Henry Sutton).

Dimensions.—Height, $5\frac{3}{8}$ in.; depth of bowl, $3\frac{1}{8}$ in.; diameter of mouth, $3\frac{1}{8}$ in.; diameter of foot, $2\frac{3}{4}$ in.

The Paten in use here is an ordinary domestic Salver of old Sheffield-plate, with plain centre and gadroon edge, on three feet. 8 in. in diameter.

An old pewter Flagon is missing from this Church.

LLANGYBI—S. CYBI

A plain silver Chalice, with inverted bell-shape bowl, supported by a baluster stem on a splayed foot. The bowl is inscribed—

"Ex dono / om^{iii} Thos Wynne"

and on the other side the sacred letters I.H.S. and a cross, which were engraved some years subsequent to the date of the Cup. The initials AB are very faintly pounced on the bowl. On the foot, which is inscribed, "LLan Gyby," is a shield of arms: *a chevron between three fleurs-de-lys, a crescent, impaling a chevron between three bulls' heads caboshed*, with two palm branches below. (PLATE XIV., No. 2.)

Marks.—Dublin date-letter for 1638-9; maker's mark, H above W, in plain shield (? William Hampton, Warden of the Goldsmiths' Company of Dublin); and Irish harp, crowned.

Dimensions.—Height, $6\frac{1}{2}$ in.; depth of bowl, $3\frac{3}{8}$ in.; diameter of mouth, $3\frac{3}{8}$ in.; diameter of foot, $3\frac{1}{4}$ in.

The donor, Thomas Wynne, was of Coed Caegwyn, Llanarmon. His wife was Jane, daughter of William Bulkeley, of Porthamel, Anglesey. He died March 26th, 1747.

A large, plain, old Sheffield-plate Paten.

LLANIESTYN—S. IESTYN

CHALICE AND PATEN-COVER.—The silver Chalice is plain, with a deep beaker-shape bowl, slightly gilt inside, supported by a truncated stem on a moulded foot. It is encircled by this inscription in one line, near the lip—

"As oft as ye shall eate this bread, and drinke this Cup, ye shew the Lord's death till he come.—1 Cor. ii. 21."

And by this other inscription in one line lower down the bowl—

"The guift of Roger Jones, Cittizen of London, borne in ye parish of Llaniestyn in yᵉ Countey of Carnarvon, 1634."

The plain silver Paten-Cover has a double circular depression, with a narrow raised border. On the foot is engraved a Dragon, with the donor's initials, R.I. (PLATE IX., No. 1.)

Marks.—London date-letter for 1634-5. Maker's mark, R, with rose under.

Dimensions.—Height of Chalice, $7\frac{9}{16}$ in.; depth of bowl, $4\frac{1}{2}$ in.; diameter of mouth, $3\frac{5}{8}$ in.; diameter of foot, $3\frac{11}{16}$ in. Paten-Cover is $4\frac{1}{16}$ in. in diameter, and $1\frac{1}{2}$ in. high.

FLAGON.—A plain plated Flagon, with I.H.S. engraved in front.

An old Flagon, Paten, and Dish, of pewter, have disappeared since 1837.

LLANLLECHID—S. LLECHYD

CHALICE.—A tall, plain silver Chalice, with beaker-shape bowl, the stem of which is divided in the centre by a plain knop, and moulded foot. It is engraved with the Christian emblems, I.H.S., a cross and three nails in glory. Inscribed—

"The Gift of Iohn Iones D.D.
to the Church of LLanllechyd
in Carnā̄r: shire Anno 1712."

Marks.—London date-letter for 1712-13. Maker's mark, WE with anchor between (Jas. Wethered).

Dimensions.—Height, 9 in.; depth of bowl, $5\frac{1}{4}$ in.; diameter of mouth, $4\frac{1}{4}$ in.

PATEN-COVER.—The silver Paten-Cover belonging to the above Chalice has the same inscription engraved on the flat edge, and the same Christian emblems on the foot.

Marks.—The same as on Chalice.

Dimensions.—Diameter, 6¾ in.; height, 1⅝ in.

FLAGON.—A tall, plain silver Flagon, cylindrical body, a plain moulding encircling the lower part of body, wide, spreading moulded foot; domed cover, surmounted by a vase-shape knob; scroll thumb-piece. Inscribed—

> " The Gift of John Jones D.D. to the Church of
> LLanllechyd, A.D. 1719."

Marks.—London date-letter for 1719-20. Maker's mark (indistinct), probably Wm. Fawdery.

Dimensions.—Height to top of cover, 11¼ in.

The donor of these was the second son of Rowland Jones, of Plas-gwyn, Pentraeth, Anglesey. He was Dean of Bangor 1689-1727. He gave a Silver Chalice and Paten-Cover to Gyffin Church, and a silver Chalice and Paten and a Flagon to Aber Church.

PATEN-COVER.—There is a small, plain silver Paten-Cover, on a foot, which is inscribed—

> " LLanllechid."

Diameter, 3 1/16 in.

The Chalice has disappeared.

Marks.—Chester date-letter for 1744-5. Maker's mark, RR in an oblong.

There is also in this Church a Communion Service, in plain old Sheffield-plate, consisting of a tall Chalice, gilt inside, on a slender stem; a Paten on foot; a tall Flagon, with domed cover; and a small circular Dish, all inscribed—

> " The Gift of
> The Rev^d. William Wynn Coytmor
> Doctor of Divinity
> of Coytmor, in this Parish.
> January 25th 1808."

Dimensions.—Chalice, 8¼ in. high; Paten, 7 in. diameter; Flagon, 11½ in. high; Dish, 6⅛ in. in diameter.

LLANLLYFNI—S. RHEDYW

CHALICE.—A tall silver Chalice, with plain V-shape bowl, on tall slender baluster stem resting on a splayed foot. Inscribed near lip—

> " LLann LLyfni 1617."

PLATE XXIV.

COEDANA, ANGLESEY.
Elizabethan Silver Chalice and Paten-Cover.
Date : 1578.

Under foot, the initials, RG, GR, are engraved in a rough manner.

Marks.—London date-letter for 1616-17. Maker's mark, MW in monogram (Jackson, 1602-3).

Dimensions.—Height, 8¾ in.; depth of bowl, 3¾ in.; diameter of mouth, 3½ in.; diameter of foot, 3¾₁₆ in.

PATEN.—A pewter Paten, the Christian symbols, I.H.S. and a cross, engraved in the centre, and inscribed—

"ELLIS THOˢ Rᴿ ILⁿ llyfni * Roᵀ W * Rɪᴰ G * Wardens * 1767."

The edge is moulded. The foot has gone.
Diameter, 7⅜ in. No marks.

PATEN OR ALMS DISH.—A circular pewter Plate or Dish, the symbols I.H.S. and cross engraved in the centre, and this inscription on the rim—

"E × T × Rᴿ ILⁿ llyfni × RW * RG * WARDˢ 1767."

Marks.—A crowned X; a bird's leg and claw, with LONDON in a label beneath; and three other marks in small separate shields—(1) three talbots' heads; (2) a bird's leg and claw; (3) one talbot's head.
Diameter, 9⅛ in.

ALMS DISH.—A larger pewter Dish, with same symbols engraved in the centre and this inscription on the rim—

"EILIS THOˢ Rᴿ ILⁿ llyfni * Roᵀ W * Rɪᴰ G * WARDENS * 1767."

Same marks as on the previous dish. Diameter, 10¾ in.

BAPTISMAL BOWL.—A circular pewter Bowl, with low moulded base.
Marks.—X crowned, and H× and other illegible letters in a label.
Diameter, 9¼ in.; depth, 3⅝ in.; diameter of base, 3¾₁₆ in.

The inscriptions engraved on the pewter vessels represent the names of the Rector, Ellis Thomas, and the two Churchwardens.

LLANNOR—HOLY CROSS

CHALICE.—A large silver Chalice, with deep, inverted, bell-shape bowl, on a short stem divided by a moulding, resting on a moulded foot. Inscribed—

"Llannor Parish G.I : W.P. Wardens. 1713."

No marks. Date, *circa* 1710.
Height, 8 in.

PATEN.—A large plain silver Paten with foot, and raised moulded border, ¾ in. wide. On it is engraved this inscription—" The Gift of Henry William Lord Bishop of Bangor, to the parish of Llannor Carnarvonshire, A.D. 1815." In the centre are engraved the Christian symbols, I.H.S., a cross and three nails in glory, and this Welsh scriptural inscription—" Os bwytty neb o'r bara hwn, efe a fydd byw yn dragywydd. S. Joan. vi. 51." It is also engraved with the arms of the See of Bangor, conjoined with those of the donor, Bishop Majendie (Bishop of Chester 1800-9, of Bangor 1809-30)—*or, on a mount vert a tree between a serpent erect and a dove close*, surmounted by a mitre.

Marks.—London date-letter for 1717-18. Maker's mark, Lo, in black letters (Seth Lofthouse).

Diameter, 9¾ in.; height, 1¾ in.

PATEN.—A new plain silver Paten, inscribed—" Llannor Church, Don: by B. T. Ellis Esq. Advent 1902. T. E. Jones, Vicar."

FLAGON.—A new silver Flagon, with globular body, inscribed—" To the glory of God. Presented to Llannor Church by B. T. Ellis Esq Xmas 1899. W. E. Jones, Vicar."

LLANRHYCHWYN—S. RHYCHWYN

A fine silver Chalice with V-shape bowl, gilt inside, decorated with grapes and foliage in low relief, on a matted surface, the surbase fluted. The tall, slender stem, which is slightly engraved with acanthus foliage, rests on a fluted splayed foot with a delicate ovolo moulding on the edge. On the plain lip is this inscription, pounced—

" Ex dono Randall LLoyd."

A human skull is faintly pounced on the plain shield on the bowl.

Marks.—London date-letter for 1614-15. Maker's mark AB, conjoined, in a shaped shield (Jackson, 1602-3).

Dimensions.—Height, 7½ in.; depth of bowl, 3¼ in.; diameter of mouth, 3⅝ in.; diameter of foot, 3⅛ in. (PLATE XXIX., No. 1.)

LLANRUG—S. MICHAEL

An Elizabethan silver Chalice with Paten-Cover. The Chalice has a beaker-shape bowl, engraved near the top with the usual plain, double strap-work band, interlacing three times, and enclosing the conventional sprays of foliage, a small sprig carried above and below each intersection.

Lower down the body are three rows of engraved hyphens. The stem follows the usual lines, and has a plain moulding at each end, with a flat, plain compressed knop between two narrow collars in the centre. On the shoulder of the foot are three rows of hyphens, as on the bowl, and on the extreme edge an egg and dart moulding. The Paten-Cover, which has lost its foot, has a reeded edge, and on the shoulder are rows of engraved hyphens. Date, *circa* 1575.

The only mark is the bird's head, erased, turned dexter-wise, peculiar to this diocese. (PLATE V., No. 1.)

Dimensions of Chalice: height, $6\frac{7}{16}$ in.; depth of bowl, $3\frac{1}{16}$ in.; diameter of mouth, 3 in.; diameter of foot, $3\frac{1}{4}$ in.

There is also in this Church a pewter Tankard, with sloping cylindrical body, moulded base, domed cover, and scrolled handle. Probable date, *circa* 1730.

An electro-plated Flagon and Paten.

LLANWNDA—S. GWYNDAF HÊN

CHALICE.—A massive silver Chalice, with tapering beaker-shape bowl. A plain collar, separated from the bowl by a narrow concave moulding, is at the top of the truncated stem, which has a moulded edge and two incised lines. It is inscribed—

"LLanunda. I*H."

The engraving of the name of the parish is contemporary with the date of the Chalice, but the initials are later.

Belonging to this Chalice is a Paten-Cover with a foot, on which is engraved the date, 1633, within an incised circle.

Marks.—London date-letter for 1633-4. Maker's mark, an escallop shell in a shaped shield (Jackson, 1628-9).

Dimensions.—Chalice, $8\frac{1}{4}$ in. high; bowl, $4\frac{3}{8}$ in. deep; mouth, $4\frac{3}{4}$ in. in diameter; foot, $4\frac{3}{8}$ in. in diameter. Paten-Cover, $4\frac{5}{8}$ in. in diameter; $1\frac{3}{8}$ in. high. (PLATE XXXI., No. 1.)

The "large pewter Flagon and small pewter Chalice," regularly mentioned in the parish terriers from 1793 until 1837, are no longer here.

LLANYSTUMDWY—S. JOHN THE BAPTIST

CHALICE.—A plain silver Chalice with deep, beaker-shape bowl, gilt inside, on short slender stem, inscribed—" H. J. and E. O. Ellis Nanney of GWYNFRYN to the PARISH CHURCH LLANYSTUMDWY 1890. In memory of their dear Son, Owen Gerald Ellis Nanney, who died July 6, 1887. Aged 8."

Marks.—London date-letter for 1890-1.

Height, $7\frac{1}{8}$ in.

PATEN.—A large, plain silver Paten, with narrow moulded edge, on truncated stem. Inscribed on back—" David and Henrietta Ellis Nanney of GWYNFRYN to the CHURCHWARDENS and INHABITANTS of LLANYS-TYNDWY, 1814."

Marks.—London date-letter for 1814-15. Makers' mark, $\frac{P\ B}{W\ B}$ in a square (Peter and Wm. Bateman).

Dimensions.—Diameter, $8\frac{7}{8}$ in.; height, $2\frac{5}{8}$ in.; diameter of foot, $4\frac{1}{2}$ in.

FLAGON.—A tall silver Flagon with globular body, encircled by four plain bands, on a short foot, and with a scroll handle. It has the same inscription and same date-letter as on the Chalice.

Height, $10\frac{3}{4}$ in.

The terriers for 1793, 1814, and 1817, mention a silver Chalice with a cover, dated 1191, a pewter Flagon, and a pewter Paten, which have, however, disappeared. The date on the Chalice was probably 1691.

MEILLTEYRN—S. PETER AD VINCULA

CHALICE AND PATEN-COVER.—The silver Chalice is plain, with beaker-shape bowl, the lip curved, supported by a long truncated stem on a moulded foot, the bowl inscribed—

" Meilltryn Cup renewed by Arthur Williams Esq 1703."

The Paten-Cover is plain, with narrow border, and with a short foot of the usual type.

Marks.—London date-letter for 1703-4. Maker's mark, DI, a cherub above and a sprig (?) below (Isaac Dighton).

Dimensions.—Height, $6\frac{1}{16}$ in.; depth of bowl, $3\frac{1}{4}$ in.; diameter of mouth, $3\frac{3}{16}$ in.; diameter of foot, $3\frac{3}{8}$ in.

NEVIN—S. PETER

Plain electro-plate Chalice, Paten and Flagon.
Britannia-metal Cup.
An old Sheffield-plate Salver, $8\frac{1}{2}$ in. in diameter, in bad condition.

PLATE XXV.

No. 2.

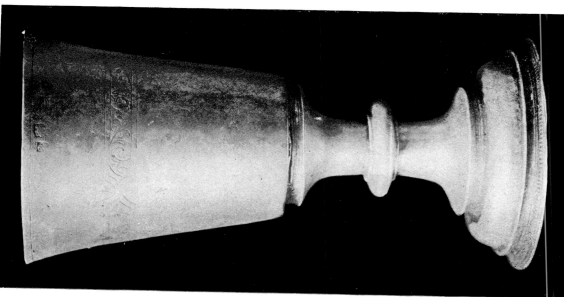

No. 3.

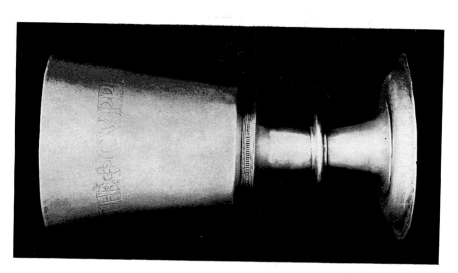

No. 1.

CAERHUN, CARNARVONSHIRE.
SILVER CHALICE, DATED 1574.
PROBABLY RE-MADE AT THE END OF THE
SEVENTEENTH CENTURY.

RHOSCOLYN, ANGLESEY.
ELIZABETHAN SILVER CHALICE.
DATE : 1574-5.

LLANBEDR-Y-CENIN, CARNARVONSHIRE.
ELIZABETHAN SILVER CHALICE.
DATE : 1576.

There is also an old silver Paten-Cover, $4\frac{3}{16}$ in. in diameter and $1\frac{1}{4}$ in. high, with London date-letter for 1679. This doubtless belonged to the old Chalice, now lost, described in the parish terriers between 1793 and 1837 as bearing this inscription—" The Gift of Mr. Robert Parry, Cittyson of London, the son of Mr. John Parry of Nevinne 1679." A pewter Flagon and Dish have also disappeared.

PENLLECH—S. MARY

CHALICE.—A plain silver Chalice with deep beaker-shape bowl, on a short truncated stem.

Marks.—London date-letter for 1710-11. Maker's mark illegible.

Dimensions.—Height, $7\frac{5}{16}$ in.; diameter of mouth, $4\frac{1}{2}$ in.; of foot, $4\frac{1}{8}$ in.

PATEN.—An old Sheffield-plate Salver, plain centre, with gadroon border, on three feet, 8 in. in diameter.

PENMACHNO—S. TYDDYD

CHALICE.—A large plain silver Chalice, with deep beaker-shape bowl, the lip curved, a plain rounded knop in the middle of the stem, the foot moulded. A shield of arms—*a chevron gu. between three fleurs-de-lis*, with scrolled and scaled mantling, is engraved above this inscription—

" Ex dono Roderici LLoyd Ar:
huius Ecclesiæ Impropriatoris
Anno dom: 1713."

Marks.—London date-letter for 1712-13. Maker's mark, WA, with anchor between, in shaped shield (Jos. Ward).

Dimensions.—Height, $9\frac{1}{16}$ in.; depth of bowl, $5\frac{1}{4}$ in.; diameter of mouth, $4\frac{1}{4}$ in.; diameter of foot, $3\frac{7}{8}$ in. (PLATE XXIII., No. 2.)

PATEN-COVER.—The plain silver Paten-Cover has a shallow depression, with the same arms engraved in the centre, and this inscription on the rim—" The Gift of Mr. Roderick LLoyd to the parish of Penmachno in the County of Carnarvan. Anno 1713." The Christian symbols, I.H.S., a cross and nails in glory, are engraved on the foot.

Marks.—As on Chalice.

Dimensions.—Diameter, $6\frac{7}{16}$ in.; height $1\frac{1}{2}$ in.

The donor was of Hafodwryd, in this parish. He built and endowed the Almshouses at Penmachno. His brother, Lewis Lloyd, was Rector of Llanarmon and Llangybi.

N

A small set for private Communion, consisting of a plain silver Chalice, 3⅝ in. high, with egg-shape bowl and moulded lip on a truncated stem with reeded edge, inscribed—" Rhôdd Syr R. W. Vaughan Bar: i 'Blwyf Penmackno 1815." (" The Gift of Sir R. W. Vaughan, Bart., to the Parish of Penmachno, 1815 "); a silver Paten-Cover, 2¾ in. in diameter, with reeded edge, and with the same inscription and the Christian symbols, I.H.S., a cross and three nails in glory, engraved on the foot; and a plain, square glass Bottle, 4 1/16 in. high, with silver top, the edge gadrooned, engraved with the same symbols.

Marks.—On Chalice and Paten: London date-letter for 1814-15. Maker's mark, RG, in an oblong (Robt. Garrard). (PLATE XXXIV., No. 1.)

The donor was Sir Robert Williams Vaughan, second Baronet, of Nannau and Hengwrt, M.P. for Merionethshire 1792-1836. He married Anna Maria, sister and co-heiress of Sir Thomas Mostyn, Bart., and with her acquired some farms in the parish of Penmachno. He and his wife gave a silver Flagon to Llanfachreth, and he presented a silver Paten to Dolgelley.

PENMAENMAWR—S. DAVID

A silver Communion Service, consisting of a plain Chalice, with inverted bell-shape bowl, supported by a stem divided by a large plain knop, and resting on a circular foot 8½ in. high; a plain Paten with wide, flat rim, 7 in. in diameter; and a plain Flagon with globular body, a cross on the cover, the handle scrolled, the foot circular, with moulded edge, 10½ in. high. Each piece is inscribed—

" RHODD
EGLWYS DEWI SANT . PENMAENMAWR
ER SERCHUS GOF AM MARY JONES Y FICERDY
A.D. 1904."

Marks.—London date-letter for 1904-5. Maker's mark, $^H_W{}^E$ in trefoil.

PENMAENMAWR—S. SEIRIOL

A massive silver Communion Set, consisting of two Chalices, 8½ in. high, with plain bowls, on which are engraved the Christian symbols, I.H.S., a cross and three nails in glory; the stems octagonal, with knop in centre. The stems and the octagonal feet are engraved with a Gothic architectural design. Two Patens, with twelve-sided rims, and with the Christian symbols as on the Chalices engraved in the circular depression in the centre, the feet octagonal, 8½ in. in diameter, 3½ in. high; and a Flagon, with octagonal body, engraved with the same architectural design as on the Chalices, the Christian symbols engraved on both sides; an octagonal vase-shape knob, covered with acanthus leaves, on the cover; height, 13½ in.

Marks.—On Chalices and Patens: London date-letter for 1853-4. Makers' mark, CTF and GF (C.T. and G. Fox). Flagon: Date-letter for 1843-4. Makers' mark, J A & G A in quatrefoil.

This service was given by the late eminent statesman, the Right Honble. W. E. Gladstone.

PENMORFA—S. BEUNO

CHALICE.—A large, plain silver Chalice with beaker-shape bowl, curved at the lip, supported by a stem with moulding in centre, and resting on a moulded foot. It is inscribed in large, bold, script lettering—

"Sir Robert Owen, 1698."

Marks.—London date-letter for 1697-8. Maker's mark, PA, in shaped shield (Thos. Parr).

Dimensions.—Height, 8⅜ in.; depth of bowl, 4½ in.; diameter of mouth, 4⅜ in.; diameter of foot, 4¼ in.

PATEN-COVER.—Plain silver Paten-Cover, with flat rim, incised with three lines, the edges of foot similarly incised. It is inscribed as Chalice.

Marks.—Same as on Chalice.

Dimensions.—Diameter, 6¼ in.; height, 1⅛ in.

This Chalice and Paten-Cover were bequeathed by Sir Robert Owen, son of William Owen, of Clennenau and Porkington, and grandson of the famous Welsh Royalist, Sir Robert Owen. He was knighted in 1678, was M.P. for Merioneth 1681, and for Carnarvon from 1689 until his death on the 30th March, 1698. (PLATE XXIII., No. 3.)

ALMS DISH.—A plain silver Salver with shaped shell border on three feet, engraved in the centre with the Christian symbols, I.H.S., a cross and three nails in glory, and inscribed on the back—"A gift to the Church of Penmorfa from the family of Kesail Gyvarch, 1760."

Marks.—London date-letter for 1753-4. Maker's mark, DM, in script capitals in a shaped shield (probably Do'thy Mills).

Diameter, 9½ in.

FLAGON.—A plain silver Tankard-Flagon, a plain moulding encircling the body near the moulded base; a spout, domed cover, scroll thumb-piece, and scrolled handle terminating in a heart-shape shield. Inscribed under base—" THE GIFT OF RICHARD GREAVES OF WERN TO PENMORFA CHURCH 1893."

Marks.—London date-letter for 1893-4. Makers' mark, $\frac{S\ B}{F\ W}$ in quatrefoil.

Dimensions.—Height, exclusive of cover, 6⅛ in.; with cover, 7½ in.

The disappearance of a small silver Chalice and Paten, inscribed— " The Gift of Anne Jones of Clenneney *alias* Parkia to the Church of Penmorfa 1703," mentioned in the parish terriers from 1803 until 1837, is noted with regret.

PENRHOS—S. CYNWYD

A pewter Goblet, 6 in. high, nineteenth century.

A pewter Dish, stamped—" B. GRAYSON & SON, SHEFFIELD."

PENTIR—S. CEDOL

CHALICE.—A plain silver Chalice, with exceptionally deep beaker-like bowl, encircled at the base with a rope moulding, supported by a very short vase-shape stem, on a plain splayed foot. Inscribed—

" Pentir Chappel,
1694."

Above the inscription the sacred letters, I.H.S., in roman capitals, surmounted by a cross, are engraved. (PLATE X., NO. 2.)

Marks.—Date-letter illegible. Maker's mark, SR, with cinquefoil below, in plain shield (Jackson, 1672-3). Probable date, *circa* 1685.

Dimensions.—Height, 5¼ in.; depth of bowl, 3¾ in.; diameter of mouth, 3 5/16 in.; diameter of foot, 3⅜ in.

PATEN.—A plain silver Paten, flat depression, moulded edge, standing on a foot. The sacred letters, I.H.S., are engraved.

Marks.—London date-letter for 1707-8. Maker's mark, Gi, with mullet above, in trefoil.

Dimensions.—Diameter, 6⅝ in.; height, 1¼ in.

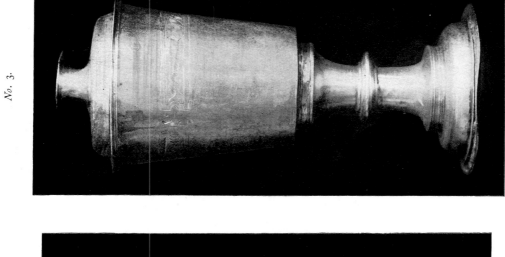

No. 3.

LLANFFINAN, ANGLESEY.
ELIZABETHAN SILVER CHALICE AND
PATEN-COVER.
DATE : 1574.

PLATE XXVI.

No. 2.

LLANIESTYN, ANGLESEY.
ELIZABETHAN SILVER CHALICE.
DATE : *circa* 1575.

No. 1.

LLANGOED, ANGLESEY.
ELIZABETHAN SILVER CHALICE.
DATE : *circa* 1575.

PATEN-COVER.—A small, plain, silver Paten-Cover, with flat edge, on a short truncated foot.

Mark.—TR, conjoined, in shaped shield, repeated twice. No date-letter.

Dimensions.—Diameter, $4\frac{3}{16}$ in.; height, 1 in. Date, *circa* 1700.

PEN-Y-GROES

A small silver set of Chalice, Paten and Flagon. London date-letter for 1880-1.

PISTYLL

CHALICE.—A plain silver Chalice with beaker-shape bowl, supported by a baluster stem on a splayed foot. Marks illegible. Date, *circa* 1640.

Height, $5\frac{3}{8}$ in.; depth of bowl, $2\frac{5}{8}$ in.; diameter, 3 in.

PATEN.—A plain, plated Salver with gadroon edge, 8 in. in diameter.

PORTMADOC—S. JOHN'S

The Communion Service here is of electro-plate.

PRENTEG

A silver Chalice, with V-shape bowl, gilt inside, chased and engraved with floral festoons and with two pointed oval cartouches, one containing the sacred monogram I.H.S., a beaded knop in centre of stem, which rests on a circular foot, slightly engraved, with beaded edge.

London date-letter for 1787-8. Maker's mark, TD, in plain cartouche (Thos. Daniell).

Height, $6\frac{3}{8}$ in.

A circular Salver, chased with roses, foliage and scrolls, shaped scroll and shell border, on three scrolled feet, the sacred monogram, I.H.S., engraved in centre.

London date-letter for 1827-8. Maker's mark, W·B, with pellet between, in double-lobed shield.

Diameter, 8 in.

A plated Flagon.

PWLLHELI

CHALICE.—A plain silver Chalice, with inverted bell-shape bowl, supported by a tall stem moulded in the centre, and resting on a moulded foot.

Marks.—Chester date-letter for 1755-6. Maker's mark, RR, in a shaped shield (Richd. Richardson).

Dimensions.—Height, $7\frac{3}{8}$ in.; depth of bowl, $3\frac{5}{8}$ in.; diameter of bowl, $3\frac{3}{4}$ in.; diameter of foot, $3\frac{7}{8}$ in.

PATEN.—A plain silver Paten on three ball feet.

Marks.—London date-letter for 1877-8. Maker's mark, SS in an oblong.

Diameter, 6 in.

FLAGON.—A very large Jug with beaker-shape bowl, gilt inside, slightly curved, encircled by a plain rounded moulding, supported by a stem, divided in the middle by a plain knop, and resting on a moulded foot. It has a long spout, reaching to the bottom of bowl, and a scroll handle with a small bead knob on its shoulder.

Marks.—London date-letter for 1635-6. Maker's mark, GG with pellets, etc., in plain shield.

Dimensions.—Height, $9\frac{11}{16}$ in.; depth of bowl, $5\frac{1}{2}$ in.; diameter, 5 in.; diameter of foot, $5\frac{3}{8}$ in.

This Jug and the Chalice came from the old Church of Deneio.

In the old terrier for 1776 a pewter Flagon and Plate are mentioned. These have, however, disappeared.

RHIW—S. AEL

CHALICE AND PATEN-COVER.—The Chalice is plain, with beaker-shape bowl on a trumpet-shape stem, and is inscribed—

" Rhiw
This was Provided by
Fredericke Wynne Warden
Anno Dni 1672."

The Paten-Cover is of the usual form with a short foot.

Marks.—London date-letter for 1671-2. Maker's mark, G B in a shaped shield.

Dimensions.—Chalice: 6 in. high; 3⅝ in. diameter. Paten-Cover is 4 $\frac{7}{16}$ in. in diameter, and ¾ in. high.

The donor, Frederick Wynn, of Bodwythog, was the son of John Wynn, of Bodvean, and is buried in this Church.

An old Sheffield-plate Salver with gadroon border, 9 in. diameter.

S. ANN'S

The Communion Plate here is of old Sheffield-plate, engraved with a baron's coronet and the initials P.C.

S. THOMAS'S—LLANDWROG

A silver set, consisting of a Chalice, 7½ in. high; a Paten on foot, 7½ in. in diameter; a Flagon, 12 in. high; and an Alms Dish, 7½ in. high; each inscribed—" Presented to St. Thomas's Church, Llandwrog, By the Hon. Thos. John Wynn of Glynllifon, Christmas Day 1856."

London date letter for 1856-7. Makers' mark, $^{C\ T\ F}_{G\ F}$

TREFLYS—S. MICHAEL AND ALL ANGELS

A small plain silver Chalice with beaker-shape bowl, supported by a moulded stem on a moulded foot. It has been roughly engraved—

" TREFLYS."

No marks. Date, probably seventeenth century.

Height, 6 in.; depth of bowl, 3¼ in.; diameter of mouth and foot, 3 in.

An old Sheffield-plate Dinner-plate.

TREFRIW—S. MARY

A silver Chalice, with plain inverted bell-shape bowl, supported by an unusually short baluster stem, on a moulded base. Inscribed—

" The Cupp of Trefriw 1701."

Marks.—London date-letter for 1700-1. Maker's mark, Ro, in a heart (Hugh Roberts).

Weight marked, 11 oz. 17 dwt.

Dimensions.—Height, $7\frac{1}{16}$ in.; depth of bowl, $3\frac{7}{8}$ in.; diameter of mouth, $3\frac{1}{2}$ in.; diameter of foot, $3\frac{1}{4}$ in.

An old pewter Flagon and Plate have disappeared from this Church.

TREMADOC

A plain silver Chalice with bell-shape bowl, gilt inside, hexagonal stem, divided by a large knop, sexfoil foot.

London date-letter for 1898-9. Makers' mark, $\begin{smallmatrix} W.G \\ J.L \end{smallmatrix}$

Height, 8 in.

A plain silver Paten on truncated foot.

London date-letter for 1899-1900. Same maker as Chalice.

Diameter, $6\frac{7}{8}$ in.

A plain glass Flagon, with silver handle and mounts.

London date-letter for 1895-6.

Height, $9\frac{1}{4}$ in.

This set was given in memory of the late Miss Nesta Breese by her brothers, sister and sister-in-law.

TYDWEILIOG—S. CWYFAN

The old silver Chalice and Paten-Cover here were originally similar to the Elizabethan Chalice and Paten-Cover in the neighbouring Church of Bryncroes, and were by the same maker, IL, whose mark is stamped on the Paten-Cover. It has, however, been "restored," and an entirely new bowl added to it; and the whole is gilt. The stem is in its original condition, and has an ovolo moulding at the top and bottom, and on the edge of the foot is an egg and dart moulding. The Paten-Cover has three rows of hyphens incised on the shoulder, and one row on the edge, and the foot is engraved with the date, $\begin{smallmatrix} \text{ANO} \\ \text{1574} \end{smallmatrix}$ and a sprig below, within an incised circle.

Height of Chalice, $6\frac{1}{8}$ in.

Paten-Cover is $3\frac{1}{8}$ in. in diameter.

FLAGON.—A plain, tall, cylindrical silver Flagon, inscribed—

"Tydweiliog Church, from M. F. W. 1898."

(Mrs. Wynne Finch.)

London date-letter for 1891-2.

Height, 9 in.

A plated Chalice and Paten.

WAENFAWR—S. JOHN THE EVANGELIST

CHALICE.—A plain old silver Chalice, with deep beaker-shape bowl, on a short truncated stem with moulded edge. Belonging to it is a Paten-Cover, with flat raised rim, $4\frac{11}{16}$ in. in diameter. There are no marks on either piece.

Date, *circa* 1690.

Dimensions.—Height, $6\frac{5}{8}$ in.; depth of bowl, $4\frac{1}{8}$ in.; diameter of mouth, $3\frac{3}{4}$ in.; foot, 4 in.

It has been suggested that this old Chalice and Paten-Cover were brought from the mother Church of Llanbeblig for use in the school-room before the erection of the present Church.

YNYSCYNHAIARN—S. CYNHAIARN

CHALICE AND PATEN-COVER.—The silver Chalice is plain, with an inverted bell-shape bowl, supported by a high truncated stem with moulded base. The sacred symbols, I.H.S., etc., in glory, engraved on the bowl. Under the foot is this inscription—

"Ex Dono W.P. arm."

The Paten-Cover has a shallow depression and the old foot has been replaced with a cross.

Marks.—London date-letter for 1740-1. Maker's mark, RT, in script capitals, with rose above, in a shaped shield. The weight, 11 oz. $11\frac{1}{2}$ dwt., is marked.

Height of Chalice, 9 in.

The donor is believed to have been William Price, of Penmorfa and Rhiwlas, who married Mary, daughter of the ninth Viscount Hereford.

PATEN.—An old Sheffield-plate Dinner-plate with gadroon border, inscribed—

"Ynyscynhaiarn 1821."

No trace can be found of the old pewter Flagon and Paten mentioned in the terriers between 1780 and 1834.

O

BRYNCOEDIFOR, MERIONETHSHIRE.

COMMONWEALTH SILVER CHALICE.
DATE : 1655-6.

SILVER PATEN.
DATE : 1719-20.

No. 2.

LLANELLTYD, MERIONETHSHIRE.

ELIZABETHAN SILVER CHALICE AND PATEN-COVER.
DATE : 1591-2.

SILVER FLAGON-JUG.
DATE : 1738-9.

MERIONETHSHIRE

ABERDOVEY—S. PETER

CHALICE.—A plain silver Chalice, with short beaker-shape bowl, the edge moulded, on tall slender stem, divided by a flat knop, resting on a moulded foot. The letters I.H.S., a cross and three nails in glory, are engraved, and it is inscribed under the foot in script—" The gift of W. W. E. Wynne, Esqᴿᵉ, of Peniarth, to Aberdovey Church, 1839."

Marks.—London date-letter for 1838-9. Maker's mark, I·T, with pellet between, in double-lobed shield.

Dimensions.—Height, 9¾ in.

PATEN.—A plain silver Paten, engraved in the centre with the same device as on Chalice, and with the same inscription on foot.

Marks.—The same as on Chalice.

Dimensions.—Diameter, 8½ in.; height, 2¼ in.

A glass cruet with silver top.

ABERGYNOLWYN—S. DAVID

CHALICE.—A silver Chalice of medieval design, the bowl inscribed in black letters—" Calicem Salutaris accipiam et nomen Domini invocabo." The hexagonal stem, with large knop in centre, rests on a sexfoil foot.

Marks.—London date-letter for 1878-9. Maker's mark, BB in an oblong shield.

Height, 7⅜ in.

PATEN.—A plain silver Paten, the centre occupied with the engraved device, I.H.S., a cross and three nails in glory, and the border engraved in black letters—" Agnus Dei qui tollis peccata mundi da nobis tuam pacem."

Marks.—London date-letter for 1879-80.

Diameter, 5½ in.

A glass Flagon with silver mounts.

BARMOUTH—S. JOHN

Two silver Chalices, the bowls engraved with a band of vandyke ornament enclosing fleurs-de-lis, with a surbase of vine leaves, etc., standing on stems divided by large knops, with bosses, on plain sexfoil feet.

London date-letter for 1890-1. Maker's mark, $^{J.W}_{F.C.W}$ in trefoil.
Height, 7⅞ in.

Two silver Patens, one inscribed on the border—" In God in Christ
in Love "; the other—" Love is Born of God."
Same date-letter and makers' mark as on Chalices.
Diameter, 7 7/16 in.

Silver Flagon, the body globular, with a band of vandyke ornamentation, as on the Chalices, and six bosses, surrounding the centre. The
lip and spout engraved with vine leaves, etc.; plain scroll handle; cross
on cover; sexfoil foot, which is engraved underneath—" In loving
memory of my Father, James Dyson Perrins, E.M.D."
Same marks as on Chalices and Patens.
Height, 12½ in.

The Chalices and Patens were given in memory of James Dyson
Perrins by his widow and children.

BARMOUTH—S. DAVID

A plain silver Chalice, with beaker-shape bowl, a plain collar under
the bowl, like the one at Rhosbeirio in Anglesey; standing on a truncated stem with moulded edge. I.H.S., cross and nails in glory have
recently been engraved on it, probably at the time the gift was made.
The bowl, which has been newly gilt inside, is inscribed—

" The offering of
M. A. R."

Marks.—London date-letter for 1633. Maker's mark, I·B, with
pellet between, an illegible device underneath, in shaped shield.
Dimensions.—Height, 6 15/16 in.; depth of bowl, 3¾ in.; diameter of
mouth, 3⅝ in.; of foot, 3 9/16 in.

Plain silver Paten, inscribed—" In Memoriam Annae Beatricis
Foster, cujus animae propitietur Deus. A.D. 1886."
London date-letter for 1883-4. Maker's mark, $^{H.E}_{W}$ in trefoil.
Diameter, 5 7/16 in.

Plain old Sheffield-plate Salver, the edge moulded, standing on three
floreated feet. 9¼ in. in diameter.

Two glass Flagons with plated mounts.

PLATE XXVIII.

No. 1.

No. 2.

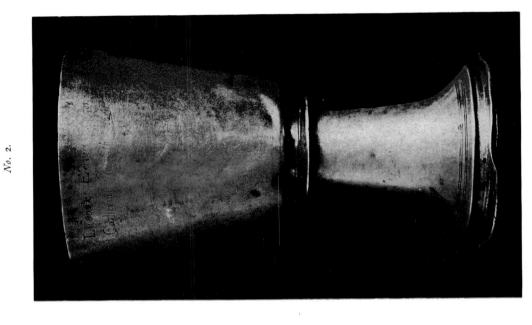

RHOSBEIRIO, ANGLESEY.

CHARLES I. SILVER CHALICE.

DATE: 1630.

MALLWYD, MONTGOMERYSHIRE.

CHARLES I. SILVER CHALICE.

DATE: 1627-8.

BLAENAU FESTINIOG—S. DAVID

CHALICE.—A tall silver-gilt Chalice, with a small, plain, inverted bell-shape bowl, which is engraved with I.H.S. in glory, and the lower half of which is enclosed in a pierced framework, consisting of a cross, symbols of the Crucifixion, and floreations. It is stamped G.M., and is of foreign workmanship, probably of the eighteenth century. This is supported by a tall, fine, richly-decorated stem, in the centre a flattened circular knop chased with foliation, a smaller knop below it, chased with acanthus leaves, with edges formed of the same leaf. The foot is circular, and is boldly embossed with acanthus leaves and the edge with laurel leaves; above the foot is a fluted collar. No marks. The stem and foot are of two distinct periods of workmanship, the stem being the earlier, and probably English.

Dimensions.—Height, $10\frac{1}{4}$ in.; depth of bowl, $3\frac{7}{8}$ in.; diameter of bowl, $3\frac{3}{8}$ in.; diameter of foot, 5 in.

PATEN.—A plain silver-gilt Paten, engraved with I.H.S. in glory in the centre; diameter, $6\frac{1}{8}$ in.

FLAGON.—A silver-gilt Flagon, divided into four prominent flutings, with quatrefoil mouth, foot and cover; scrolled thumb-piece; a disc, formed of the letters I.H.S. in glory, applied under the spout; an erect cross on the cover.

Marks.—London date-letter for 1841-2.

Dimensions.—Height to top of cross, $12\frac{1}{4}$ in.; exclusive of cross, 11 in.

ALMS DISH.—A small silver-gilt Alms Dish with narrow moulded edge, the sacred symbols, I.H.S., a cross and three nails in glory, engraved in the centre.

London date-letter for 1842-3. Maker's mark, R·H. in an oblong.

Diameter, 9 in.

BRITHDIR—S. MARK

An Italian Chalice of gilt metal, with a shallow, inverted bell-shape bowl of plain gilt silver (?), enclosed in a surbase of engraved acanthus. The stem is hexagonal, and on it are enamelled quatrefoils, and it is divided by a large embossed knop, foliated, with six circular discs, originally enamelled, of the Saviour, Saints, and Ecclesiastics, and a shield of arms: three tortoises with a star above. The foot is sexfoil, with V-shape projections at the angles, which are slightly engraved with quatrefoils, etc.

Probable date, late eighteenth century.

Dimensions.—Height, $7\frac{5}{8}$ in.

A plain silver-gilt Paten with a cross engraved on the rim. $5\frac{1}{4}$ in. in diameter.

London date-letter for 1897-8.

Marks.—C. K. Krall.

BRYNCOEDIFOR—S. PAUL

CHALICE.—A very small, plain silver Chalice, of the Commonwealth period, with a short beaker-shape bowl, curved out at the lip, standing on a baluster stem on a splayed foot.   The date, 1680, pounced under the foot, and this inscription is engraved on the back—

"S^t. Paul's Bryncoedifor,"

probably engraved at the time of the gift of this Chalice at the consecration of this Church, some fifty-five years ago.

Marks.—London date-letter for 1655-6.   Maker's mark, a capital letter M in a heart.

Dimensions.—Height, $4\frac{1}{8}$ in.; depth of bowl, 2 in.; diameter of bowl, $2\frac{7}{8}$ in.; diameter of foot, $2\frac{5}{8}$ in.

PATEN.—A small, plain silver Paten with moulded edge, standing on a truncated foot, the edge moulded.   Engraved with a shield of arms: Quarterly, 1-4, *ermine on a saltire...a crescent*, 3-4, *or a lion rampant...; in the honour point a martlet.*   Crest: *a boar passant fretty.*

Marks.—London date-letter for 1719-20.   Maker's mark, SL, in shaped shield.

Dimensions.—Diameter, 5 in.; height, $1\frac{5}{8}$ in.

The foregoing Chalice and Paten were given either by Richard Richards, Esq., or Richard Meredyth Richards, Esq., of Caerynwch, the son and grandson respectively of the Right Hon. Sir Richard Richards, Knt., Lord Chief Baron, who married Catherine Humphreys, heiress of Robert Vaughan Humphreys, Esq., of Caerynwch. (PLATE XXVII., No. 1.)

CHALICE.—A silver Chalice of medieval form, with an inscription on the bowl, in black letters—"Calicem salutaris accipiam et nomen Dni invocabo." The letters I.H.S. engraved on the foot, and this inscription under the foot—

> " A. H. R.
> Ecclesiæ Bryncoedivor
> D.D."

Marks.—London date-letter for 1849-50. Maker's mark, I·K, in an oblong (J. Keith).

Dimensions.—Height, 7¾ in.; diameter of bowl, 4½ in.; diameter of foot, 5 in.

PATEN.—A silver Paten, with the *Agnus Dei* engraved in the sexfoil centre, and this inscription in black letters on the border—" Agnus Dei qui tollis peccata mundi miserere nobis."

Marks.—London date-letter for 1849-50. Maker's marks, same as on Chalice.

Dimensions.—6¾ in. in diameter.

FLAGON.—A silver Flagon, the body globular, with inscription in large black letters engraved round the centre—" Te laudamus tibi benedicimus."

Marks.—London date-letter for 1848-9. Same maker's mark as on Chalice and Paten.

Dimensions.—Height, 9⅛ in.; diameter of base, 3½ in.

This silver set was given by the Honble. Mrs. Arthur Douglas (*née* Richards of Caerynwch), wife of the late Bishop of Aberdeen.

BRYNCRUG

A silver-gilt Chalice, with plain bowl, encased in a surbase of chased acanthus foliage, the knop on stem and the sexfoil foot set with various coloured stones.

London date-letter for 1881-2.

Height, 8⅜ in.

PATEN.—A small, plain, flat silver-gilt dish, with moulded edge, transformed from a piece of plate bearing the London date-letter for 1743-4.

Diameter, 6 in.

FLAGON.—A glass Flagon, with silver-gilt mounts and sexfoil foot, set with stones.

London date-letter for 1881-2.

Height, 10¼ in.

P

CAERDEON

A plain electro-plate Chalice.

A small, circular silver Paten, with plain depressed centre and an embossed floreated border, 6⅝ in. in diameter.   No marks.

CORRIS—HOLY TRINITY

CHALICE.—A silver Chalice, the bowl engraved with a foliated design, an ornamental knop on the stem, the foot quatrefoil shape.   Height, 7⅞ in.
Birmingham date-letter for 1886-7.

PATEN.—A silver Paten, the *Agnus Dei* engraved in the centre, the border engraved with a foliated design, the foot quatrefoil shape, diameter, 8 1/16 in.
Birmingham date-letter for 1894-5.

FLAGON.—A silver Flagon with globular body, a band of vine foliage encircling the centre, I.H.S. in glory engraved thereon, the foot quatrefoil shape.   Inscribed—" To the Glory of God and in Affectionate Remembrance of William Birley, of The Larches, and Charles Birley, of Bartle Hall, both in the County of Lancaster, this Communion Service, consisting of Flagon, Chalice, Paten & Plate, is presented by the Braich Goch Slate Quarry Company to the Church of Holy Trinity, Corris.   The Feast of Sᵗ. Michael and All Angels. A.D. 1894."
Birmingham date-letter for 1894-5.
Height, 11¾ in.

ALMS DISH.—Very similar in design to the Paten, and with the same marks.   Diameter, 9⅛ in.

DOLGELLEY—S. MARY

CHALICE.—A large, plain silver Chalice, with deep, beaker-shape bowl, the lip curved out, a plain moulding in centre of stem, the foot moulded.   Inscribed—

" The Communion Cupe of Dolgelle
Maurice Iones Rectʳ.
J O } Church Wardens
G H }   1683."

Marks.—London date-letter for 1683-4.   Maker's mark (indistinct), probably RG in beaded oval.

Dimensions.—Height, 9 in.; depth of bowl, $5\frac{1}{8}$ in.; diameter of mouth, $4\frac{1}{2}$ in.; diameter of foot, $4\frac{1}{16}$ in.

PATEN-COVER.—The Paten-Cover belonging to this Chalice has a wide flat rim with slightly moulded edge.   The foot, which has an incised line near the edge, is engraved with the letters I.H.S., a cross, three nails and a heart in glory.

Marks.—The same as on Chalice.

Dimensions.—Diameter, $5\frac{7}{8}$ in.; width of rim, $1\frac{3}{16}$ in.; height, 1 in.

PATEN.—A large, plain silver Paten, with narrow moulded edge, standing on a truncated foot, the edge moulded.   Inscribed on the back, in script lettering—

" To The Parish Church of Dolgelleu From Its Sincere
Friend Rob. Williames Vaughan, October 1819."

Marks.—London date-letter (indistinct) probably 1709-10.   Maker's mark, Pa, a vase above, pellet below, in shaped shield (Humphrey Payne).

Dimensions.—Diameter, $8\frac{5}{8}$ in.; height, $2\frac{1}{4}$ in.

The donor of this Paten was Sir Robert Williames Vaughan, second Bart., of Nannau and Hengwrt.   He and his wife gave a silver Flagon to Llanfachreth Church in 1803.

FLAGON.—A tall, plain massive silver Flagon, with cylindrical body, slightly tapering, the edge of lip moulded, a moulding along lower part of body, which rests on a wide splayed and moulded base.   The cover, which is domed and moulded, and surmounted by a short circular knob, has a double volute thumb-piece, and the scrolled handle terminates in a plain shield.   On the body is engraved the following inscription below the conventional device formed of the letters I.H.S., a cross and three nails in glory—

" Dicavit Deo
Elizeus Lewis Cler.
In Usum Eccles. Parochiat
De Dolgelle
Com Mervin
In qua dei filius factus fuit."

Under the foot—" Anno 1724."

Marks.—London date-letter for 1723-4.   Maker's mark, Ne (Ant. Nelme).

Dimensions.—Total height, 12½ in.; height of body, 10⅜ in.; diameter of mouth, 4 in.; diameter of foot, 6⅞ in. (PLATE XXI.)

CHALICE.—A new plain silver Chalice, with cross engraved on the bowl, and the sacred letters I.H.S. on the circular foot. This inscription engraved in black letters under the foot—

" Presented to the Parish Church of
Dolgelley by Maria Tomes, of New York,
in memory of her Mother, 1866."

Marks.—London date-letter for 1853-4. Maker's mark, $^{E}_{B}{}^{C}$ in trefoil.
Height, 7½ in.

PATEN.—A plain silver Paten, with cross engraved on the rim, 6$\frac{7}{16}$ in. in diameter.
Marks.—London date-letter for 1871-2; same maker's mark as on Chalice.

A small silver-mounted glass Flagon, with London date-letter for 1888-9, and maker's mark, TP in an oblong shield.

FESTINIOG—S. MICHAEL

CHALICE.—A very small, plain silver Chalice, with inverted bell-shape bowl, supported by a stem, divided by a moulding, and resting on a moulded foot.
Marks.—Chester date-letter for 1782-3. Maker's mark, RR in an oblong (third Richd. Richardson).
Dimensions.—Height, 5⅜ in.; depth of bowl, 2¾ in.; diameter of mouth, 2¾ in.; diameter of foot, 3⅛ in.

FLAGON.—A large old pewter Flagon, with tapering cylindrical body, moulded lip, domed cover, surmounted by a tall knop, a moulding encircling the body near the lip and another near the base, which is wide and spreading. It is stamped with four marks in small shields—CB, a lion, a leopard's head, and fleur-de-lys, and an X above. Inside is a crowned X.
Dimensions.—Height to top of knob, 11½ in.; body, 8¾ in.; diameter of mouth, 3⅞ in.; diameter of foot, 6¼ in.

A large set of Chalice, Paten and Flagon in electro-plate.

No. 3.

LLANDUDNO.
JAMES I. SILVER CHALICE.
DATE : 1607-8.

PLATE XXIX.

No. 2.

HOLYHEAD.
JAMES I. SILVER CHALICE.
DATE : 1610-11.

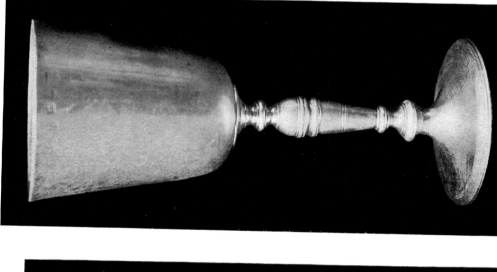

No. 1.

LLANRHYCHWYN, CARNARVONSHIRE. ;
JAMES I. SILVER-GILT CHALICE.
DATE : 1614-15.

HARLECH—S. TANWG

A plain silver Chalice with short beaker-shape bowl, supported by a baluster stem on a splayed foot, which has the initials, HB, roughly engraved underneath. (PLATE XIV., No. 1.)

Marks.—London date-letter for 1664-5. Maker's mark illegible.

Dimensions.—Height, $5\frac{1}{4}$ in.; depth of bowl, $2\frac{11}{16}$ in.; diameter of mouth, $3\frac{1}{2}$ in.; diameter of foot, $3\frac{3}{8}$ in.

Note.—This came from the old Church of Llandanwg.

Two plated Patens.

A large old pewter Dish, 12 in. in diameter, in very bad condition.

LLANABER—S. MARY

A new silver Chalice, of medieval design, with a plain bowl, on which a cross is engraved; hexagonal stem, divided by large knop; sexfoil foot, which is inscribed—

"In usum Eccles. de Llanaber 1860."

London date-letter for 1859-60. Makers' mark, E B & J B in quatrefoil (E. & J. Barnard).

Height, $7\frac{1}{2}$ inches.

A plain silver Paten, a cross engraved in centre, standing on a sexfoil foot; inscribed—"In usum Ecclesiæ de Llanaber (Com: Mervin) hanc patenam cum calice lubens obtulit Robertus Owen. S. Th. Bac. Coll: Jesu Oxon, Socius dilectorum suorum intra sacram aream conquiescentium non immemor. A.D. 1860."

Same marks as on Chalice. Diameter, $6\frac{3}{4}$ in.

This interesting old Church was in possession of a "small silver Chalice with a top," probably Elizabethan, "one pewter Flagon, and two pewter Plates," in 1801, 1808, and 1811, but all trace of these is lost.

LLANBEDR—S. PETER

CHALICE.—A plain silver Chalice with beaker-shape bowl, curved at the lip, plain stem on a moulded foot, inscribed—

"Robert Wynn Rector of Llanbeder."

Marks.—London date-letter for 1715-16. Maker's mark, LO in monogram (Matthew Lofthouse).

Dimensions.—Height, 7½ in. ; depth of bowl, 4½ in. ; diameter, 4 in. Robert Wynn was Rector from 1711 till 1729.

PATEN.—A plain old Sheffield-plate Dinner-plate with gadroon border.

LLANDECWYN—S. TECWYN

A pewter Chalice and Paten of late eighteenth century date.

A large old pewter Dish, with wide flat rim, of late seventeenth century, stamped with four marks, a buckle, TF, a lion and a leopard's head crowned.

LLANDDWYWE—S. DDWYWAN

CHALICE.—A very tall, plain silver Chalice, with deep bowl, with curved out lip, standing on a stem with a plain moulding in the centre, on a moulded foot.
Marks.—London date-letter for 1732-3. Maker's mark, EV, annulet above and below, in an oval (probably Edw. Vincent).
Dimensions.—Height, 10¾ in. ; depth of bowl, 5⅜ in. ; diameter of mouth, 4⅜ in.

PATEN-COVER.—The silver Paten-Cover belonging to this Chalice is plain, with flat sunk centre, and has the usual form of foot.
Marks.—Same as on Chalice.
Dimensions.—Diameter, 5$\frac{5}{16}$ in. ; height, 1$\frac{9}{16}$ in.

ALMS DISH.—A silver dish, resembling a domestic Salver without feet, circular in shape, with a plain flat centre and a shaped border, I.H.S. and cross in glory engraved in the centre, while this inscription is engraved in script lettering in a circle on the back—" Elizabeth Jones The Doner Gives this to LLandduwa Church 1731." The weight, 17 oz. 1 dwt., is marked on it.
Marks.—London date-letter for 1710-11. Maker's mark, Ho, in oblong (Ed. Holaday).

A silver Flagon, weighing about 34 ozs., was sold about the year 1870 to purchase a harmonium for this Church!

LLANEGRYN—S. EGRYN

CHALICE.—A new silver Chalice of medieval form, hexagon stem, divided by large knop, on a sexfoil foot. The bowl inscribed in black letters—"Calicem salutaris accipiam et nomen Domini invocabo."

London date-letter for 1854-5. Makers' mark, E B & J B (E. & J. Barnard).

Height, $7\frac{1}{2}$ in.

PATEN.—A silver Paten, with I.H.S. engraved in the sexfoil depression and this inscription in black letters on the border: "Agnus Dei qui tollis peccata mundi da nobis tuam pacem."

London date-letter for 1856-7. Maker's mark, same as on Chalice. Diameter, $5\frac{7}{8}$ in.

LLANELLTYD—S. ILLTYD

CHALICE.—Elizabethan silver Chalice, in a perfect state of preservation, with an exceptionally deep beaker-shape bowl, considerably curved. Running round the bowl is an engraved band, $\frac{3}{8}$ in. wide, inscribed in Lombardic capitals—

"✠ THE COMVNION CVPE OF LLANILLTID."

The inscription is preceded by a small cross, and the two first words are separated by a small quatrefoil, a small, plain circle dividing the other three words, and the background of the inscribed band is very faintly matted. The stem, which is of unusual shortness, is divided by a plain rounded knop, and rests on a high domed foot with a fine egg and dart moulding.

Marks.—London date-letter for 1591-2. Maker's mark, which is almost illegible, is probably RE in an oblong shield.

Dimensions.—Height, $6\frac{15}{16}$ in.; depth of bowl, $4\frac{1}{4}$ in.; diameter of mouth, $3\frac{5}{8}$ in.; diameter of foot, $3\frac{3}{8}$ in.

PATEN-COVER.—The Paten-Cover of this Chalice has a reeded edge, and is encircled on the shoulder with a band of engraved laurel leaves; the foot is plain. (PLATE XXVII., No. 2.)

Marks.—The same as on Chalice.

PATEN.—A large, plain silver Paten, with a narrow moulded edge, standing on a truncated foot, moulded. The conventional device, formed of the letters I.H.S., a cross and three nails in glory, is engraved in the centre and surrounded by this inscription in script lettering—" The Gift of Willm. Evans A: M: Rector of Barthomley in Cheshire Son of Evan Williams of the Parish of Dolgelley to the Chapel of LLanelltud 1739."

Marks.—London date-letter for 1738-9. Maker's mark, RB in an oblong.

Dimensions.—Diameter, 9⅛ in.; height, 2⅜ in.

FLAGON.—The Flagon in use here takes the form of a plain, domestic silver Jug, of globular form, with moulded tapering spout, scrolled handle, moulded lip, standing on a short moulded foot. The same device and inscription as on the Paten are engraved on the body.

Marks.—The same as on Paten.

Dimensions.—Height, 8⅝ in.; diameter of mouth, 4 in.; diameter of foot, 5 in.

A small set for private Communion, consisting of a plain silver Chalice with egg-shape bowl, on short foot, a small silver Paten on foot, and a square glass Bottle, with plain silver top. The Chalice and Paten are engraved with the letters I.H.S., a cross and three nails in glory, and this inscription—

" William Williams. Gweinidog
1809
William Williams . Gweinidog
Edward Jones } Wardeniaid."
Rice Edwards }

Marks.—On Chalice and Paten: London date-letter for 1809-10. Maker's mark, RG, in an oblong.

Marks.—On mount of bottle: London date-letter for 1809-10. Makers' mark, $^{T \cdot P}_{E \cdot R}$ with pellet between in quatrefoil.

Dimensions.—Chalice: height, 2⅝ in.; diameter of mouth, 1⅞ in.; foot, 1¾ in. Paten: diameter, 2⁵⁄₁₆ in.; height, 1 in. Bottle, 4 in. high.

A similar set is at Llanfachreth Church, Merionethshire.

LLANENDDWYN—S. ENDDWYN

CHALICE.—A plain silver Chalice, with deep beaker-shape bowl, curved outwards at the lip, standing on a short stem, divided by a plain moulding or flattened knop, on a moulded foot. Inscribed—

" The Parish of LLanenddwyn.
Churchwardens Hugh Jones
D: Hum: 1628."

Marks.—London date-letter for 1627-28. Maker's mark, RA, with slipped flower below, in plain shield (Jackson 1638-9).

Dimensions.—Height, $7\frac{5}{8}$ in.; depth of bowl, $4\frac{3}{8}$ in.; diameter of mouth, $3\frac{1}{2}$ in.

FLAGON.—A very tall, old pewter Flagon, cylindrical body, with a moulding along the lower part; scrolled handle; an acorn on the summit of the domed cover; open, scrolled thumb-piece, with arched top; and a moulded base.

Marks (four).—I & H; a griffin's head erased; three escallop shells on a horizontal bar; and a leopard's head; all in small shaped shields.

Dimensions.—Height, $12\frac{1}{8}$ in.

This Flagon closely resembles the pewter Flagon at Llanfachraeth in Anglesey, and bears the same marks.

PEWTER PLATES.—Two circular plates, $9\frac{3}{8}$ in. in diameter, one of which is engraved with these initials, WP   WH, probably representing the names of Churchwardens.

LLANFIHANGEL-Y-PENNANT—S. MICHAEL

CHALICE.—A plain silver Chalice, with beaker-shape bowl, rounded off at the base, standing on a thick stem, plainly moulded at the top and bottom, and incised with two lines, resting on a high rounded and moulded foot.   Inscribed—

" THE COMMVNION CVPP OF LLAN VIHANGEL Y PENNANT
Edward Owen and Ro: Griffith
Church wardens."

Mark.—The only mark is RD, with a crescent below, in a plain shield —an unknown mark.

Dimensions.—Height, $7\frac{1}{4}$ in.; depth of bowl, 4 in.; diameter of mouth, $3\frac{1}{4}$ in.; diameter of foot, 3 in.

PATEN-COVER.—The silver Paten-Cover belonging to this Chalice has a shallow depression, with a flat rim incised with three lines, the date, 1625, engraved on the foot.

Dimensions.—Diameter, $3\frac{7}{8}$ in.; height, $\frac{7}{8}$ in.   (PLATE IX., No. 3.)

The Chalice, though not dated, is of the same date as the Paten-Cover, 1625, as they both bear the same maker's mark.

Q

PATEN.—A plain silver Dish, circular and flat, with moulded edge. Inscribed on the back—

" THE COMMUNION PLATE
of
LLANFIHANGEL-Y-PENNANT
Merionethshire, 1815."

London date-letter for 1814-15.   Makers' mark, $_{WB}^{PB}$ in a square.

LLANFACHRETH—S. MACHRAETH

CHALICE.—A plain silver Chalice, with inverted bell-shape bowl, on a stem, moulded in the centre, resting on a moulded foot.   The Christian symbols, I.H.S., a cross and nails in glory, engraved on one side, and this Welsh inscription on the other—

" Y cwppan hwn a newidiwyd am un arall
gan Blwyfolion Llanfachreth 1809,
William Williams, Gweinidog
Griffith Lewis ⎫ Wardeniaid."
David Jones ⎭

(" This Cup was exchanged for another by the parishioners of Llan- fachreth, 1809 ")—then follow the names of the Rector and Wardens.
Marks.—London date-latter for 1808-9.   Maker's mark, RG, in an oblong cartouche.
Height, 7¾ in.; depth of bowl, 4⅜ in.; diameter of mouth, 3¾ in.; diameter of foot, 4 in.

PATEN.—A plain silver Paten, with narrow moulded edge, on a truncated moulded foot, inscribed—

" A Gift to Llanfachreth Church
July 1785."

Marks.—London date-letter for 1785-6.   Maker's mark, EI, in an oblong cartouche (Edwd. Jay, *ent* 1773).
Diameter, 7 in.; height, 1⅝ in.

FLAGON.—A tall, plain silver Flagon with tapering cylindrical body, the body above the splayed base encircled by a moulding, the edge of domed cover and the lip moulded, and the scrolled handle terminating

PLATE XXX.

No. 3.

BOTTWNOG, CARNARVONSHIRE.

ELIZABETHAN SILVER CHALICE AND PATEN-COVER.

DATE : 1575.

No. 2.

RHOIDWDDGEIDIO, ANGLESEY.

ELIZABETHAN SILVER CHALICE.

DATE : 1574-5.

No. 1.

LLANDYFRYDOG, ANGLESEY.

ELIZABETHAN SILVER CHALICE AND PATEN-COVER.

DATE : *circa* 1575.

in a large plain shield. The Christian symbols, I.H.S. and a cross in glory, are engraved, and also this Welsh inscription—

"Rhôdd Syr Robert Williames Vaughan Bar.
ac Anna Maria ei Wraig
i Blwyf Llanfachreth
yn Sir Feirionnydd
1803."

("The gift of Sir R. Williames Vaughan, Bart., and Anna Maria, his wife, to the Parish of Llanfachreth, in the County of Merioneth, 1803.")

Marks.—London date-letter for 1793-4. Maker's mark, EF, in an oblong cartouche (probably Ed. Fennell).

Dimensions.—Height, exclusive of cover, $8\frac{15}{16}$ in.; with cover, $10\frac{3}{8}$ in.; diameter of mouth, $3\frac{3}{4}$ in.; diameter of base, 6 in.

The donors, Sir Robert Williames Vaughan, second Baronet, of Nannau and Hengwrt, and his wife, Anna Maria, daughter of Sir Thomas Mostyn, Bart., gave a small silver set for private Communion to Penmachno Church, and he himself presented a silver Paten to Dolgelley.

A small set for private Communion, consisting of a plain silver Chalice with egg-shape bowl on short truncated foot, engraved with I.H.S., a cross and nails in glory, and inscribed—

"Plwyf Llanfachreth
1809
William Williams, Gweinidog
Griffith Lewis ⎱
David Jones ⎰ Wardeniaid."

Height, $2\frac{3}{4}$ in.

Marks.—London date-letter for 1808-9. Maker's mark, RG in an oblong.

A Paten on foot, the same Christian symbols engraved on the centre, and the same inscription on the back. Same marks as on Chalice. Diameter, $2\frac{5}{16}$ in.; and a square-shape glass bottle, with plain silver top, stamped with London date-letter for 1808-9 and makers' mark, $\substack{\text{T·P}\\\text{E·R}}$ in a quatrefoil. Height, $3\frac{7}{8}$ in. (PLATE XXXIV., No. 3.)

LLANFAIR-JUXTA-HARLECH—S. MARY

CHALICE.—A plain silver Chalice with inverted bell-shape bowl, supported by a baluster stem on splayed foot, the edge of which is incised with three lines.

Marks.—London date-letter for 1639-40.   Maker's mark, RW, with mullet below, in shaped shield.

Dimensions.—Height, $7\frac{3}{16}$ in.; depth of bowl, $3\frac{1}{2}$ in.; diameter, 4 in.

PATEN.—A plain electro-plate Paten on three feet.

FLAGON.—Plain electro-plate.

There is also a large old pewter Dish, in bad condition, stamped with four marks in separate shields.

LLANFIHANGEL-Y-TRAETHAU—S. MICHAEL

An electro-plate Chalice, Paten, and a glass Cruet.

The old silver Chalice, mentioned in the terriers between 1801 and 1831, appears to have been replaced by this modern electro-plated Chalice.

LLANFROTHEN—S. BROTHEN

CHALICE.—A tall silver Chalice, with plain inverted bell-shape bowl, gilt inside, and engraved with the sacred monogram, I.H.S. and a cross. Inscribed on edge of the circular foot—

" J. Williams Ellis A.B. Brondanw."

London date-letter for 1859-60.   Maker's mark, WS, in an oblong. Height, $9\frac{1}{2}$ in.

PATEN.—Plain silver Paten, on truncated foot, inscribed—

" Offrwm i allor yr Arglwydd yn Eglwys
Llanfrothen, gan J. Williams Ellis, Brondanw, 1844."

London date-letter for 1843-4.   Diameter, $8\frac{1}{8}$ in.   Height, $3\frac{1}{4}$ in.

There is also here an interesting old pewter Porringer with two handles and an inverted bell-shape bowl, encircled by a plain moulding, on a low moulded foot, stamped with four small marks in separate shields —T & H, a griffin's head erased, escallops on a bar, and a leopard's head.

Probable date, end of the seventeenth century.

Height, $4\frac{1}{4}$ in.; diameter about $3\frac{3}{4}$ in.

An old pewter Jug, with tapering cylindrical body, short spout, scrolled handle. Inscribed in roman capitals—

"THE GIFT OF RICHD HUMPHREYS GENᵀ
TO THE CHURCH OF LLANFROTHEN 1698."

Cover missing. Height, 8½ in.
The donor of the Jug was the father of Humphrey Humphreys, Bishop of Bangor 1689-1701, who had been Rector of this place in 1670.

LLANGELYNIN—S. CELYNIN

CHALICE.—A plain silver Chalice, inscribed—

" 1843
LLANGELYNIN CHURCH
Revᵈ. T. Jones, A.B. Minister
T. Owen ⎫
J. Lewis ⎭ Churchwardens."

Height, 7⅝ in.

PATEN.—A small plain silver Paten of concave form, inscribed—

" EG: GELYNIN SANT
Meirion 1904."

Birmingham date-letter for 1904-5. Diameter, 6³⁄₁₆ in.

ALMS DISH.—A plain, circular, electro-plated dish.

A large old pewter Flagon, a moulding encircling the tapering cylindrical body; domed cover; pierced scroll thumb-piece; an acanthus leaf applied to shoulder of the scrolled handle; the foot splayed.
No marks.
Height, exclusive of cover, 9½ in.; with cover, 10½ in.

A large circular pewter dish, stamped with the name DUNCUMB, and LONDON, in a scroll. Diameter, 12 in.

The Chalice appears to replace a "silver goblet with a cover to it, weighing seventeen ounces," mentioned in the terriers for 1801 and 1817.

LLANYMAWDDWY—S. TYDECHO

A plated Communion set.

An old pewter Plate, inscribed—

"LLANYMAWDDWY."

9½ in. in diameter. Date, *circa* 1725.

The parish terriers from 1749 until 1792 mention a silver Chalice and a pewter Flagon, but both have, unhappily, disappeared.

MAENTWROG—S. TWROG

CHALICE.—A plain silver Chalice with hexagonal stem, divided by a large pierced knop of medieval design, resting on a sexfoil foot, on which is engraved the symbols of the Crucifixion. It is inscribed— "RHÔDD Iohn Roberts (Hen Weinidog ymhlas Tan y Bwlch) i Eglwys Maen Twrog 1743."

Marks.—London date-letter for 1878-9. Maker's mark, W.C. Height, 6 in.

The old Chalice was, unfortunately, melted in 1878, on the ground that its shape was "inconvenient" (!) and the original inscription reproduced on this new Chalice.

PATEN-COVER.—This is the original silver Paten-Cover belonging to the destroyed Chalice. It has a foot and is quite plain, with the Christian symbols I.H.S. and a cross in glory engraved in the centre, and with the same inscription as on the Chalice.

Marks.—London date-letter for 1738-9. Maker's mark illegible.
Dimensions.—Diameter, 5⅛ in.; height, 1 3/16 in.

FLAGON.—A glass Flagon with plain silver handle and mounts. London date-letter for 1878-9. Maker's mark, $^{H\,E}_{W}$ in trefoil.

PENNAL—S. PEDR MEWN CADWYNAU

CHALICE.—A plain silver Chalice, with beaker-shape bowl, slightly curving out at the lip, the stem divided by a moulding, the foot moulded. Inscribed—

"PENAL 1734."

PLATE XXXI.

No. 1.

LLANWNDA, CARNARVONSHIRE.

CHARLES I. SILVER CHALICE AND PATEN-COVER.

DATE : 1633.

No. 2.

LLANGEINWEN, ANGLESEY.

SILVER PATEN.   JAMES I. SILVER CHALICE AND PATEN-COVER.

DATE : 1736.   DATE : 1614-15.

Marks.—London date-letter for 1733-4. Maker's mark, HE in script capitals, with mullet above and below, in shaped shield—the same mark appearing on the Chalice at Penegoes.

Dimensions.—Height, $7\frac{13}{16}$ in.; depth of bowl, $4\frac{1}{4}$ in.; diameter of mouth, $3\frac{1}{2}$ in.; diameter of foot, $3\frac{1}{2}$ in.

PATEN.—A charming, small, square, silver Salver, with plain flat centre, shaped corners, gadrooned border, standing on four feet. Inscribed at the back—

" The Gift of
M^{rs}. Mary Pryse of Esgirweddan
PENAL * CHURCH
1743."

Marks.—London date-letter for 1728. Maker's mark illegible.
Dimensions.—$7\frac{5}{8}$ in. square.

FLAGON.—A tall, new, silver Flagon, $14\frac{1}{2}$ in. high, with plain upright cylindrical body, on moulded foot, a cross surmounting cover. I.H.S. and cross in glory engraved on body. Inscribed—

" Eglwys
Sant Pedr
Mewn Cadwynau."
(" The Church of S. Peter in chains.")

Marks.—Sheffield date-letter for 1877-8. Maker's mark, H. W. & Co.

There is also in this Church a private Communion set of electro-plate.

PENRHYNDEUDRAETH—HOLY TRINITY

CHALICES.—Two small, plain silver Chalices with inverted bell-shape bowls, gilt inside, moulded lips, on slender stems moulded in the centre; plain circular feet. I.H.S. in monogram engraved on the bowls.

Marks.—London date-letter for 1857-8. Maker's mark, G·I, with pellet between, in an oblong.
Height, $6\frac{7}{8}$ in.

PATEN.—A plain silver Paten, with narrow moulded edge, I.H.S. in monogram engraved in the centre, supported by a truncated moulded foot.

Marks.—Same as on Chalices.
Diameter, 7 in.; height, 2 in.

FLAGON.—A tall silver Flagon with cylindrical body, a moulding encircling the lower part, the base moulded, a cross surmounting the domed cover, I.H.S. in monogram engraved under the spout; shell thumb-piece.

Marks.—Same as on Chalices and Paten.

Height with cross, 12 in.; exclusive of cross, 10 in.

TALYLLYN—S. MARY

CHALICE.—A plain silver Chalice, with bell-shape bowl, moulded lip, supported by a stem with wide moulding in the centre, and resting on a moulded foot, inscribed—" The Gift of John Owen Curate of Tâlytlyn 1729."

Marks.—Chester mark, date-letter indistinct. Maker's mark, RR, addorsed, in a shaped shield (Richd. Richardson).

Dimensions.—Height, $7\frac{3}{8}$ in.; depth of bowl, $3\frac{3}{4}$ in.; diameter of mouth, $3\frac{1}{2}$ in.; diameter of foot, $3\frac{7}{8}$ in.

PATEN.—A small, plain silver Paten, inscribed—

" The Church of S^t. MARY TALYLLYN 1899."

Diameter, $5\frac{1}{4}$ in.
London date-letter for 1899-1900.

A plain plated dish.

An old pewter Flagon and Paten have disappeared from this Church.

TOWYN—S. CADFAN

CHALICE (No. 1).—A small, plain silver Chalice, of medieval form, a cross engraved on the bowl, the stem hexagonal and divided by a large knop, the foot sexfoil, and I.H.S. engraved on one lobe. It is inscribed underneath the foot—

" Renovat impeus Jer: Griffith A.M. Vic^r. Towyn Ano 1774. Titus Lewis B.D. de Towyn Vicarius et Ruralis de Estimaner Decanus renovat A.D. 1888."

This Chalice was, unfortunately, entirely re-made in another form in 1888, on the ground that its former shape was " inconvenient."

CHALICE (No. 2).—Silver-gilt Chalice, with plain shallow bowl, supported by a stem divided by a decorated knop, and resting on a sexfoil foot engraved with scrolls and a diamond pattern, and an applied boss on each lobe. Inscribed under foot—" To the Glory of God and in memory of William Parry and Jane his wife of Bryngarreglwyd in this parish, given by their Daughter, Michaelmas 1883."

Marks.—London date-letter for 1883-4. Maker's mark, IF in a double-lobed shield.

Height, 8½ in.

PATEN (No. 1).—A plain silver-gilt Paten with same inscription and marks as on Chalice No. 2. Diameter, 6½ in.

PATEN (No. 2).—A plain silver Paten; diameter, 5½ in. London date-letter for 1888-9. Maker's mark, WK, in double-lobed shield.

FLAGON.—A silver-mounted glass Flagon, same marks as on Chalice No. 2.

A large old pewter Flagon, with tapering cylindrical body, two mouldings surrounding body, one near the lip, the other towards the spreading base. A knob, surmounted by an acorn, is on the top of the domed cover; scrolled handle, and fluted thumb-piece.

Marks.—A crowned X, and CB, in a small shield.

Height of body only, 10⅛ in.; with cover and knob, 13½ in.

Another Flagon, identically similar in form, but smaller in size, stamped with same marks. Height of body, 8 in.; total, 11¼ in.

A pewter Plate, 9 in. in diameter.

Described in the terrier for 1801 are the following pieces of plate, then in possession of this Church, but now no longer there:—" A silver Case with this inscription: ' Rhodd David Jones i Blwyf Towyn 1793 '; a silver Chalice of Pryce Maurice Vicar of Towyn, 1790."

TRAWSFYNYDD—S. MADRYN AC ANHUN

CHALICE.—A very large, massive silver Chalice, the beaker-shape bowl considerably curved outwards at the lip; a large, flattened knop, with narrow moulding round its centre, in the middle of the stem, which stands on a spreading moulded base. Inscribed, in large script lettering—

" Ad Hoc Poculum Emendum
Johannes Tudor A.M.
Septem Libras Legavit A.D. 1733
Griffinus Frater
Tres Aureos Contulit."

R

Marks.—London date-letter for 1736-7. Maker's mark, EP, with lion rampant above, in shaped shield (Edw. Pocock).

Dimensions.—Height, 12 in.; depth of bowl, 6⅛ in.; diameter of mouth, 5 in.; diameter of foot, 5 5⁄16 in.

PATEN-COVER.—The Paten-Cover belonging to this Chalice has a plain flat centre, with a narrow moulded rim, the edge of foot also moulded. The foot is inscribed, in script capitals—

"J : T
G : T } D.D."

Marks.—The same as on Chalice.

Dimensions.—Diameter, 5⅞ in.; height, 1⅜ in.

CHALICE.—A smaller Chalice, with plain V-shape bowl, gilt inside, engraved with a crest, a sun in splendour, within a foliated wreath; another similar wreath (empty) on the opposite side; the edge of foot reeded; hexagonal base.

Marks.—London date-letter for 1797. Maker's mark illegible.

Dimensions.—Height, 7 in.; depth of bowl, 4 in.; diameter of mouth, 3½ in.

ALMS DISH.—A large Alms Dish of old Sheffield-plate, with fluted border, standing on three very short feet. 11¾ in. in diameter.

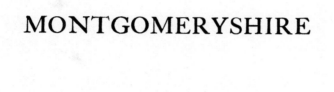

MONTGOMERYSHIRE

PLATE XXXII.

CEMMAES, MONTGOMERYSHIRE.
SILVER CHALICE AND COVER.
DATE : 1720-1.

BANHADLOG

CHALICE.—A tall silver Cup, with inverted bell-shape bowl, moulded edge, supported by a high baluster stem, on a moulded foot. The sacred emblems, I.H.S., a cross and three nails in glory, are engraved. It is inscribed on the foot in script letters—

" Presented to Banhadlog Chapel by
Rev^d. Arthur Trewman, M.A. Curate
1848."

London date-letter for 1840-1. Maker's mark, probably WC in an oblong.

Height, 8 in.

PATEN.—A plain silver Paten, moulded edge, supported by a moulded foot. The sacred emblems, I.H.S. and a cross in glory, are engraved, probably at a later date.

London date-letter for 1714-15. Maker's mark illegible.

Diameter, $6\frac{3}{16}$ in.; height, $1\frac{3}{4}$ in.

CARNO—S. JOHN THE BAPTIST

CHALICE.—A plain silver Chalice, with low, beaker-shape bowl, supported by a baluster stem on a splayed foot, inscribed—

" The Parish cup of Charno in the Countie of Montgomery
1676
Churchwardens
E M * H R."

Marks.—London date-letter for 1652-3. Maker's mark illegible.

Dimensions.—Height, $6\frac{1}{4}$ in.; depth of bowl, $3\frac{1}{8}$ in.; diameter of mouth, $3\frac{3}{4}$ in.; diameter of foot, $3\frac{5}{8}$ in.

This and the small Chalice at Bryncoedifor are the only pieces of Commonwealth silver plate in this Diocese.

PATEN.—A plain silver Paten, inscribed—" A thank offering for Peace. By the Congregation of S^t. John the Baptist, Carno, May 31st, 1902."

London date-letter for 1902-3.

Diameter, $5\frac{13}{16}$ in.

A plated Flagon, given by Rev. J. Dixon, 1895.

A plated Paten on foot.

A circular pewter Plate, $9\frac{3}{8}$ in. diameter. No marks.

CEMMAES—S. TYDECHO

CHALICE.—A tall silver Chalice with cover, of graceful proportions, the bowl, which is rounded at the bottom, has a moulded lip, and a little lower down a plain narrow moulding is carried round the body. The centre is engraved with the familiar device of the letters I.H.S., a cross and three nails in glory, and below this the following inscription in script lettering—

"This Challice & Cover is yᵉ Gift of Mʳˢ.
Bridget Mostyn of Aberhirieth to yᵉ
Parish ᵒᶠ Cemes, for yᵉ use of yᵉ Altar 1720."

The bowl stands on a baluster stem, resting on a high moulded foot. The tall cover is moulded and surmounted by a flame-like ornament in silver gilt.

Marks.—London date-letter for 1720-1. Maker's mark illegible.

Dimensions.—Total height to top of cover, 13¼ in.; Chalice only, 9 in.; depth of bowl, 4⅛ in.; diameter of mouth, 4 in.; diameter of foot, 4 in. (PLATE XXXII.)

PATEN.—A large plain silver Paten, with moulded edge, standing on a truncated foot. The letters I.H.S., a cross and three nails, in a halo, are engraved in the centre. Weight marked, 14 oz.

Marks.—London date-letter for 1707-8. Maker's mark, SH, with a rose (?) above and an illegible device below, in a lozenge—probably for Alice Sheene.

Dimensions.—Diameter, 8⅞ in.; height, 3 in.

An old pewter Flagon has disappeared from this Church since 1856.

DAROWEN—S. TUDYR

CHALICE.—An Elizabethan silver Chalice, with tapering beaker-shape bowl, engraved with a double strap-work band, ⅞ in. wide, intersecting three times and filled with short oblique lines, enclosing the conventional sprays of foliage. The stem, which is divided by a plain compressed knop between two narrow collars, has a plain reeded moulding at the top and bottom, and rests on a plain moulded foot.

No marks. Date, *circa* 1575.

Dimensions.—Height, 7 in.; depth of bowl, 3½ in.; diameter of mouth, 3⅜ in.; diameter of foot, 3½ in. (PLATE XXII., No. 1.)

PATEN.—A plain silver Paten, with plain moulded edge, a decorated cross engraved in the centre. Inscribed on back—

> " Richard Jones . Rector of Darowen
> Hugh Pughe ⎫
> Tho⁵. Peters ⎭ Ch : Wardens 1882."

Marks.—London date-letter for 1878-9. Makers' mark, $^{T\ C}_{E\ C}$ in a square.

Diameter, $6\frac{9}{16}$ in.

A glass Cruet with silver top.

The terriers between 1749 and 1791 include a pewter Flagon and a Plate, but these have since disappeared.

DYLIFE

A plated Chalice with two handles.

A plain plated Paten.

LLANBRYNMAIR—S. MARY THE VIRGIN

CHALICE.—An Elizabethan silver Chalice, with beaker-shape bowl, engraved with a wide, plain, double strap-work band, $\frac{3}{4}$ in. in width, intersecting three times, filled with conventional sprays of foliage, delicately engraved, a large spray of foliage carried above and below each intersection. Above the band, "LLAN · BRYN * MAIRE" is engraved in roman capitals, doubtless contemporary with the date of the Chalice. The plain stem has lost its central knop. The edge of the rounded foot is plainly moulded. (PLATE XXII., No. 2.)

Marks.—London date-letter for 1595-6. Maker's mark illegible.

Dimensions.—Height, $6\frac{3}{8}$ in.; depth of bowl, $3\frac{3}{16}$ in.; diameter of bowl, $3\frac{1}{8}$ in.; diameter of foot, $3\frac{1}{16}$ in.

CHALICE.—A small new silver Chalice, engraved with the letters I.H.S., a cross and three nails in glory, and with this inscription on the foot—

> "LLANBRYNMAIR, A.D. 1883."

London date-letter for 1882-3. Maker's mark, $^{H\ E}_{W}$ in trefoil. Height, $7\frac{1}{16}$ in.

PATEN.—A small new silver Paten, engraved with the *Agnus Dei* and a cross, and with the same inscription as on the new Chalice.

Marks.—The same as Chalice.

Diameter, 5¾ in.

FLAGON.—A very large old pewter Flagon, with two scrolled handles (broken). No cover. The foot badly damaged.

A small silver-mounted glass Cruet.

LLANDINAM—S. LLONIO

CHALICE.—A plain silver Chalice, with V-shape bowl, on baluster stem resting on a splayed foot with moulded edge.

Marks.—London date-letter for 1607-8. Maker's mark, TR, in monogram, in a shaped shield.

Dimensions.—Height, 8¾ in.; depth of bowl, 4¼ in.; diameter of mouth, 4⅜ in.; diameter of foot, 3½ in.

PATEN.—A plain silver Paten, with moulded edge on a truncated foot, moulded. Inscribed on the back in script letters—" Presented to the Parish Church of Llandinam by Mrs. Brome, of Berthddu, 1851."

London date-letter for 1849-50.

Dimensions.—Diameter, 8 in.; height, 2½ in.

FLAGON.—A tall, plain silver Flagon, upright cylindrical body, resting on a wide splayed foot.

London date-letter for 1902-3.

Height, 12 in.

LLANGURIG—S. CURIG

CHALICE.—A plain silver Chalice, with beaker-shape bowl, the lip curved, a narrow moulding in centre of stem, the foot moulded.

Marks.—London date-letter for 1734-5. Maker's mark, R·G in quatrefoil with T above and C below.

Dimensions.—Height, 8 in.; depth of bowl, 4¼ in.; diameter of mouth, 4 in.; diameter of foot, 3⅞ in.

PATEN-COVER.—The Paten-Cover of this Chalice has a moulded edge and a foot. Same marks.

Diameter, 5 in.; height, 1⅜ in.

A silver Communion set, consisting of a Chalice, 7¼ in. high, with a gilt band of trefoil ornaments around the bowl, the knop on stem decorated with gilt arabesques and set with six amethysts *en cabochon*— a sexfoil foot with a border of gilt arabesque decoration. Inscribed—

PLATE XXXIII.

No. 1.

No. 2.

LLANFIGAEL, ANGLESEY.

ELIZABETHAN CHALICE AND PATEN-COVER.

DATE: 1574-5.

LLANFFLEWIN, ANGLESEY.

ELIZABETHAN CHALICE AND PATEN-COVER.

DATE: 1574-5.

"THIS CHALICE, PATEN AND FLAGON WAS GIVEN TO THE CHVRCH OF LLANGURIG BY MISS HINDE-LLOYD OF GLOCHFAEN . 1879." A Paten, with a Pelican in her piety engraved in the centre, diameter, $6\frac{9}{16}$ in.; and a Flagon, 12 in. high, with globular body, a gilt band of arabesque ornament encircling it, and set with four large carbuncles, on a circular foot, which is inscribed underneath—"RHODD MAIR CHARLOTTE HINDE-LLOYD O'R CLOCHFAEN I EGLVYS LLANGVRIG 1879."

The Chalice and Paten have the London date-letter for 1878-9, and the Flagon for 1879-80.

LLANIDLOES—S. IDLOES

CHALICE (No. 1).—A plain old silver Chalice with beaker-shape bowl, curved out lip, short truncated stem. Inscribed—

"Ex dono Bridgette Evans wid."

Date, *circa* 1685. The only mark is RL with slipped flower below, in plain shield.

Dimensions.—Height, $7\frac{7}{8}$ in.; depth of bowl, $4\frac{7}{8}$ in.; diameter of mouth and foot, $4\frac{3}{16}$ in.

CHALICE (No. 2).—A silver Chalice, vase-shape bowl, with surbase of embossed acanthus leaves, moulded lip; an ornamental collar of acanthus leaves, etc., under the bowl; edge of foot embossed with egg and tongue and acanthus moulding. Inscribed—

"Presented
TO THE REVD. J. DAVIES
by his Parishioners
And given by him to the Parish Church of
Llanidloes for the Communion Service
1st January 1838."

London date-letter for 1836-7. Makers' mark, $_{J\ W}^{E\ E}$B in quatrefoil (E. E. J. & W. Barnard).

Dimensions.—Height, $6\frac{1}{4}$ in.; depth of bowl, $3\frac{7}{8}$ in.; diameter, $3\frac{1}{2}$ in.; diameter of foot, $3\frac{1}{4}$ in.

CHALICES (Nos. 3 AND 4).—Two new silver Chalices, of modernised medieval design, trefoil feet with pointed angles; applied gilt crucifixes on the foot.

London date-letter for 1880-1. Maker's mark, IF, in double-lobed shield.

Height, 6 in.

S

PATENS.—Two new silver Patens, 6 in. in diameter. Same date-letter and marks as on Chalices.

FLAGON.—A silver Flagon, globular body, trefoil foot with pointed angles, a cross surmounting the cover. Same marks as on Chalices (Nos. 3 and 4) and Patens. Height, 11 in.

LLANWNOG—S. GWYNOG

A very large plain silver Chalice, with beaker-shape bowl, lip slightly curved out, a narrow moulding in centre of stem, moulded foot. Inscribed, in an oval cartouche, in script letters—

"A Gift to
The Parish of
lLanwonog in Com
Mountgomery
Anno Dom.
1707."

Marks.—London date-letter for 1707-8. Maker's mark, CH, with rose under, in shaped shield.

Dimensions.—Height, 10⅛ in.; depth of bowl, 6 in.; diameter of mouth, 5⅛ in.; diameter of foot, 4⅜ in.

PATEN-COVER.—The Paten-Cover of this Chalice is plain, with a narrow moulded edge, and has a foot which is engraved with the same inscription as above.

Marks.—The same as on Chalice.

Dimensions.—Diameter, 6½ in.; height, 1¼ in.

The list of Benefactions on a board in the vestry refers to this gift thus: " Hester Pryce widdow and Relict of Matthew Pryce of Park Esqʳ gave a large silver Chalice and Salver to the use of this Church in yᵉ year of our Lord, one thousand seven hundred and seven." She was the twelfth daughter of John Thelwall, of Bathafarn Park, Denbighshire, and her husband, who died in 1699, is described as Chancellor, and M.P. for Montgomery in the two last Parliaments of Charles II.

PATEN.—An old pewter Paten, with moulded edge, supported by a truncated stem, stamped with a mark, a vase of flowers between two scrolls with a name (illegible) on one side. Inscribed on edge of foot—

"RW : DO : CW."

Date, *circa* 1705.

Dimensions.—10 in. in diameter, 3¼ in. high.

These initials probably represent the names of the Church-wardens.

LLANWRIN—S. UST AND DYFNIG

CHALICE.—A large, plain silver Chalice, with large beaker-shape bowl, the lip slightly curved, standing on a stem divided in the centre by a moulding, on a moulded foot. Inscribed in script lettering—

"The Communion Cup of LLanŵryn."

Marks.—London date-letter for 1714-15. Maker's mark, Ne in oblong.
Dimensions.—Height, $8\frac{5}{8}$ in.; depth of bowl, $4\frac{3}{4}$ in.; diameter of mouth, $4\frac{1}{4}$ in.; diameter of foot, $3\frac{3}{4}$ in.

PATEN-COVER.—The silver Paten-Cover belonging to this Chalice is plain, with a moulded edge, and has the customary form of foot.
Marks.—The same as on Chalice.
Dimensions.—Diameter, $5\frac{1}{8}$ in.; height, $1\frac{3}{8}$ in.

There is also a small old Sheffield Salver, plain centre, with shaped shell and scroll border, on three claw and ball feet, $7\frac{1}{4}$ in. in diameter.

A large old pewter Dish, circular.

MACHYNLLETH—S. PETER

CHALICE.—A large, plain silver Chalice, with beaker-shape bowl, slightly curving out at the lip; a plain moulding in the centre and at the top of the stem, which rests on a moulded foot. Inscribed in script—

"A.D. 1709 Abhinc maneat intemeratus hic Calix in Ecclesia de Machynlleth infra Diœces Asaph et Com: Montgom: Divino Solum Cultui Sacer."

Marks.—London date-letter for 1708-9. Maker's mark illegible.
Dimensions.—Height, $9\frac{1}{8}$ in.; depth of bowl, 5 in.; diameter of mouth, $4\frac{5}{8}$ in.; diameter of foot, $4\frac{1}{4}$ in.

PATEN.—A large, plain silver Paten, with moulded edge, standing on a truncated and moulded foot. Inscribed on back, in script—"The Legacy of yᵉ Reverend Thomas Parry, Clerke, Doctor of Lawes, late Rector of Machynlleth, to that Parish Church Anno Dm. 1704."
Marks.—London date-letter for 1713. Maker's mark, LO in monogram, in oval (Matthew Lofthouse, entered 1705).
Dimensions.—Diameter, $9\frac{5}{8}$ in.; height, $2\frac{5}{8}$ in.

CHALICES.—Two new silver Chalices, of modern medieval design, with Latin inscriptions engraved on the bowls, standing on sexfoil feet, inscribed—

" St. Peter
Machynlleth."

Marks.—London date-letter for 1879-80.   Maker's mark, wBJ. (W. & J. Barnard.)
Dimensions.—$6\frac{11}{16}$ in. high.

FLAGON.—A silver Flagon, inscribed—" This Service for Holy Communion is Presented to S^t. Peter's Church, Machynlleth, By the Marquess & Marchioness of Londonderry and Lady Edwards, Easter Sunday, 1880."
London date-letter for 1878-79.   Same maker's mark as on Chalices.

PATEN.—Silver Paten on foot, the monogram I.H.S. in glory engraved in centre.   Same marks as on Flagon.   Diameter, 7 in.

The disappearance of an old pewter Salver, described in the old terriers as marked " Churchwardens 1747 . Richard Lewis and William Pugh," and an old pewter Flagon, is to be regretted.

MACHYNLLETH—CHRIST CHURCH

A silver Chalice, of modern medieval design, with plain bowl, on sexfoil foot.
London date-letter for 1850.   Maker's mark, I·K, with pellet between, in oblong.   Height, $8\frac{3}{8}$ in.

MALLWYD—S. TYDECHO

CHALICE.—A plain silver Chalice with beaker-shape bowl, slightly curved, inscribed—" MALLWYD 1628," in large roman capitals near the lip.   The thick stem, which rests on a rounded, moulded foot, is divided by a rounded knop between two collars.
Marks.—London date-letter for 1627-8.   Maker's mark, TE, in monogram, in a shaped shield.

Dimensions.—Height, $6\frac{7}{16}$ in.; depth of bowl, $3\frac{7}{16}$ in.; diameter of mouth, $3\frac{3}{8}$ in.; diameter of foot, $3\frac{1}{8}$ in.   (PLATE XXVIII., No. 1.)

The Church of Mallwyd was provided with this Chalice during the incumbency of the eminent Welshman, Dr. John Davies, author of a Welsh dictionary and other important literary works, who, during the long period of forty years that he held this benefice, did so much for this parish, providing it with three bridges, built the Rectory, presented the three bells to the Church, and in all probability gave this Chalice, though there is no inscription or record in definite proof of the conjecture.

CHALICE.—A plain silver Chalice, with an inverted bell-shape bowl, an incised line along the lip, the top of the slender truncated stem and the edges of the foot, reeded.   Inscribed—

" Mallwyd Church."

Marks.—London date-letter for 1797-8.   Maker's mark, GB in an oblong (probably Geo. Baskerville).

Dimensions.—Height, $7\frac{5}{8}$ in.; depth of bowl, $4\frac{1}{2}$ in.; diameter of mouth, $3\frac{7}{8}$ in.; diameter of foot, $3\frac{3}{4}$ in.

PATEN.—A plain silver Paten, with moulded edge.   The letters I.H.S., in glory, engraved in the centre.   This inscription is engraved on the foot, which has moulded edges—

" Mallwyd
Church
1798."

Marks.—London date-letter for 1798-9.   Maker's mark, GB, as on Chalice.

Dimensions.—Diameter, $6\frac{5}{8}$ in.; height, $1\frac{5}{8}$ in.

The Rector from 1783 until 1799 was the Rev. Edward Williams, M.A.

FLAGON.—A tall plain silver Flagon with cylindrical body, a moulding carried round the lower part, just above the spreading moulded foot; a low, slightly-domed cover, with a pierced scroll thumb-piece, the scroll handle terminating in a heart-shape shield.   Engraved in front of body— INRI above the familiar device of letters I.H.S., a cross and three nails in glory.   This inscription is also engraved thereon, in script lettering—

" Hunc calicem eucharisticum
altari Ecclesiæ de Mallwyd,
dedicavit &c. donavit A. P.
ejus Ecclesiæ Rector, Anno 1773."

Marks.—London date-letter for 1773-4. Maker's mark, S·E, in script capitals, a pellet between, in an oblong.

Dimensions.—Total height, 8¾ in.; height of body only, 7½ in.; diameter of mouth, 3½ in.; diameter of foot, 5½ in.

This silver Flagon, which is a copy of a Flagon of an earlier period, of about the middle of the seventeenth century, was the gift of the Rev. Anthony Pool, of Cae Nest, Merionethshire, Rector of Mallwyd from 1755 to 1783, and is described in the parish terrier for the year 1774 as " a quart silver Flagon, value £11 2s. 6d., weight, 29 oz. 6 dwts." The " old pewter Flagon for the wine, and a pewter Plate for the Bread at the Sacrament," mentioned in the same terrier, and also in 1730, and again in 1791, have disappeared.

PENEGOES—S. CADFARCH

CHALICE.—A plain silver Chalice, with beaker-shape bowl, curving out slightly at the lip, the stem divided by a moulding, standing on a moulded foot.   Inscribed—

" A.D. 1728
Pertinet ad Ecclesiam de Pen Egwest
alias Llan Gadfarch Hic CALIX."

Marks.—London date-letter for 1728-9. Maker's mark, H.E., in script capitals, with mullet above and below, in shaped shield, as on the Chalice at Pennal.

Dimensions.—Height, 6⁷⁄₁₆ in.; depth of bowl, 3⅝ in.; diameter of mouth, 3¼ in.; diameter of foot, 3⅛ in.

CHALICE.—An old pewter Cup, with tall body, standing on a low moulded foot, two scrolled handles, plain mouldings surrounding the body near the top and the foot.   It is without pewter marks.   Probable date, 1750.

Dimensions.—Height, 7⅛ in.

PATEN.—An old pewter Paten, plain flat centre, with a fluted border, standing on a truncated foot with fluted edge, the junction of the foot

PLATE XXXIV.

No. 2.

LLANDEGAI, CARNARVONSHIRE.
SILVER SET FOR PRIVATE COMMUNION.
DATE : 1819-20.

No. 4.

CARNGIWCH,
CARNARVONSHIRE.
MINIATURE SILVER CUP.
DATE : *circa* 1690.

No. 1.

PENMACHNO, CARNARVONSHIRE.
SILVER SET FOR PRIVATE COMMUNION.
DATE : 1814-15.

No. 3.

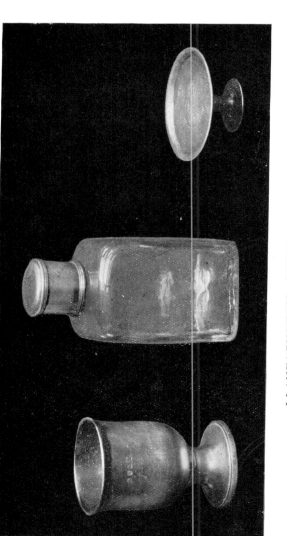

LLANFACHRETH, MERIONETHSHIRE.
SILVER SET FOR PRIVATE COMMUNION.
DATE : 1808-9.

with the plate being similarly fluted. The mark stamped on it is the name WILL BANCKS in scrolls, with a griffin rampant between—the mark repeated twice.

Dimensions.—Diameter, $8\frac{1}{8}$ in.; height, 3 in.; diameter of foot, $4\frac{1}{8}$ in.

ALMS DISH.—An old pewter Alms Dish, in the form of an ordinary flat circular plate, $9\frac{1}{4}$ in. in diameter, stamped with four marks: an animal, probably a dog, courant; M & C°. in a plain label; X; and a floral device.

An electro-plated Flagon and Paten.

PENSTROWED—S. GWRHAI

An interesting Elizabethan silver Chalice, with Paten-Cover. The bowl is beaker-shape, and is engraved with a double strap-work band, incised with lines and intersecting three times. The space inside is without the conventional sprays of foliage so frequently found on Elizabethan Chalices. Above the band, PEN STROIDE, in irregular Roman capitals, of contemporary date, is engraved. The stem is plainly moulded at the top and bottom, and is divided by a small, plain, compressed knop or moulding. The edge of the rounded foot has plain moulding. On the shoulder of the rounded Paten-Cover, which has a reeded edge, is an engraved band filled with three rows of incised lines or hyphens; and on the short foot is the engraved date, 1576, on a plain oblong label, and an incised line along the edge. As this Chalice bears no London hall mark, or maker's mark of any description, it is supposed that it emanated from one of the provincial silversmiths, and from the proximity of this parish to Chester and Shrewsbury, it may be that one of the craftsmen of either of these important guilds of goldsmiths, established there in the middle ages, produced this interesting example of Elizabethan plate. (PLATE XXII., NO. 3.)

Dimensions.—Chalice: height, $5\frac{3}{16}$ in.; depth of bowl, $2\frac{11}{16}$ in.; diameter of mouth and foot, $2\frac{3}{4}$ in. The Paten-Cover is 3 in. in diameter and $1\frac{1}{4}$ in. in height.

A small new silver Paten, plain, bearing the London date-letter for 1898-9.

A circular pewter Plate, stamped with a bird's leg and claw issuing from a coronet, an X, and YATES & BIRCH BIRMINGHAM. Diameter, $9\frac{5}{8}$ in.

Another pewter Plate, with moulded edge, stamped with a Tudor rose and royal crown, twice repeated; $8\frac{3}{8}$ in. in diameter.

TREFEGLWYS—S. MICHAEL

CHALICE.—A tall, plain silver Chalice, with beaker-shape bowl, slightly curved at the lip, supported by a plain stem with moulding in the centre, and resting on a moulded foot.

Marks.—London date-letter for 1734-5. Maker's mark indistinct.

Dimensions.—Height, $8\frac{1}{4}$ in.; depth of bowl, $4\frac{3}{8}$ in.; diameter of mouth, $3\frac{5}{8}$ in.; diameter of foot, $3\frac{7}{16}$ in.

PATEN.—An old pewter Paten with flat rim, stamped with two marks, three talbots' heads erased, in a shield, and LONDON, in a scroll.

Diameter, $9\frac{5}{16}$ in.

There is also a new electro-plated set of Chalice, Paten, Flagon and Alms Dish.

ADDENDA et CORRIGENDA

Page 6.—BEAUMARIS. The arms on the Alms-dish or Credence Paten, with Chinese subjects, are *a chevron between three bulls' heads cabossed impaling three battering rams barwise in pale headed and garnished.*

Page 34.—LLANFIHANGEL-YSCEIFIOG. For " pomegranates " substitute " vines " (twentieth line.)

Page 42.—LLANRHYDDLAD. There is an old silver Paten-Cover, probably belonging to the Chalice and of the same period.

WORKS CONSULTED

Cripps' *Old English Plate.*

Massé's *Old Pewter.*

J. T. Evans' *Church Plate of Pembrokeshire.*

Halliday's *Llandaff Church Plate.*

G. Eyre Evans' *Antiquities of Cardiganshire.*

J. Starkie Gardner's *Old Silver Work.*

Williams' *Eminent Welshmen.*

Burke's *General Armoury.*

W. H. St. John Hope on " Mazer Bowls," *Archæologia.*

W. H. St. John Hope and T. M. Fallow on " Mediæval Chalices and Patens," *Archæological Journal*, vol. xliii.

H. C. Moffatt and Archdeacon Stanhope's *Church Plate of Herefordshire.*

F. Haslewood's *Church Plate of Suffolk.*

C. A. Markham's *Church Plate of Northampton.*

E. Freshfield's *Communion Plate of City of London Churches.*

,,   ,,   ,,   *County of London.*

,,   ,,   ,,   *Middlesex.*

R. S. Ferguson's *Church Plate of the Diocese of Carlisle.*

J. E. Nightingale's *Church Plate of Dorset.*

,,   *Church Plate of Wilts.*

A. Trollope's *Church Plate of Leicestershire.*

T. Burn's *Old Scottish Communion Plate.*

Breese's *Calendars of Gwynedd.*

Rowland's *Mona Antiqua*.

Angharad Llwyd's *Anglesey*.

Nicholas' *County Families of Wales*.

Myrddin Fardd's *Gleanings from God's Acre*

Brown Willis's *See of Bangor*.

Foster's *Alumni Oxoniensis*.

Wood's *Athenæ Oxon*.

Dugdale's *Monasticon*.

Lewis Dwnn's *Visitation*.

Strype's *Archbishop Parker*.

Dictionary of National Biography.

Bangor Diocesan Calendar.

Archæologia Cambrensis, Wales, Byegones, Y Brython, Cymru.

MS. Books of Pedigrees, Taicroesion, Bardd Coch, Eben Fardd.

INDEX OF PLACES

CARNARVONSHIRE

MERIONETHSHIRE

MONTGOMERYSHIRE

BEMROSE AND SONS LIMITED, DERBY AND LONDON.

Selected from the Catalogue of
BEMROSE & SONS LTD.

Memorials of the Counties of England.

MEMORIALS OF OLD OXFORDSHIRE.

Edited by the Rev. P. H. DITCHFIELD, M.A., F.S.A., Editor of "Memorials of Old Buckinghamshire." Dedicated by kind permission to the Right Hon. the Earl of Jersey, G.C.B., G.C.M.G. With numerous Illustrations. Demy 8vo, cloth extra, gilt top. Price **15/=** net.

> "This beautiful book contains an exhaustive history of 'the wondrous Oxford,' to which so many distinguished scholars and politicians look back with affection. We must refer the reader to the volume itself . . . . and only wish that we had space to quote extracts from its interesting pages."—*Spectator.*

MEMORIALS OF OLD DEVONSHIRE.

Edited by F. J. SNELL, M.A., Author of "A Book of Exmoor," &c. Dedicated by kind permission to the Right Hon. Viscount Ebrington, Lord Lieutenant of the County. With numerous Illustrations. Demy 8vo, cloth extra, gilt top. Price **15/=** net.

> "Is a fascinating volume, which will be prized by thoughtful Devonians wherever they may be found . . . richly illustrated, some rare engravings being represented."—*North Devon Journal.*

MEMORIALS OF OLD HEREFORDSHIRE.

Edited by Rev. COMPTON READE, M.A., Author of "Vera Effigies," "A Memoir of Charles Reade, D.C.L.," &c. Dedicated by kind permission to Sir John G. Cotterell, Bart., Lord Lieutenant of the County. With numerous Illustrations. Demy 8vo, cloth extra, gilt top. Price **15/=** net.

> "Another of these interesting volumes like the 'Memorials of Old Devonshire,' which we noted a week or two ago, containing miscellaneous papers on the history, topography, and families of the county by competent writers—the Dean of Hereford, Mr. H. F. J. Vaughan, of Humphreston, the Rev. A. T. Bannister, and others—with photographs and other illustrations."—*Times.*

MEMORIALS OF OLD HERTFORDSHIRE.

Edited by PERCY CROSS STANDING, Author of "The Battles of Hertfordshire," &c. Dedicated by kind permission to the Right Hon. the Earl of Clarendon, G.C.B., Lord Chamberlain. With numerous Illustrations. Demy 8vo, cloth extra, gilt top. Price **15/=** net.

> " . . . The book, which contains some magnificent illustrations, will be warmly welcomed by all lovers of our county and its entertaining history."—*West Herts and Watford Observer.*

> " . . . The volume as a whole is an admirable and informing one, and all Hertfordshire folk should possess it, if only as a partial antidote to the suburbanism which threatens to overwhelm their beautiful county."—*Guardian.*

MEMORIALS OF OLD HAMPSHIRE.

Edited by the Rev. G. E. JEANS, M.A., F.S.A., Author of Murray's "Handbook to Hampshire." Dedicated by kind permission to His Grace the Duke of Wellington, K.G. With numerous Illustrations. Demy 8vo, cloth extra, gilt top. Price **15/=** net.

> "'Memorials of the Counties of England' is worthily carried on in this interesting and readable volume."—*Scotsman.*

MEMORIALS OF OLD SOMERSET.

Edited by F. J. Snell, M.A., Author of "A Book of Exmoor," &c., and Editor of "Memorials of Old Devonshire." Dedicated by kind permission to the Most Hon. the Marquess of Bath. With numerous Illustrations. Demy 8vo, cloth extra, gilt top. Price **15/=** net.

Among the contributors are:—The Rev. Canon Scott Holmes, W. Tyte, Rev. Canon Church, H. St. George Gray, Rev. D. P. Alford, Rev. C. W. Whistler, and other eminent writers.

MEMORIALS OF OLD WILTSHIRE.

Edited by Alice Dryden, Editor of "Memorials of Old Northamptonshire." With numerous Illustrations. Demy 8vo, cloth extra, gilt top. Price **15/=** net.

Among the contributors are :—Sir Alexander Muir-Mackenzie, Bart. ; J. Alfred Gotch, F.S.A., F.R.I.B.A. ; Rev. Canon Wordsworth ; the Lord Bishop of Bristol ; Rev. J. Charles Cox, LL.D , F.S.A. ; Harold Brakspear, F.A.S., F.R.I.B.A. ; M. Jourdain, and other eminent writers.

The following volumes are in preparation :—

With numerous Illustrations. Demy 8vo, cloth extra, gilt top. Price to subscribers before publication, **10/6** each net. *Prospectuses will be sent on application.*

Memorials of Old Kent. Edited by P. H. Ditchfield, M.A., F.S.A., and George Clinch, F.G.S.

„ „ **Shropshire.** Edited by T. Auden, F.S.A.

„ „ **Essex.** Edited by A. Clifton Kelway.

„ „ **Warwickshire.** Edited by Alice Dryden.

„ „ **Yorkshire.** Edited by T. M. Fallow, M.A., F.S.A.

„ „ **Gloucestershire.** Edited by W. P. W. Phillimore, M.A., B.C.L.

„ „ **Lincolnshire.** Edited by Canon Hudson, M.A.

„ „ **Nottinghamshire.** Edited by W. P. W. Phillimore, M.A., B.C.L.

„ „ **Norfolk.** Edited by H. J. Dukinfield Astley, M.A., D. Litt., &c.

„ „ **Dorset.** Edited by T. Perkins, M.A., F.R.A.S.

LONGTON HALL PORCELAIN.

Being further information relating to this interesting fabrique, by William Bemrose, F.S.A., Author of "Bow, Chelsea, and Derby Porcelain." Illustrated with 27 Coloured Art Plates, 21 Collotype Plates, and numerous line and half-tone Illustrations in the text. Bound in handsome "Longton-blue" cloth cover suitably designed. Price **42/=** net. *Prospectus will be sent on application.*

"This magnificent work on the famous Longton Hall ware will be indispensable to the collector." —*Bookman.*

"The collector will find Mr. Bemrose's explanations of the technical features which characterize the Longton Hall pottery of great assistance in identifying specimens, and he will be aided thereto by the many well-selected illustrations."—*Athenæum.*

THE VALUES OF OLD ENGLISH SILVER AND SHEFFIELD PLATE. FROM THE FIFTEENTH TO THE NINETEENTH CENTURIES.

By J. W. Caldicott. Edited by J. Starkie Gardner, F.S.A. 3,000 Selected Auction Sale Records ; 1,600 Separate Valuations ; 660 Articles. Illustrated with 87 Collotype Plates. 300 pages. Royal 4to, cloth. Price, **42/=** net. *Prospectus will be sent on application.*

" . . . A most elaborate and painstaking work, which no collector of silver could afford to be without."—*Scotsman.*

"A most comprehensive and abundantly illustrated volume . . . Enables even the most inexperienced to form a fair opinion of the value either of a single article or a collection, while as reference and reminder it must prove of great value to an advanced student."—*Daily Telegraph.*

"A finely-got-up book, copiously and well illustrated, giving detailed auction records and other information of value to buyer, seller, and owner."—*Times.*

HISTORY OF OLD ENGLISH PORCELAIN AND ITS MANUFACTORIES.

With an Artistic, Industrial and Critical Appreciation of their Productions. By M. L. SOLON, the well-known Potter Artist and Collector. In one handsome volume. Royal 8vo, well printed in clear type on good paper, and beautifully illustrated with 20 full-page Coloured Collotype and Photo-Chromotype Plates and 48 Collotype Plates on Tint. Artistically bound. Price **52/6** nett.

> "Mr. Solon writes not only with the authority of the master of technique, but likewise with that of the accomplished artist, whose exquisite creations command the admiration of the connoisseurs of to-day."—*Athenæum*.

> 'Like the contents and the illustrations, the whole get-up of the book is excellent to a degree which is not often met with even in English books. . . . a real mine of information and a beautiful work of art."—*Tonindustrie-Zeitung, Berlin*.

> "Written in a very clear and lucid style, it is a practically exhaustive account of the evolution of English Porcelain."—*Connoisseur*.

MANX CROSSES :

Or The Inscribed and Sculptured Monuments of the Isle of Man, from about the end of the Fifth to the beginning of the Thirteenth Century. By P. M. C. KERMODE, F.S.A.Scot., &c. The inscribed and sculptured stones treated in this work belong to the system of Early Christian Sepulchral Monuments in the British Isles, to which attention has been more particularly directed of late years. The illustrations are from drawings specially prepared by the Author, founded upon rubbings, and carefully compared with photographs and with the stones themselves. In one handsome Quarto Volume $11\frac{1}{8}$ in. by $8\frac{5}{8}$ in., printed on Van Gelder hand-made paper, bound in full buckram, gilt top, with special design on the side. Price to subscribers, **42/=** net. The edition is limited to 400 copies. [*In the Press.*

OLD ENGLISH GOLD PLATE.

By E. ALFRED JONES. With numerous illustrations of existing specimens of Old English Gold Plate, which by reason of their great rarity and historic value deserve publication in book form. The examples are from the collections of Plate belonging to His Majesty the King, the Dukes of Devonshire, Newcastle, Norfolk, Portland, and Rutland, the Marquis of Ormonde, the Earls of Craven, Derby, and Yarborough, Earl Spencer, Lord Fitzhardinge, Lord Waleran, Mr. Leopold de Rothschild, the Colleges of Oxford and Cambridge, &c. Royal 4to, buckram, gilt top. Price to subscribers, **21/=** net. [*In the Press.*

THE OLD CHURCH PLATE OF THE ISLE OF MAN.

By E. ALFRED JONES. With many illustrations, including a pre-Reformation Silver Chalice and Paten, an Elizabethan Beaker, and other important pieces of Old Silver Plate and Pewter. Crown 4to, buckram. Price, **12/6** net.

LLANDAFF CHURCH PLATE.

By GEORGE ELEY HALLIDAY, F.R.I.B.A., Diocesan Surveyor of Llandaff, with 59 Illustrations in line and half-tone. Royal 8vo, cloth. Price **12/6** net.

> "A thoroughly good contribution to the history of Church Plate."—*Reliquary*.

GARDEN CITIES IN THEORY AND PRACTICE.

By A. R. SENNETT, A.M.I.C.E., &c. Large Crown 8vo. Two vols., attractively bound in cloth, with 400 Plates, Plans, and Illustrations. **Price 21/=** net.

> " . . . What Mr. Sennett has to say here deserves, and will no doubt command, the careful consideration of those who govern the future fortunes of the Garden City."—*Bookseller*.

THE ART OF THE OLD ENGLISH POTTER.

By M. L. SOLON. An Account of the Progress of the Craft in England from the earliest period to the middle of the eighteenth century. The work forms a handsome volume in imperial quarto, printed on Dutch hand-made paper, with 50 Plates etched on copper by the Author. Only 250 copies were printed, and the plates destroyed after publication. Messrs. Bemrose & Sons Ltd. have a few copies left, which are offered at **105/=** each net.

Second Edition, Revised. With an Appendix on Foreign imitations of English Earthenware. Illustrated by the Author. Demy 8vo, cloth, price **10/6** ; large paper, **21/=**.

SOME DORSET MANOR HOUSES, WITH THEIR LITERARY & HISTORICAL ASSOCIATIONS.

By SIDNEY HEATH, with a fore-word by R. Bosworth Smith, of Bingham's Melcombe. Illustrated with forty drawings by the Author in addition to the numerous rubbings of Sepulchral Brasses by W. de C. Prideaux, reproduced by permission of the Dorset Natural History and Field Club. Dedicated by kind permission to the Most Hon. the Marquess of Salisbury. Royal 4to, cloth, bevelled edges. Price to subscribers, **30/-** net. [In the Press.

DERBYSHIRE CHARTERS:

In Public and Private Libraries and Muniment Rooms. Compiled with Preface and Indexes for SIR HENRY HOWE BEMROSE, Kt., by ISAAC HERBERT JEAYES, Assistant-Keeper in the Department of MSS., British Museum. Royal 8vo, cloth, gilt top. Price **42/-** net.

DERBY: ITS RISE AND PROGRESS.

By A. W. DAVISON, illustrated with 12 plates and 2 maps. Crown 8vo, cloth. Price **5/-**.

"A volume with which Derby and its people should be well satisfied."—*Scotsman.*

JOHN N. RHODES: A YORKSHIRE PAINTER, 1809-1842.

By WILLIAM H. THORP. Illustrated by 19 Plates of Reproductions of J. N. Rhodes' Oil Paintings, Sepia Drawings, and Crayon Sketches, four of which are in colour. Crown 4to, artistically bound in cloth. Price **10/6** net. *The edition is limited to 400 copies.*

ACROSS THE GREAT ST. BERNARD.

The Modes of Nature and the Manners of Man. By A. R. SENNETT, A.M.I.C.E., &c. With Original Drawings by HAROLD PERCIVAL, and nearly 200 Illustrations. Large Crown 8vo, attractively bound in cloth. Price **6/-** net.

"A Book which we recommend as heartily to those for whom it will be a memorial of Switzerland as to those who will find in it the revelation of beauties and wonders they have not been privileged to behold."—*Glasgow Herald.*

THE CORPORATION PLATE AND INSIGNIA OF OFFICE OF THE CITIES AND TOWNS OF ENGLAND AND WALES.

By the late LLEWELLYNN JEWITT, F.S.A. Edited and completed with large additions by W. H. ST. JOHN HOPE, M.A. Fully Illustrated, 2 vols., Crown 4to, buckram, **84/-** net. Large paper, 2 vols., Royal 4to, **105/-** net.

"It is difficult to praise too highly the careful research and accurate information throughout these two handsome quartos."—*Athenæum.*

THE RELIQUARY: AN ILLUSTRATED MAGAZINE FOR ANTIQUARIES, ARTISTS, AND COLLECTORS.

A Quarterly Journal and Review devoted to the study of primitive industries, mediæval handicrafts, the evolution of ornament, religious symbolism, survival of the past in the present, and ancient art generally. Edited by J. ROMILLY ALLEN, F.S.A. New Series. Vols. 1 to 12. Super Royal 8vo, buckram, price **12/-** each net. Special terms for sets.

"Of permanent interest to all who take an interest in the many and wide branches of which it furnishes not only information and research, but also illumination in pictorial form."—*Scotsman.*

TRACES OF THE NORSE MYTHOLOGY IN THE ISLE OF MAN.

A Paper read before the Isle of Man Natural History and Antiquarian Society. By P. M. C. KERMODE, F.S.A.Scot., &c. Demy 8vo. Illustrated with 10 plates, paper cover. Price **2/6**.

"This brochure is undoubtedly a very valuable addition to our scanty knowledge of an obscure yet extremely fascinating subject."—*Reliquary.*

London :
Bemrose & Sons Ltd., 4, Snow Hill, E.C.;
AND DERBY.